*To Shannon Norb[?]
With much love, respect and appreciation –*

Dan E Perry
7/3/08
Rom 1:16

MORE THAN I DESERVE

More Than I Deserve

The writing of this book was given to me by the grace of God. It is now my privilege to pass it on to you as a gift, free of any charge or obligation. It would, however, give me great pleasure for you to make a donation of any amount to one of the following three worthy causes:

4) Faith Fellowship Church (for: the Building Fund)
   2278 Paul's Path Road, Kinston, NC 28504
5) The Salvation Army (for: use in Kinston, NC)
   P.O. Box 1479 Kinston, NC 28503-1479
6) Son Set Ministries (for: the Refuge)
   P.O. Box 5247, Kinston, NC 28503-5247

"… Freely you have received, freely give." Matt. 10:8

I pray that as you read "More Than I Deserve", the Lord will bless you and your family in the same fashion He has blessed me in the writing of it.

Dan E. Perry, Attorney
P.O. Box 1475
Kinston, NC 28503-1475

MORE THAN I DESERVE

≈ Dan E. Perry ≈

CHAPEL HILL
PRESS, INC.

Copyright © 2008 Dan E. Perry

All rights reserved. No part of this book may be used, reproduced
or transmitted in any form or by any means, electronic or mechanical,
including photograph, recording, or any information storage or
retrieval system, without the express written permission
of the author, except where permitted by law.

ISBN: 978-1-59715-051-4

Second Printing

Dedication

This book is dedicated
To the Glory of God
And to His Son, Jesus the Christ,
And to the Holy Spirit;

And to the cherished honor of my dear wife,
Margaret Marston Taylor Perry,
And our three children:
Elizabeth, Daniel, and Radford;

And in loving memory of my parents,
Ely Jackson Perry and
Elizabeth Ann Seipp Perry;
and my two older brothers:
Warren Seipp Perry and
Ely Jackson Perry Jr.

Intention and Disclaimer

My intention and purpose is to present the events in my life as fairly and accurately as I can recall them before my memory begins to fade and take its toll. I realize some of the details may not be 100 percent correct. Some of my earliest recollections and memories are admittedly hazy because of the passage of time. Be that as it may, they have lingered in my mind all these years. A number of memories have never before been shared with anyone. In essence, I believe them all to be correct, at least for the most part. It is my intention to portray my successes and accomplishments truthfully and without false modesty. How else can the reader know who I really am unless he gets the full story? I want to tell it like it is. Likewise, regarding my failures and short comings, I think it is important to let them be known (at least for the most part) without restriction. Frankly, several of my failures are hard to admit in writing for the "whole world" to know. But in keeping with the general theme of telling my life's story, it would be incomplete without telling the whole truth. By the time the reader finishes the last page of my journey through this life, I hope he will have a good idea of who Dan Perry is—where I've been and where I'm going. For sure, it all has been much more than I deserve.

Contents

Foreword .... *ix*
Acknowledgements .... *xi*
Introduction .... *xiii*

Part I ❧ Recollections and Memories *1*

Chapter i ❧ Birth and Early Childhood *3*

Chapter ii ❧ On to Grammar School *17*

Chapter iii ❧ Family Life at 908 West Road *27*

Chapter iv ❧ On to High School *37*

Chapter v ❧ Family Trips *47*

Chapter vi ❧ Five Unforgettable Speed Rides *51*

Chapter vii ❧ Camp Morehead—A Great Experience *57*

Chapter viii ❧ My Interest in Sports *71*

Chapter ix ❧ Woodberry Forest School for Boys *83*

Chapter x ❧ Sports at Woodberry *101*

Chapter xi ❧ Friends and Woodberry Activities *111*

Chapter xii ❧ Morehead City—My Second Home *123*

Chapter xiii ❧ Undergraduate Years at Carolina *129*

Chapter xiv ❧ Fraternity Life at UNC *139*

Chapter xv ❧ Special Friends *155*

Chapter xvi ❧ Graduation from Carolina *163*

Chapter xvii ❧ After Graduation *171*

Chapter xviii ❧ My Army Years *183*

Chapter xix ❧ Back to Civilian Life *209*

Chapter xx ❧ Twenty-seven Months in Blue Heaven *221*

Part ii ❧ My Search for Truth and Spiritual Growth *245*

Chapter xxi ❧ Living at Home with Mother and Daddy *247*

Chapter xxii ❧ The Lord Finally Provided *257*

Chapter xxiii ❧ My Search Continues *277*

Chapter xxiv ❧ Trying to Put It All Together *297*

Chapter xxv ❧ Family Life at 1305 Perry Park Drive—1975–2002 . . . . . *309*

Chapter xxvi ❧ Precept Bible Study Comes to Kinston *317*

Chapter xxvii ❧ Our Split with Gordon Street *323*

Chapter xxviii ❧ Life Takes on New Meaning *339*

Chapter xxix ❧ Looking Back at Golf *347*

Part iii ❧ 21 Lessons I've Learned Along the Way *375*

Foreword

As I write these words and prepare to tell my story, I am reminded that it is mainly for the benefit of my wife and children as well as nephews and nieces and in-laws. Hopefully, my friends and acquaintances will also find it of some interest and value. Anything beyond that is strictly the Lord's business.

I believe the Lord will lead me not only to share "facts and figures" and experiences, but also some of my innermost thoughts and feelings that have made me who I am today. I'm sure I will be referring to names and situations, which hopefully will not embarrass anyone.

Maybe it would be beneficial to look at this whole story as a journey into the life of Dan Perry. Who is he? Where did he come from and where is he going? What is his purpose for being here? Hopefully, this book will answer at least some of these questions.

DEP
4/1/06

Acknowledgements

My first thanks goes to my wife, Margaret, for putting up with me during these almost sixteen months it has taken to write my story. She has been a true sounding board, adviser, encourager, and editor. Also Barbara Ruth and Barbara have been most helpful in helping me recall certain memories, along with Z.A Collins and Cooper Taylor. Finally, a special tribute goes to Linda Murray who spent hours upon hours, deciphering my voluminous pages of messy writing and typing and retyping my many corrections, additions, and deletions. Thanks also to Edwina Woodbury of the Chapel Hill Press for her expertise, advice, and encouragement.

Introduction

… Or How All This Got Started

On Thursday March 30, 2006, at about 6:05 A.M., I had just finished my morning routine of journaling and daily reading of my chronological Bible. For some reason, I picked up Jesse McDaniel's autobiography, *A Long Life with a Good Wife*. My wife, Margaret, had read the book two or three months before and had put it in my desk among all the other books and clutter. I had never read it, although I had leafed through the pages to get a flavor for Jesse's style of writing. My thought was to read it at some convenient time, "when I got around to it." You see, I'm not known to be much of a reader of books for pleasure; I seem to be more of a "studier" than a reader.

But on this particular morning, I started reading Jesse's book from the beginning, and almost immediately I began to get a clear understanding from the Lord. He seemed to be speaking to my spirit: "Dan, this is the time. You've put it off long enough. Your time has come to write your own life's story."

A couple of years ago, Margaret felt the need to preserve some recollections of her childhood and family background so that our children could look back and remember their heritage from her side of the family. She took time to tape-record some funny stories and family history, which our daughter Elizabeth typed and copied for distribution among our three children. Margaret has encouraged me to do the same, but being the procrastinator that I am, I simply have not gotten around to it—until now.

What Next …?

"O.K., Lord, if you really want me to do this, you've got to show me how. This is my first time at writing a book or manuscript or whatever this thing is called."

Some years ago, two of Kinston's finest leaders Felix Harvey and Roy Poole had each written their life's story—and then my long time golfing buddy Ray Rouse wrote his book, *They Didn't Sell Ice On Sunday.* Even son Daniel wrote *Go West, Young Dan*, an account of his travels out West after graduating from college. Now Jesse McDaniel's autobiography had recently been published. Maybe the Lord really was telling me, "Yes, Dan it's your turn. The time is right. So go ahead and get started."

But How…?

I remember from the Bible how God showed Noah how to build the ark, with what materials and exact dimensions; and how He gave Moses detailed instructions as to how to build His tabernacle; and how He led Solomon to build the temple, exactly like He wanted. I realize I am not worthy to be mentioned in the same breath with Noah, Moses, and Solomon—but at the same time, I believe the Lord is going to show me exactly what He wants me to say and how to say it.

What's My Message…?

The Lord seems to be telling me this is not only going to be the story of my life, but He wants me to go beyond that. He wants me to tell my story with the underlying message being to pave the way and set the stage for God to move in the lives of the readers. He wants this book to be an instrument or vehicle by which at least one person will be drawn to see the need to accept His Son, Jesus, as Lord and Savior, and then to grow and mature in the likeness of His only begotten Son. I believe the Lord is going to show me how my story and the overall context of this book should unfold and be used for His glory.

PART I

Recollections and Memories

JULY 2, 1931–DECEMBER 31, 1961

Chapter I

BIRTH AND EARLY CHILDHOOD

I was born July 2, 1931, at 908 West Road in Kinston, North Carolina. I was the youngest of three sons born to Ely Jackson Perry and Elizabeth Ann Seipp Perry. My oldest brother, Warren, recalled it was early on a Sunday morning. My uncle, Dr. Clifton F. West, was the attending physician. My mother said that the first words she heard Dr. West say after the delivery were, "I'm not going to tell her." Then she heard someone else say, "Well, I'm sure not going to tell her!"

Shortly after that the truth was revealed. She had given birth to her **third son**! The problem was she had always wanted a little girl! They had already picked out the name "Elizabeth." Now her hopes were shattered! What were they going to do? They had no choice but to switch to plan B. According to plan A, if it was a little girl, they would name her Elizabeth Ann Seipp Perry and Plan B, if it was a boy, they would name him after my daddy's father, Daniel Elijah Perry. But there was a contingency. If it was a boy, they would have the birth certificate read: "Dan E. Perry," with the idea in mind that if they later had a little girl they would name her Elizabeth and change the birth certificate to read "Daniel Elijah Perry," and all would be well. But what if they didn't have a little girl, what then? Well, would you believe that Mama later told me she planned to change the Dan E. Perry to Dan *Elizabeth* Perry? That's right! According to my own dear mother, my real name was Dan Elizabeth Perry, although she would call me "Dan." Can you believe that? You can believe that, as I was growing up, I never let any of my friends know my middle name was technically Elizabeth. I guess you might say that my official name (according to my mother) for some twenty-six years was Dan Elizabeth Perry, although I always signed my full name as Daniel Elijah Perry. It wasn't until the North Carolina Bar Examiners noticed the discrepancy in my signature and birth certificate that the matter was finally settled. I had to go through a court proceeding to change my name officially to Daniel Elijah Perry to conform to my signature before I was allowed to take the bar exam to become a lawyer. So much for my name!

Some of My First Remembrances

"They say" you are at least two years old before you can begin remembering things, so I guess I must have been at least two. Amazingly enough, I remember the first time I realized who my middle brother was. I remember we were playing in the nursery, and it came to me all of a sudden, like a light coming on, that the bigger boy I was playing with was my brother. He was not just another little boy. He was my brother! Everyone knew him as "Bud" and not as we later called him, Ely Jr. He was five years older than I (born June 4, 1926). My oldest brother, Warren, was seven years older than I (born March 25, 1924).

It's interesting to note that everybody in Kinston whose name was "Bud" or "Buddy" was so named by Abi Metts, a well-known black nurse. She had the reputation of being *the* nurse to get when newborns came into the world. Those were the names she gave all of "her children." Not only was there Bud Perry, but also Bud Wooten, Buddy Taylor, Buddy Wallace, Buddy Storm, Buddy Hill, and several others.

The first nurse I can remember was Irene Hart. She was a very nice, black teenager who stayed overnight in our home from time to time, and was our official babysitter. We played together and I enjoyed her company. It's interesting to note that her boyfriend drove a black hearse when he came to see her at 908 West Road. His name was Robert Swinson Jr. of Swinson Funeral Home. They later married and their grandson, Robert Swinson, IV, is now serving on the Kinston City Council.

- I also faintly remember my across-the-street neighbor, Z. A. Collins Jr.

- being put in my crib (we must have been at least two) and later being told that Z. A.'s daddy, Zollie, said something like, "Boy, they'd make a good boxing pair, wouldn't they!"
- I also have a vague recollection of getting my face and hands all messed up while mother was feeding me in my high chair.
- The first Christmas I can remember Mama was talking about writing a letter to Santa Claus. Warren and Bud could write a little something, but Mama had to write mine. After explaining who Santa Claus was she asked me, "What do you want Santa Claus to bring you?" All I can remember was toys and candy. We all hung our stockings, with a little help from Mama. My own little sock was way too small, so Mama had to borrow one of Warren's for me.

The Night I Saw Santa Claus

A Christmas or so later, I remember the excitement of going to bed early to try to go to sleep so Santa Claus would come. It was dark all around me, but I got up and looked out the window, up into the clear starry sky. I was thinking if I looked real hard maybe, just maybe, I could see Santa Claus and his sleigh flying around up there. Much to my amazement, my wildest dream came true! There he was, if only for a brief moment, streaking across the sky like a comet! Yes, I actually saw Santa Claus! He and his sleigh and reindeer zipped from my right to my left at about a 60-degree angle in the sky. I remember it was only in the "twinkling of an eye," but I saw him! I did! I know I did! I can still remember the feeling and the excitement I experienced in telling Mama and Daddy on Christmas Day. They both shared my excitement because they knew I was telling the truth.

"The Night before Christmas"

One of our earliest family traditions, which continued for several years, was Mama gathering Warren, Bud, and me around her on the couch and reading, "The Night before Christmas." When the time came for her to read that story, we knew Christmas was getting close. I enjoyed the pictures about as much as

I did hearing the poem read. I could just visualize the whole story unfolding from beginning to end. In fact, it didn't take me long before I could "read" the caption under each page. I had it all memorized. Oh, they thought I was so smart! Look at Dan read. Why, he hasn't even started school yet and he can already read! "The Night Before Christmas," originally known as "A Visit From St. Nicholas," by Clement Moore has stayed with me all through the years, even to this very day. It is still a part of my Christmas celebration. Secular as it may be, it still has spiritual overtones in my life.

908 West Road

My birthplace and childhood home was 908 West Road. Z. A. (Zollie Albert) Collins lived at 909 West Road and Charles Wickham lived at 907 West Road. Z. A. was always "the little boy who lived across the street," and we played together every day. "Charlie Wick" was about three years younger than Z. A. and I; so we were really the "big boys" in the neighborhood while Charlie Wick was the "little boy" who lived next to Z. A. My first memory of Charlie Wick was while the Wickhams were building their house. We (the Perrys, Collins, and Wickhams) were in Z. A.'s front yard just standing around watching Charlie Wick run around in the yard. He must have just started to learn to run, because he would run a few steps and fall, get up and run some more and fall. I remember asking his daddy why he kept falling. "What's wrong with him?" Mr. Wickham tried to explain to me in his own quiet way, "He's tripping himself. One foot gets caught in the other. He's just learning. He'll get better."

Face Men

Z. A. and I used to play "Face Men" with Charlie Wick—or I should say we would play "Face Men" *against* Charlie Wick. Z. A. and I were into comic books—"Superman," "Captain Marvel," and all the others. For some reason, we called all of them "Face Men." I became known as "The Red Tornado," but I can't remember who Z. A. was. But anyway, Captain Marvel was my real hero. I had Mama make me a Captain Marvel cape; it really looked exactly like the one Captain Marvel wore. I had a pair of long johns, which Mama dyed red to match Captain Marvel's outfit, and for all practical purposes I became Captain Marvel (at least as far as Z. A. and I were concerned). We even tried to create some kind of smoke to appear when I said "SHAZAM" (like Billy Batson would say in the comic book), but we never could get it to work. That didn't make any difference to us. I still became Captain Marvel when I said "SHAZAM," and our greatest pleasure was to fool Charlie Wick. Z. A. would hold his attention while I disappeared around the corner, said "SHAZAM," hurriedly put on my disguise and reappear before their very eyes as Captain Marvel himself. Charlie Wick never let on that he knew it was really Dan Perry. After a brief appearance as Captain Marvel, I would very cleverly disappear around the corner and reappear as one of the neighborhood boys. Boy, did we have ol' Charlie Wick fooled! Z. A. and I would later enjoy talking about our great deception and lay out our next strategy.

We even had plans for me to appear on the roof of my house with my hands on my hips, with my cape gently flowing in the breeze. Below, Z. A. would be talking to Charlie Wick, then suddenly exclaim excitedly, "Look, there's Captain Marvel!" But as you can imagine, our plan never materialized. Mama somehow caught wind of it all and nixed our plan. Besides that, when I went to check it out, it was not a very practical thing to do. It was just too much of a chore to go through the window to get to the roof. It was apparently too hard to do, even for a big six-year-old. But, to this day I can still see in my mind's eye the picture of Captain Marvel standing majestically on the roof top with legs spread apart, hands on hips, cape flowing in the breeze, and peering down at the crowd as they all stood there in utter amazement. What a thrill that was (and still is)!

The Spinach Episode

One day when we were about five or six, I crossed the street to visit Z. A. His maid, "Lucy" (I believe that was her name), had fixed us lunch. Both Zollie and Big Roland were gone for some reason, and Z. A. and I were all alone in his cubbyhole breakfast room, about the size of ours. We were sitting on opposite sides of the table. The only food I remember on my plate was spinach.

Z. A. kept telling me it was the food Popeye ate. It was supposed to be good for you, and better than that, it would give you muscles and make you strong. Lucy was in the kitchen. I took a bite of spinach. Uuh! I didn't like it! Z. A. didn't either. The next thing I knew, he was throwing a bit of the green stuff against the wall behind me, and I was throwing it against the wall behind him. He would throw some, and I would throw some. He would throw some and I would throw some. We did that until all our spinach was gone. Both walls were a mess! To our surprise, most of it stuck. I can't remember what happened next. I guess Lucy must have cleaned it up because we, or at least I, never heard anything from Mr. or Mrs. Collins.

Playing with Matches

If you think Z. A. and Dan were bad boys with the spinach episode, wait until you hear this.

One day, we couldn't have been over four or five, possibly six, Z. A. came over and showed me something I had never seen before. It was a pack of safety matches. He wanted to show me how it worked. We were careful not to be too close to home, because we didn't want anyone to see us. I remember we ended up under the old persimmon tree, which was a whole block away behind my house at the edge of Carey Road. It was almost seventy years ago, but I still can remember it with at least some vague clarity. Z. A. flipped opened the pack, and after several tries, finally struck a match and placed it under a leaf, but it went out. After about four or five unsuccessful tries, Z.A. came to the conclusion that it was too damp because of the morning dew, or maybe the previous night's drizzle.

We certainly didn't want to give up because we were exploring new horizons. The anticipated thrill led me to suggest, "Why don't we go to my house where it's dry? It'll probably work there." So we scampered back to my house with our devilish little scheme. I don't remember seeing Mama at all. We went into the nursery, and after a few minutes of messing around, I found a piece of hemp rope about ten to twelve inches long. That would be perfect! The edges were stringy, and besides that, it was very dry. Naturally, we didn't want anybody to see us, so I suggested we go in the closet and close the door. We'd be safe there. Nobody would see us. At first we had to crack the door so Z. A. could see how to strike the match. He was able to light several matches, but they all went out after a few seconds.

Finally, we did manage to get a little glow to appear on the rope for a few seconds, but that was about it. No matter how hard we tried, all our efforts failed. We just couldn't get the blaze we wanted to see. So, we shut the closet door and innocently played in the nursery, fully confident that the incident was over and maybe we would try again later under more ideal circumstances.

It wasn't long before I heard Mama saying something from the kitchen, something about smelling smoke. I remember it not even registering with me as to what she was talking about. Z. A. and I were just innocently playing with our toys, having a good time.

Mama hurriedly came into the nursery, sniffing around as she exclaimed, "I smell smoke, where is it coming from?" I still didn't connect our dastardly deed with her smelling smoke. But I could tell she was beginning to panic. What was this all about? Why was she so excited? Why was she interrupting our playtime? Then it happened! After checking in all the corners of the room, she flung open the closet door. Much to my surprise, a massive gush of smoke came pouring out of the closet. Then it occurred to me. Did Z. A. and I have anything to do with all that smoke? Then I began to realize that, yeah, I'll bet you those matches and that hemp rope could have something to do with it.

Mama rushed back to the kitchen to get a pan of water and whatever else she could find to alleviate the problem. Z. A. and I stood back in holy horror. Finally, Mama was able to get everything under control. The whole house now smelled like smoke. I don't remember how long it took for her to ask the ultimate question of the two little boys who had been so quietly playing and minding their own business. I don't remember her exact question, but it was something like, "Do you know anything about this?" She had checked out the floor of the nursery closet and there was the evidence: a small piece of hemp rope with one end charred and blackened, with a whole bunch of burned matter lying around with the empty match cover, all in plain view.

When she showed us the black burned spot in the middle of the floor, I knew our goose was cooked!

I don't remember too much about any display of great anger Mama showed. In fact, I'm thinking that in her own loving and gentle way, she sent me to my room to think about what we had done; and she sent Z. A. home to "tell your mama all about it." Z. A. ended up getting a spanking when his daddy came home. I never got a spanking for it, but I do remember my daddy making it perfectly clear that I could have burned our house down and that I was never to do anything like that again. Daddy's little talk put me to shame and must have been effective, because even though Z. A. and I did many other "bad things" as a pair of little boys, at least we never played with matches again!

The Rock Throwing Incident

Another stupid and childish thing Z. A. and I did happened several years later. We went to a party one time at Betsy Britt's house when she lived on the Westside of North Queen Street, somewhere in the area where the Mutual Savings and Loan building would later be located. I believe it may have been the same house in which Marion and Lillian Parrott started their married life together. Anyway, there were both boys and girls at the party, so I guess we must have been at least eleven or twelve. Z. A. and I got bored, and we went outside to check things out. Evidently, there was some new construction going on because I remember a pile of sand and some small rocks right next to the road. We were just talking and passing the time, and, as boys will do, we picked up some rocks and began throwing them—at no target in particular—just throwing rocks (I believe "pebbles" might be a better term). I remember seeing an occasional car go by, and somehow I was challenged to see if I could hit a moving car. I figured I would probably miss, so I saw no reason not to try it. One of my first targets was a car going north in the far lane. I remember throwing a rock or two at one or two other cars. Z. A. joined in and we both were having a bit of innocent fun—or at least we thought it was innocent. We didn't think too much about it until we noticed a car slowly approaching us. It stopped next to where we were, and a man got out. I don't remember his being particularly mad, for he seemed rather calm. His first words were, "Do you boys know you hit my car back there?" We didn't deny it, but I remember being dumbfounded. How could that be? He said a few more words of warning and caution and then he popped the question of all questions to us: "Who is your daddy?" Thankfully, I could remember his name, even though I was scared to death—"Ely Perry." Then looking straight at Z. A. with a little more emotion, he asked him the same question, "and who is your daddy, young man?" Z. A. was also somehow able to give the correct answer—"Zollie Collins." He asked us where we lived, and with that I was really beginning to get worried. I could just picture him taking us both home and knocking on the door and asking to speak to Ely Perry. We were both in shock, and any words we spoke after that were almost inaudible. I remember praying an inward prayer: "Please don't let him tell my daddy." I didn't know what I'd do if he told my daddy. "Please don't let him tell my daddy," I begged again! Well, the Lord must have heard me because his only other words to us were but a final warning, "and don't you ever do anything like that again!" I'm glad Daddy went to his grave without ever knowing of my foolish rock-throwing episode. There was a certain kindness, yet firmness, about that man that left a lasting impression on me. I must have learned a good lesson, for I never had any desire to throw rocks at a moving car again.

More Early Memories

One of the things I remember about the Great Depression during the early 1930s is the W. P. A. I think it was officially called the "Works Progress Administration," which was one of President Roosevelt's programs designed to give employment to the jobless. I remember seeing a bunch of men leaning on shovels while another man shoveled dirt in the front of our house on West Road before it was paved. Progress was slow so we nicknamed the W. P. A. the "We Poke Along."

I remember when downtown Queen Street was cobblestone and later was bricked before it was paved. There were two monuments in the middle of

Queen Street. One was a Civil War soldier, which was located on top of the hill in the middle of the intersection of Summitt Avenue and Queen Street; the other was an obelisk in the intersection of Caswell Street and Queen Street. I remember how Daddy would frequently take us on a family-after-supper outing and drive from one end of Queen Street to the other so as to circle the monuments. I understand from local historian Bill Rowland, that the Civil War soldier was captioned, "Through the Eyes of a Soldier." It was moved in about 1938 to the east side of the intersection of Queen Street and Highland Avenue near the swimming pool, and later moved to its present location at the Ram Neuse site on Highway 70 West.

In the process of moving the obelisk monument to its present location on the grounds of the St. John's Masonic Lodge on north Queen Street, the top part broke into three main pieces. They can be seen there today.

Greene's Barber Shop

My first few haircuts were given to me by Daddy. About all I remember is that he used hand clippers and they pinched my neck. When I was old enough to get a "real big boy" haircut in the middle 1930s, Mama would drop Warren, Bud, and me off at Greene's Barber Shop in the 100 block of East Gordon Street. The going rate at the time was 25 cents, and she would give each of us a quarter to take care of the bill. Greene's was owned by Mr. Jim Cogdell who worked the far end chair. There were five chairs, all the barbers were black, and back then they had the reputation of being the most popular barbershop in town. I ended up settling in with Clarence Maye, and over a period of many years we became good friends. He was always cordial and pleasant with all his customers and our close relationship extended well into my adult years until his death sometime in the 1970s. When he became sick with cancer, I remember visiting him at the University Hospital in Chapel Hill. After Clarence's death, I went to James Aitch, who was also an excellent barber and friend. I continued with James until we moved our law office from 106 West Gordon Street in 1986 to the Kinston Plaza Shopping Center.

Afterwards, I started going to P. H. Pigford at the Model Art Barber Shop at the Plaza. I hated to leave James on East Gordon Street, because Greene's Barber Shop had always been a way of life for me. But convenience won out, and I've been with P. H. ever since. He has the reputation of being an excellent barber and the hardest working of them all. Monday through Saturday, he's usually working on the job from 7:30 in the morning until 11 o'clock at night. Obviously, he loves his work! I'm confident in saying that he gives more haircuts than any other barber in town. Back in the 1930s when I was paying 25 cents at Greene's Barber Shop, Jim Cogdell's young son Jimmy (later also known as "Jim") was the shoeshine boy. He was probably three or four years older than I, red headed, and very popular with all the customers. When he became old enough, he followed in his father's footsteps and became an excellent barber until his death in the 1970s. Recently, while I was reminiscing with P. H. Pigford about Greene's Barber Shop and its heydays in the 1930s, 1940s, and 1950s (and beyond), he confirmed its popularity. He said he thought it may have first opened its door sometime in the late 1920s. By the way, I think I'm correct in saying that some time in the late 1960s, Jim Cogdell's brother, Harold, became the first black police officer in Kinston.

Saturday Afternoon Movies

As Z. A. and I grew up in the 1930s and 1940s, Saturday afternoon cowboy movies were a big part of our lives. Every Saturday we looked forward to having either his mother or my mother drive us to the Carolina Theater. After we were old enough and could be trusted, we would usually ride our bicycles if the weather was good. The custom was for all our friends to meet at the movies, or "picture show" as we often called it. The theater would be full of young folks, yelling and screaming at the bad guys and pulling for the good guys to catch them. Some of our heroes were Johnny Mack Brown, Bob Steele, and Red Ryder. They were the good guys who wore white hats and were always after the bad guys. Two of my least favorites were Gene Autry and Roy Rogers. They were good guys, but they were just not rough enough and tough enough to be real cowboys—and besides that they were always playing a guitar and singing songs. My idea of a true cowboy didn't include singing. Although Jesse James was a bad guy, I always seemed to pull for him to get away (and he did up until the very last). One of the big drawing cards that created interest and excitement was the serials, which were continued each week. We couldn't wait to get back the following Saturday to see how the Lone Ranger escaped from being thrown over the cliff, or how "Copper Head," who was tied to the conveyor belt, freed himself from being split from head to foot as he approached, ever nearer, the twirling chain saw.

Z.A.'s Version of "Haircuts and Movies"

After writing about some of my early memories, I decided to send a copy to Z.A. to see if he agreed with my recollections. He didn't make any changes, but he was kind enough to suggest I add a couple of paragraphs that he entitled "Haircuts and Movies." Actually, my two sections on "Greene's Barber Shop" and "Saturday Afternoon Movies" were written after his reminder. Here is Z.A.'s version written from my perspective as he suggested:

Back in 1944 when we were 13 years of age, our mothers had decided to allow us to ride our bikes downtown to get our haircuts. Once a month, we would head out on this trip, which was about two miles away. Haircuts cost 35 cents all over town, but I had found a barber who would cut hair for 25 cents. I told Z.A. about this, so when our mothers gave us 35 cents to get our haircuts, we would head for the cheap barber shop. With the remaining 10 cents, we decided to go to the movies, which cost 9 cents. With the one cent left over, we would buy a tootsie roll. Our mothers always asked us why it took so long to get a haircut and we said we ran into friends and played around with them, and forgot about the time.

I remember when Z.A. and I saw the movie *National Velvet* starring Elizabeth Taylor and Mickey Rooney. It was about horses in a steeplechase race in Ireland. It was a great movie. The horses ran on this beautiful, grassy racetrack and jumped over these hedges. We just loved it. On the way back home on our bikes, we decided that we would get our ponies and use my front yard to race since I had a hedge on one end of the front yard. It worked out perfectly. We would run up and down the entire length of my yard and jump the hedge and turn around and do it again, over and over again! When mother got home several hours later and came out front, she said, "Stop this right now!! You have destroyed my front yard; it looks like it has been plowed up for spring planting, and the hedge is beyond repair. Z. A., you take that pony home, and I am going to call your mother and tell her what you two boys have done. Dan, you take the pony back to the stable and go to your room indefinitely!!" You might say that was the end of our steeplechase days.

Chapter II

ON TO GRAMMAR SCHOOL

My formal school education began in the fall of 1937. I had reached the ripe age of six on July 2. Z. A. was six on May 30th, so we were both ready for this new stage in our lives. I remember Mama taking me to the Harvey School auditorium on the first day, where teacher assignments were made. I was excited when Mama told me I had gotten Mrs. Guthrie. Everybody said she was really good. Z. A. and I would be in the same class. We called them "rooms" back then and not "classes." Yes, we would be in the same room at school. "Hot dog!" We were really excited!

I remember Mrs. Guthrie introducing herself to the class and telling us (about 20 of us) how happy she was to be our teacher. She said that we would be learning to read and write, and we were all going to have a good time together. We didn't stay long that first morning, but she said she would see us the next morning at 9 o'clock. She said she would have on the same yellow dress in case we forgot what she looked like.

The next day, Z. A. and I rode our bicycles to school. I was real impressed because he knew exactly where to go and how to get there. I'm sure I would have gotten lost if it hadn't been for him. We were now schoolboys!

These are some of my recollections of the first grade:
- Although I pretty much knew my ABCs before first grade, I didn't understand how they formed words. The sound of the various letters and the forming of words from those letters was very interesting to me.

- The first road sign I remember reading was when Z. A. and I went with Zollie (his daddy) to the brickyard. From time to time, we would go with him on Highway 70 somewhere around Dover and play around while Zollie took care of business at the brickyard. It was a lot of fun seeing them put soft clay bricks in the kilns and taking them out all red and hard. That was a learning experience for us. The first time we went to the brickyard after starting school, Zollie asked us what we were learning in school. "Have you learned to read yet?" Just about that time, we were approaching a "U.S. 70" road sign. Z. A. and I both met the challenge at about the same time. "Yeah, that road sign says 'us' 70!" That became one of Zollie's all time favorite stories about Z. A. and Dan learning to read. He seemed so proud of us when he would tell the story of our reading "us" 70.
- We learned to write by the Palmer System. Mrs. Guthrie had a beautiful handwriting, as she would demonstrate each letter on the blackboard. The whole alphabet, capital and small letters, was on display on cardboard around the room. She showed us how to do "push pulls" and "round rounds" to help us learn the knack of writing the Palmer way.
- Mrs. Guthrie told us about raising our hand if we wanted to ask a question or talk. If we needed to go to the bathroom, we should raise our right hand and show two fingers. She would not stop the class, but just nod her head and softly give her permission, "Yes, you may go."
- Although sometimes we maybe got a little noisy, I never remember her having a problem with discipline. But, there was one time she had to leave the room for a few minutes. She told us to be real quiet and not to leave our seats before she returned. Before she came back, Billy Ross was crawling around on one of the tables and the whole class was getting a little rowdy. Mrs. Guthrie didn't like it when she suddenly appeared… but it didn't take her long to calm everybody down.
- We studied reading, writing and arithmetic. We also had a class period for drawing. I liked to color and draw, but for some reason I never could get a top grade in drawing. I would generally get all "1's" in everything

except drawing. Most of the time I would get a 2 or a 2+. Occasionally I would get a 2 in conduct, but when Daddy would get on me, I would most of the time pull it up to a 1 or 1-. I don't think it was until the fourth grade, under Mrs. Maude Hooker, that I was able to get all 1's. That included a 1 in drawing! Daddy would give me a dime for every "1" I got on my report so I would make about 80 or 90 cents each month. I can't remember how many subjects we were graded on.

- Charlie Larkins was left-handed and it always fascinated me to see him go to the blackboard and write a "2". There was something about the way he held that piece of chalk and swirled his whole left arm around with a smooth, graceful motion. I often thought how much fun it would be to be left-handed. I even tried it several times, but it just didn't work. I was a born right-hander, and no matter how hard I tried, I couldn't make the change.
- Some friends of the family once asked me what was my favorite subject: reading or 'rithmatic or what? "No," I said with little hesitation, "I like recess the best!" Everybody always looked forward to recess so we could go out and play. We played dodge ball, kickball, tag, and several other running games. In the higher grades, we played baseball, softball, and football.

We boys were beginning to notice girls. The way Katherine Armstead kept smiling at me made me start thinking. Why was she always smiling at me? And it was a pretty smile too! She probably smiled at all the boys, but the way she seemed to focus her attention on me made me think, "I guess she must like me." I never remember being seated next to her. She was always a couple of rows away. I guess she was my first childhood sweetheart. I was quite bashful when it came to girls, but somehow I managed to return a glimpse and half smile back in Katherine's direction. Z. A. seemed to take a special liking to Dot Smith. Then there was Margie Ferrell, Ursula Spence, Evelyn Oettinger, Frances Lonon, and Yalanta Broadwell, to name a few. Z. A. and I were too interested in sports to be really interested in girls.

Miss Guthrie's husband ran Guthrie's filling station, located on the corner of Fairfield Avenue and Vernon Avenue. Mama would sometimes take me with her when driving down to the station to get a coke and some gas. Many times, Mrs. Guthrie would be there on Saturdays during the summer just to help Mr. Guthrie. I remember he would have to pump the gas in the clear tank, so you could see how many gallons you were getting. Most of the time, Mama would get 5 or 10 gallons of gas. I remember the price being 17 cents a gallon and later it went up as high as 18 cents. I think I recall some of the "old timers" remembering when it was as low as 13 cents a gallon.

One day, while playing outside at recess, Gene Potter was all excited when he told us that Lewis School had burned down. The rest of us got excited, too, as we began to think—hey, maybe Harvey school will burn down, too, and we won't have to go to school anymore. It wasn't that we hated school so much. It was just the idea and prospect of not having to go to school was that exciting, because we could play all the time and not have to worry about getting up every morning and spending all day at school. We could see in our mind's eye those children at Lewis School not having to go to school ever again. As luck would have it, we never got our wish.

Miss Hobgood and Brer Rabbit

One of the highlights of grades one through six at Harvey School was going to the school auditorium once or twice a week to hear announcements, to sing familiar songs, and to have special programs from time to time. It was always a favorite of the whole school when our Principle, Miss Hobgood, told us stories, for she was a great storyteller. I can hear her now telling us about Brer Rabbit, Brer Fox, Tar Baby, and Sis Cow and all the related characters. She had all of the sound effects down pat for each character. We loved to hear Brer Rabbit plead with Brer Fox after being caught in a trap, "Please, please, Brer Fox, do whatever you want with me, but just don't throw me in the briar patch! Oh, please don't throw me in the briar patch!" We all knew that's exactly where he wanted to be even though in Brer Fox's mind the sharp, prickly briars would surely be a horrid punishment for the little varmint, just short of death. It was always a relief when Brer Fox finally threw ole Brer Rabbit in the briar patch. He had escaped Brer Fox's clutches one more time!

The Two Times I Fooled My Teacher

Generally, I made pretty good grades in school, but not because I was all that smart. I guess I was conscientious and knew my mama and daddy were expecting me to do well, or at least my very best. I never did very well on achievement tests and I. Q. tests, but somehow I got by and must have given the impression that I was pretty smart. Most of the girls in our class were considered smarter than most of us boys. Sandy Peak was probably the smartest boy in our class in grammar school.

Z.A. nick-named Ann Bennett "Dictionary" and Barbara Ann Larkins "Encyclopedia" because they seemed to know all the right answers.

One time in the second grade, I got ahead of them all. I got the right answer. Miss Marston was telling us about Abraham Lincoln and what a great president he was. She asked the question, "Does anyone know in what state he was born?" Nobody said anything, so she continued, "Was it Virginia? Was it Tennessee? Was it Minnesota?" She named several other states, each time pausing a little to see if anyone would venture a guess. Finally she said, "Was it Kentucky?" I didn't have any idea where Abraham Lincoln was born, but I detected her facial expression as she said "Kentucky." Her eyebrows went up and her eyes got a little bigger, just enough for me to confidently and without hesitation raise my hand and almost shout, "It was Kentucky!" "Good boy, Dan. You are exactly right!" Miss Marston seemed so pleased that I had the right answer. Maybe some of the others saw it in her eyes, too, but I happened to be the one to get the answer and the approval of the teacher.

The second time I really fooled the teacher, we were in Miss Fletcher's sixth grade Geography class. Without warning, she told us to get out our pencil and paper because she was going to give us a test. She wanted to find out if we had studied our assignment. We never had much homework in those early grades, but for whatever reason, I was totally unprepared and was beginning to panic. The fact that it was to be a true/false test gave me little consolation. She passed out the ten written questions with a space to mark true or false after each one. I read the first question; then the second; then the third. I had no clue as to what the right answer was for any of them. What was I going to do? I remember grumbling something under my breath—and then I remembered the nickel I happened to have in my pocket. Rather than guessing my way through each question, I decided to flip the nickel and play heads or tails. Heads it was true and tails it was false. That was as good as I could do at this point. I'd just have to take my chances and go for it. I slyly sneaked the nickel out of my pocket. As far as I could tell, nobody saw me look down at the palm of my left hand each time before I recorded the answer. Of the ten questions asked, I was absolutely at a loss as to what any of the correct answers were. Ten questions; ten flips or shakes of the coin; and ten answers. That was the way it went. Time was up. We had to turn in our papers. It was all over. I remember leaving that classroom feeling down and dejected. It was a total disaster.

The next day when it came time for geography, Miss Fletcher stood before the class with the graded test papers in hand. She began telling us how disappointed she was with the results. Most everybody had failed. She said only one person got them all right. She continued to give us a hard time, then as she began passing out the papers, she commented that, "Dan Perry must have been the only one to have studied the assignment, because he's the only one in the class to get 100." As everyone began looking my way to express their silent congratulations, I was busy trying to hold back my feeling of shock, surprise, and amazement. Instead of appearing to say, "Who me? There must be some mistake!" I tried to fake it and show a quiet, modest confidence as if to say, "I don't want to brag, but I guess my preparation and hard work must have paid off."

Many years later I happened to be on a commercial flight on which Charlie Larkins was also a passenger. I believe Charlie was in the State Senate at the time. We sat next to each other, and he began telling me about Miss Fletcher and how sick she was. In fact, he thought her time was short. Charlie and I shared some pleasant memories about Miss Fletcher, so I was able to tell him my nickel-flipping test story. We both had a good laugh, and I told him I was going to write her a letter confessing how I fooled her on that memorable day. He gave me her address, and I wrote the letter a day or so later, telling her the whole story, detail by detail. I didn't want her to go to her grave thinking I was all that smart. I also told her how much I appreciated all her efforts as a teacher. I don't know if she got my letter or not, for I never heard anything from it. I was somehow hoping it got there in time for someone at least to read it to her before she passed on into eternity.

My Hero…Tarzan

Z. A. and I used to love to go to Tarzan movies. Johnny Weissmuller was Tarzan. The only problem was every time a Tarzan movie came to town, I would always get poison ivy. It didn't take me long to figure out the reason. After seeing a movie, Z. A. and I would find some vines to swing on across ditches, just like Tarzan. It was great fun seeing Tarzan in our imagination swinging through the woods and trees and giving his famous yell. Evidently, poison ivy was mixed up in there somewhere. I remember in the sixth grade getting it so bad on my face that my eyes were swollen shut for two days and I had to miss school. My hands and arms and legs were all affected. It was a terrible time, but at least I missed school and a few people even felt sorry for me. I heard about one classmate (I think it was George Patrick) who bragged about being immune to poison ivy. He would play around it and touch it and even rub the leaves on his arm, but he never got infected. One day he took his bragging too far! He said, "Look, I can even eat it and I won't get it!" Well, as I understand it, the next day he broke out in a terrible rash. I don't think his mouth was swollen shut, but his whole face turned red and puffy for several days. It's for sure he never tried that stunt again!

My First Broken Bone

Another time, I believe it was during the summer after the first or second grade, Z. A. and I were practicing flying through the air like our hero, Tarzan. We were in Thornton Hood's yard playing on a mimosa tree right across the street and up the hill from Z. A.'s house. There was this long limb, which stretched almost parallel to the ground. I had dived to the limb several times from a certain perch in the tree. It was great fun flying through the air after catching the limb and swinging back and forth two or three times before jumping to the ground.

As fate would have it, I jumped one too many times. My grip must have slipped because before I knew it, I was on the ground holding my left arm, in rather intense pain. I don't remember crying a lot, but I do know I went home to see if Mama would kiss it and make it well. She did what she could, but it still hurt right around the elbow area. After a few minutes, she decided to take me downtown to let Dr. West take a look at it. He was my uncle through marriage to my Aunt Susie (Daddy's sister) who lived up the hill from us and across West Road from Thornton Hood's house.

Dr. West was always available whenever anyone was sick or hurt. I remember his welcoming Mama and me and escorting us to his backroom where he had what he explained to me was an X-ray machine. He said he was going to take a picture of my arm. I didn't know what good that would do as far as helping the pain, but, anyway, I remember holding my arm against some sort of screen for a few seconds, then I sat on the table holding my arm—just waiting, not thinking about anything in particular. I heard Mama and Dr. West talking in a low voice while looking at the picture. I overheard him say something like "It's broken. You can see right here." It's a funny thing, but I thought he was talking about the X-ray machine. I thought he was telling Mama that the X-ray machine was broken, so I figured the whole trip down town was for naught. We'll just have to come back later after he's fixed the X-ray machine or gotten a new one. But then he said, "We'll have to set it." I didn't know what he was talking about, but in a few minutes he explained that it was my left elbow that was broken, and he'd have to put some "plaster of Paris" around most of my arm. It would be in a cast, so I wouldn't be able move it. He said it would take about six weeks to heal. Six weeks! You mean I'd have to have that white thing going from my mid arm almost to my wrist for six weeks? That's what he said, and that's the way it was. But all was not bad. Quite a few of my friends signed their names (as best they could, being only six or seven)—and, of course, I felt somewhat of a hero with all the sympathy I was getting.

You can well imagine after six weeks the cast was plenty dirty and almost falling apart. When Dr. West cut the cast off with surgical scissors, I remember my first reaction upon seeing my arm. It was shriveled up and looked like mere skin and bone—and dirty skin at that. It was a pitiful sight! I couldn't believe that was my arm. The dead skin was all gray and brown and almost black in places. Anyway, after cleaning it up, Dr. West told me I was going to be all right. "Just be patient," he said. Since the arm had been set in a bent position so long, it was stiff and I was unable to straighten it out. I remember it being a good long process, but finally after several days, I was able to straighten it enough to reach my pocket. I was finally getting well. I knew it wouldn't take long now. So much for my first broken bone.

Chapter III

FAMILY LIFE AT 908 WEST ROAD

A year or so after Mama and Daddy were married in 1922, they built the home place known as "908 West Road." The property was part of the Perry Farm, which Daddy, Aunt Susie, and Aunt Bliss inherited from my grandfather, Daniel Elijah Perry.

The house itself, by today's standards, was a small, modest, brick house. It started out as a two-bedroom, one-bathroom house. I think it was after I came along that they added a "sleeping porch" off of the master bedroom to accommodate their three boys. Mama's mother, whom we called "Grandmother Seipp," lived in Towson, Maryland, where Mother grew up. When she came to visit us, she would sleep in the guest room. I believe it was after the original house was built that they added a toilet and sink to the guest room because in the early days I never remember using any bathroom but the one all five of us used. It's rather amazing that I never remember anyone complaining about feeling we were cramped for space. We would just wait our turn to use the bathroom. That's the way it was back in those days.

Our main source of heat was what we called an "Arcola," an upright cast iron contraption, which burned coal. It was located on one side of the kitchen area. We also had two coal-burning fireplaces, one located in a small room we called "the playroom or nursery" and the other in the living room. The two fireplaces backed up to each other, but it was not a see-through arrangement. I'm quite convinced that none of the heat from the Arcola or two fireplaces ever reached the sleeping porch, because the main thing I remember about the sleeping porch was that it was always cold. I frankly don't remember any of us making a big deal over being cold when the outside temperature got below freezing. I never knew how cold it got on the sleeping porch. We just bundled up as best we could and kept going. In the cold of winter, Mama would put some blankets and a couple of quilts over us, and we'd get along just fine—except for our feet (or at least my feet)! Frequently, my feet and toes would feel like they were frozen. (Twenty-five years later, I remember that same "frozen feeling" while sleeping in a tent in Korea, but I'll tell you about that later.) We all just took the frigid nights and frozen feet as being in the normal course of things. Warren, Bud, and I all slept in the same bed for a while, but later Warren graduated to the guest room, and Bud and I got separate beds on the "sleeping porch."

I vaguely remember having an icebox to keep milk and other foods cold. The iceman would routinely make his rounds in a horse-drawn delivery truck and bring us blocks of ice. When we finally got an electric refrigerator, we thought we were really high class. It was a real modern convenience!

Family Time

We had a big stand-up cabinet radio that we all gathered around and listened to after supper. I can still hear the introduction of Jack Benny and the announcer saying "J-E-L-L-O—the Jello program starring Jack Benny and Mary Livingstone with Rochester...." As a family, we also listened to "Edgar Bergen and Charlie McCarthy" and "Fibber McGee and Molly." A lot of times Mama and Daddy would play gin rummy while they listened. These were family times together, which we all enjoyed.

Some of my personal radio favorites were "The Green Hornet"; "The Shadow Knows," with Lamont Cranston; "Mister District Attorney," with Lyn Doyle; and "Father Flanagan's Boys' Town." But my absolute favorite was "The Lone Ranger" and his faithful companion Tonto. I never missed hearing him if I could help it.

Those were the times when families did a lot of things together, and it was one of the reasons why all five of us in the Ely Perry family were always very close in our relationship with each other—for which I have been eternally grateful.

I well remember our small cubbyhole breakfast room and the five of us having our meals together. We always started each meal with a blessing, for Mama and Daddy, as well as Grandmother Seipp, taught us early in life that we should be thankful for everything we have and because everything comes from God. Our traditional family blessing, which we all said together, was, "God is great, God is good. Let us thank Him for our food. Amen." We later expanded it by adding the words: "By His goodness we are fed, give us God our daily bread. Amen."

We three boys grew up drinking milk, and lots of it, every day. Daddy had helped Elmer Wooten get his dairy started by buying him two or three cows. In return, Mr. Wooten would bring us six quarts of milk and a pint of cream every day, seven days a week. We would have it on our cereal each morning and have an additional glass or two with our regular breakfast of bacon and eggs, as well as drink a glass or two with our other meals. I remember many times coming home from school on a hot day and drinking a quart of milk at one sitting (most of the time, I just stood around in the kitchen drinking milk and talking with Mama). It just went right on down. I've always enjoyed drinking milk, even to this day. It still amazes me to think that the five of us consumed six quarts of milk and a pint of cream each day! Every morning those glass bottles would be sitting on our front porch. That was before pasteurized and homogenized milk, and we would have to shake the bottle so the cream on the top would be mixed with the milk.

A Love Affair That Never Ended

I have many happy memories of growing up in a loving and supportive family. Mama and Daddy loved each other, and they demonstrated their love for each other and their three boys on a daily basis. Many times I would hear Daddy say, "Look at her, ain't she pretty!…Just as pretty as a speckled pup…." He was always bragging on Mama and saying nice things about her in front of others, as well as us three boys. She was always **Number One,** and he made us feel that our whole family life revolved around her.

How They Met

One of my biggest regrets is not recording Daddy's version of how he and Mother first met and their courtship that followed. Daddy's face always lit up when he told it. Elizabeth Ann Seipp grew up in Towson, Maryland, a suburb of Baltimore. She graduated from Hood College in Frederick, Maryland, in 1921. Aunt Susie was attending college at nearby Notre Dame in Baltimore (not the one at South Bend), and somehow had met and become close friends with Mother. When Aunt Susie invited her to come to Kinston for an extended visit, she naturally wanted Elizabeth to meet her friends and show her some good ol' southern hospitality. That's where her younger brother came in. She asked Daddy to fix her up with a date with some of his friends each afternoon and night so to keep her from getting bored. So Daddy had it all arranged. He was not all that interested in going out with one of his sister's friends, so he didn't include himself in the line up of dates. Finally, the big day came for the arrival of Aunt Susie's house guest, Elizabeth Seipp. Daddy, Aunt Susie, and (I assume) several other family members were on hand at the station excitedly waiting for the train. Now, here's where the story picks up steam. Daddy says that when Mother stepped off that train, he saw the most beautiful girl he had ever seen! He couldn't believe his eyes! That was it! Love at first sight! It didn't take him long to realize he had to take immediate action. The first thing he did when he got home was to call all his friends and cancel their dates. He told them he appreciated their willingness to do him such a big favor, but other arrangements had been made and he would no longer need their services. The simple fact was he didn't want any of them butting into his private business. He wanted her all to himself. I never did know her schedule, but Daddy said he was with her "morning, noon, and night." He didn't want to let her out of his sight! An incident Daddy liked to tell was about the afternoon he had the Victrola in the parlor playing one of his favorites. When he saw Mother gracefully coming down the stairs, he met her at the foot of the steps, took her in his arms, and smoothly started dancing. He described her as being "light as a feather," and she "followed like a breeze." He was really smitten by this new girl from Baltimore, and he knew she was the one for him.

I don't know how many days Mother's visit lasted, but Daddy apparently was with her much of the time—or at least as much as he could. I don't know where Aunt Susie was all this time. Mother says that the day after her arrival back at Hood, or maybe it was a "day or so," she got a special delivery letter which started out, "A day, a week, a month, a year has passed since I last saw you." She says that for every day they were apart she got a letter each of those days, with a special delivery on Sunday. A story Mother liked to tell was about her father realizing his daughter was getting serious about her new boyfriend. He asked her to "tell me about him." Her reply was, "Well, I can't live with him, and I can't live without him." She was referring to the fact that although Daddy's persistence may have been a little overbearing at times, the bottom line was she loved him and wanted to marry him. They were married on October 14, 1922, and the rest is history. His love for her never faded. Several times, I heard him tell us boys, "I loved her the first time I saw her, and I love her even more now. She's prettier now than she's ever been."

I am grateful for the example Daddy set for us as a family. From time to time, he would tell Warren, Bud, and me, "You're to love both of us, but love your mama just a little bit more than your daddy, but I'm not far behind." Then he would hold up his thumb and index finger only a micro, indistinguishable distance apart and say, "Love your mama just a 'liiiittle' bit more than your daddy." I heard him say to us as well as others, "In all the years we've been married, we've never had an argument." Even when Mama would get a little irritated at him from time to time, I never heard her raise her voice or complain to any great extent. What an example for us boys!

Daddy was considered throughout the community to be a good businessman, and we were told how blessed we were to have a father who loved us and provided for our needs. Although I don't remember Mama bragging about Daddy the way he bragged about her, Daddy knew she was always loving and supportive of him in every way (except one). She didn't like his one bad habit, and that was chewing tobacco. From time to time, she would make it known in no uncertain terms that she didn't like it one bit!

Mama loved flowers and gardening. On many occasions, as Daddy would go to work in the spring time, they would walk out the backdoor together, look around at the garden next to the garage. She would pick him a small flower and put in his lapel, and then she would get in the car with him. He would back the old Chevrolet onto Perry Park Drive and slowly drive the fifty yards or so onto West Road, take a right and then slowly stop to kiss her goodbye. After a brief conversation he let her out to stroll back through the front yard to the house. The first time I saw them do that, I remember thinking, "Why in the world would they do that? To ride just that short distance. What was that all about?" But after a few times, I began to get the message: they were just enjoying being in each other's company. These are among my most treasured memories.

Whenever Daddy left for work he would kiss her goodbye. When he came home for lunch and supper, he would always greet her with a kiss. She was his sweetheart. and he called her "Sweetheart" in public as well as in private. When he called her on the telephone, his hello and goodbye always had a "sweetheart" in there somewhere. A few times I heard him call her "Dumps." I never could figure out what he meant by "dumps." I never asked him, but I guess he was saying "dumpling" or "sugar dumpling" or something of that nature. In any event, I'm sure it was a term of endearment meaning, "I love you, sweetheart."

I don't remember Mama (I later called her Mother) calling Daddy anything but "Ely." Although, I seldom saw her initiate any physical expression of love toward Daddy, she would always respond warmly to him. I guess she didn't need to initiate anything because he was constantly expressing his attraction toward her.

Warren, Ely, and I always got along well. I don't remember any sibling rivalry as we grew up, and our respect for each other carried on into our adult and business activities together. I do remember one time when Bud was teasing me about something and "picking" on his little brother, as he would do from time to time. I said, "I'll get you back one day. Just you wait 'til I grow up." I don't remember Warren "picking" on me like Bud used to do. Those "picking" times seemed to disappear when he outgrew the name "Bud," and became "Ely Jr." to me.

The Log Cabin out Back

Daddy used to take us all in his Chevrolet out for rides in the country to check out several farms that he had acquired. One day, he saw a rustic log cabin that attracted the attention of all of us. "Hey," we all seemed to be thinking in unison, "Wouldn't it be great to have a log cabin like that in our back yard." Of course, my thoughts were on playing cowboys and Indians. It looked exactly like some of the log cabins we had seen in the cowboy movies. Z. A. and I could really have a great time if we had a real log cabin like that to play in. It would fit into our play plans perfectly. Well, it didn't take long before Daddy stopped at the cabin and made inquiries as to who could build us such a get-away place. Shortly afterwards, Z. A. and I oversaw the construction of a nice little one-room log cabin with a big fireplace and mantle at one end. It was built in our back yard far enough away from the main house, our cowboy frontier! (Actually, it was only about 45 or 50 feet from the garage.)

Mother used the cabin to entertain her Sunday school class and other groups with cookouts. Warren and Ely Jr. had their friends over from time to time, but Z. A. and I and Robert Abbott, who had recently moved to a house nearby on Carey Road, used it to play cowboys and Indians. Robert had recently joined our neighborhood gang, and the three of us used to spend the night, and then fix our bacon and egg breakfast the next morning. We slept on army cots and had a great time. By the way, Charlie Wick was too young to join us older boys in spending the night in the cabin.

One night, we were awakened by several people talking and approaching the cabin. All of a sudden, somebody switched on the light and exclaimed, "Somebody's in here; let's get out of here!" They turned off the light and scampered away. We never found out who they were, but it sounded like some high school teenagers who were exploring around. I always figured they were some of Warren's crowd, somebody like Carl Wooten, Roland Paylor, John Hewitt, Neva Whitaker, and Joyce Wooten. I think I was about nine or ten years old at the time, so they would have been sixteen or seventeen or so, old enough to have a driver's license.

Along Came the War

I used to love to make airplane models when I was nine, ten, and eleven years old. They were made out of balsa wood, and we got them from Spears Sporting Goods down on Queen Street. One Sunday afternoon a little after five P.M., I was in the log cabin by myself working on an airplane model and listening to the Lone Ranger on the radio. It was December 7, 1941, and I was ten years old. I well remember the Lone Ranger being interrupted by a special announcement: "Early this morning the Japanese bombed Pearl Harbor!" I don't remember too much else about it, except my first thought was, "What is Pearl Harbor?" In my mind's eye I envisioned a big white pearl. I had no idea what the significance was. The following day in Miss Fletcher's fourth grade class, she had a radio and we listened to President Roosevelt's famous speech and heard him say, "December 7th, 1941, is a day that will live in infamy."

The war with Germany had been going on for a couple of years, and I remember making a scrapbook of daily clippings from the Free Press of various airplanes, not only American but also German and later Japanese airplanes.

One day while I was playing on the floor in the living room, Daddy was playing solitaire and listing to the radio. I'm not sure if it was soon after we declared war on Germany or several months preceding the war when Hitler was making the news and moving into prominence on the world scene. I do remember Daddy all of a sudden really showing his temper and yelling out, "They ought to kill him! Somebody ought to kill him!" I had never seen him, before or after, any madder than he was at that moment. I didn't have any idea what he was talking about, but I knew he meant business. Why would he want anybody to kill somebody else? This was totally out of character for him. He had taught me all about the Ten Commandments and that we should love one another and not hate. Killing? What was going on? That must have been in 1938 or 1939, when I was seven or eight, too young to have any great understanding of world affairs. It didn't take me long to begin to realize that Daddy was seeing Adolph Hitler, the dictator and madman, for what he really was—a devastating force for evil who left his sinister mark on world history.

I also remember my Aunt Susie making a fiery remark, which I didn't understand at the time. We were down at Morehead and looking at a cargo ship at the Beaufort Port. It was evidently the summer of 1941, because she exclaimed in a fit of temper, "We're sending that scrap metal over to Japan and they're going to use it to kill our boys!" As of this writing in 2006, it was some sixty-five years ago. Bob Wiley, a long-time family friend and brother of Woodard Heath, reminded me of Aunt Susie's observation just two nights ago at the Kinston Country Club. I don't know how it came up, but Bob recalled someone else making the exact same comment when seeing our scrap metal being shipped to Japan only months before December 7, 1941. Maybe Pearl Harbor was not a surprise attack after all!

Chapter IV

ON TO HIGH SCHOOL

After graduating from the sixth grade, I moved on to high school, or what we all thought of as high school—there was no middle school to attend. The seventh and eighth grades were located at Grainger High, so we just considered ourselves high school students. We had finally arrived! We were getting to be big boys and girls! It was the fall of 1943. World Was II was raging, but life went on as usual for us in school. One of my special memories during these times was the spaghetti dinners Frank Saville's mother prepared for some of Frank's friends on his birthday each year. Z. A., Douglas Baker, and I were always included. One year Frank's little brother, Bert, played the piano for us. He played by ear, and I remember thinking how much fun it would be if I could play like that. It was about that time that I started taking piano from "Cudden" Gladys.

Learning to Dance

Friday nights were taken up with either Red Devil football home games or going to dances at Emma Webb Park. Actually, it was more socializing than dancing for most of us. Cap'm Pat was head of the Kinston Recreation Department and was the one in charge of seeing that we young people were learning to mingle and develop our social skills. To get us started, we did what was called the "Virginia Reel." The boys lined up on one side and the girls on the other. Volunteer mothers were there to help out and direct traffic. Both lines moved (or marched) to the music in the same direction, some 15 to 20 feet apart, turned to the middle where boy met girl, and then proceeded hand in hand to the dance floor where we officially began our dancing careers.

I think it's safe to say that most of us boys were a little slow starting out, but it didn't take us long to begin to catch on. Evidently, the girls had already been practicing, because they seemed to know what to do, and they were eager to teach us. It wasn't long before we ventured out from the two-step to turning and twirling and all sorts of fancy steps. I remember Ursula (later Sue) Spence patiently spending extra time with me to help develop my dancing skills. After several weeks at Emma Webb Park and with a little help from others, I got so I actually enjoyed being with and dancing with girls. I was still very shy—but, nevertheless, I enjoyed it.

It was about this time that the "Simple Set" evolved. I was with Patty Crawford Pitman a couple of weeks ago (at the time of this writing) and we got to talking about old times and the Simple Set. She said there were nine girls in "the gang" that seemed to stick together and had a special relationship all through high school. I don't know how they got the name "Simple Set" because all of them were among the smartest in our class. She named them, which was a pleasant reminder for me: Kit Armstead (I still call her "Katherine"), Dot Smith (sometimes "Dorothy"), Margie Ferrell, Sue Spence (I called her "Ursula" for a long time), Betsy Britt, Frances Lonon, Patty Crawford (I called her "Patsy" for years), Estelle Fuchs, and Libby Noe. Frances Lonon and I were born one day apart. Her birthday was July 1, 1931, and mine was July 2. She is now deceased, but for many years prior to her death I would call her every July 1 to wish her a happy birthday. We would have a good time reminiscing about the good old days.

"Somebody Up There Loves Me!"

I grew up singing, "Jesus Loves Me," and with my family and church background, I've always known that God loves me and cares for me. Never has this truth been clearer demonstrated to me than one Friday night when I was rushing to get to Emma Webb Park for a dance or party. I was probably in the eighth grade. I was not wasting any time as I was riding my bicycle through the front yard of a lady who lived on the corner of Warren Avenue and Herritage Street. Instead of going to the corner and making a right-angle turn to the left, I merely cut across her yard to save time. After all, every short cut I could find was necessary when I wanted to get some place in a hurry to have fun. The path was well worn and looked like it had been there for years. I believe I had probably used it earlier in the week after school during daylight hours for a baseball game at the park. I had no fear of any problem even though it was almost dark and I could only faintly see the dimly lit area and the path I was about to turn onto. My eyes were glued to the oncoming path, what I could see of it, and I was going at a pretty fast speed. All of a sudden, and for no reason, I suddenly screeched on brakes veering to the right off the path. The next thing I knew I was on the ground wondering what in the world had happened. Why would I suddenly stop like that? There was no one else around—no cars, no nothing. As I got up, and still somewhat dazed and bewildered, the answer appeared. There in front of me was a single strand of barbed wire. Then I noticed the posts. Someone had put a barbed wire, single strand, fence around the lady's yard for the obvious purpose of keeping out intruders. She must have just put it up. As I observed the situation more closely, I could see that the height of the barbed wire appeared to be exactly where my eyes would have been had I continued on the same course I was traveling. At that point, I was deeply humbled! Being only thirteen years old, I'm not sure if I had even heard of the expression, "Praise the Lord" or "Thank you, Lord." But I do remember that deep emotion of gratitude. I knew in my young spirit that it was not luck that caused me to stop. I knew I hadn't seen the wire. There was absolutely no explanation for my having stopped on my own volition or by my own reason. It was purely a divine act of God, and I knew it in my heart. I don't remember telling Mama and Daddy or anyone else about the incident until years later. At the time, I didn't know the theological meaning of the terms "God's grace" and "God's mercy." But I did realize that I could have been severely injured and possibly blinded, had it not been for God's grace and mercy. He had been graceful and merciful to a totally helpless and unknowing young teenager, and

I have never forgotten it. That memorable experience so long ago has given extra meaning to the expression I use now on a daily basis, "Praise the Lord" and "Thank you, Lord."

The High School Band

One of my most pleasant memories about the seventh, eighth, and ninth grades was playing the clarinet in the high school band. I guess I got my start way back in about the third grade when I got a little toy instrument called a "tonnette." It was a little plastic, cigar-looking musical toy about five inches long with about eight holes on the top side and one hole on the bottom side. On it, I was able to play the scale and even a little more. I evidently had at least a little talent, for I had no trouble at all playing some simple tunes, such as "Mary had a Little Lamb," "Baa, Baa Black Sheep," and other nursery songs. It was during the War, and all the service songs were the rage. The Marines Hymn was a "piece of cake," so I got the bright idea that if Z. A. could get a tonnette we could play a duet for "show and tell" at school. Z. A. didn't have any trouble, so we displayed our talents before the class one day and everyone enjoyed it (or at least they gave us a good round of applause). On several occasions when talent was needed for entertainment for the class, someone would offer that Z. A. and Dan could play the "Marines Hymn" for us. Yes, we were famous for playing the "Marines Hymn" on our little tonnettes. I think we also may have played the "Caisson Song" and one or two others, but the "Marines Hymn" was always the crowd's favorite. Maybe that was just the one we did best.

As time went on, I got several other, more sophisticated flute-like instruments and was able to impress Daddy enough that he suggested I get a clarinet. I didn't know much about a clarinet, but after seeing a picture of one, I was thrilled at the prospect of learning how to play it. Daddy had already checked with his friend, Charlie McCullers, who was head of the Chamber of Commerce and a fellow Rotarian. He could play the clarinet and would be glad to give me a few lessons to get me started. Mr. McCullers' office happened to be next door to my daddy's law office on the second floor of the Perry-Wooten Building at the northeast corner of Queen Street and Gordon

Street. It's now sometimes referred to as the "Silver Dome Building." By the way, I remember Mama taking me to Daddy's office as a three-, four-, and five-year-old and sitting in his office window to watch the Christmas parade going up Queen Street. Of course Santa Claus was always the last in line, and I can still remember waving to him from my perch in Daddy's office window.

I think Charlie McCullers gave me about three clarinet lessons, all in his office; I'm sure it was disturbing for everyone in Daddy's office as well as anyone else in the area to hear this young up-start squeaking and squawking and making all kinds of weird sounds. Mr. McCullers was very patient with me, and soon I began to get the hang of it. He also taught me a little bit about reading music. When school started, I didn't feel like I was quite ready to go out for the band, so it was a few days later that I finally got enough nerve to show up with my clarinet for my first band practice. We met in the basement of Grainger High; Robert Rhodes was the bandmaster. He also played the violin in the choir at Gordon Street Christian Church, so we knew each other. I got along fine in getting oriented as a band member. The number one clarinetist was Alma Jenkins. She played loud and strong and led the way for the rest of us. I sat beside Aubrey Bronstein behind Alma. I think he was number two, and I was number three. Later, Don Cox joined us. I was reminded in recent conversations with Aubrey Bronstein and Hilary Daugherty of other members of the band: Cullen Daugherty, clarinet; Hilary Daugherty, George Denmark, and Doug Baker, trumpet; Louis Gooding, French horn; Guy Elliott, euphonium; Prior Mixon, snare drum; Leroy Batts, base drum; Willard Arthur, piccolo; and Rodolph Nunn, trombone. Verian Herndon and Nora Ellen Faulkner led the marching band as majorettes; Skippy Larkins (I believe) was the drum major who strutted around with his baton in front of the whole marching band.

I particularly enjoyed the parades and marching up Queen Street playing "Stars and Stripes Forever," "Washington Post March," and some of the other familiar marches. I had a great time playing for the football games and marching at half-time. We also played for a two-ring circus in one of the local warehouses as well as several concerts in the school auditorium and elsewhere, including Caswell Center. All in all, it was a lot of fun and contributed greatly to my love of music and especially the marches of John Phillip Sousa. Later Daddy also got me a saxophone. I learned to play it only halfway decently, but the clarinet was my main interest, thus my saxophone prowess faded and never really got off the ground. Warren and Ely Jr. both took a couple of guitar lessons along the way, but neither one had much musical talent for further pursuit.

Mama's Old Piano Got Me Started

I was in the eighth grade when Mama suggested I take piano lessons. It didn't take much encouragement for me to agree because I thought it would be great to be able to sit down and play for my own enjoyment as well as the entertainment of others. I could just see myself at the piano—effortlessly playing anything I wanted to, just like in the movies. But what about a piano to get me started? Mama had the answer. Her old piano was still at home in Towson, the one she played when she was a little girl. I doubt if it had been moved or even tuned since she last played it in high school. It wasn't long before it was shipped down to 908 West Road, sitting in the nursery, ready for me to begin my piano career. It was an old upright, which was not in the best of shape; in fact, I don't believe it ever could be tuned decently. A couple of the ivory keys were missing, and it never did sound too good, but it was the best we had and it certainly satisfied me to get me started. I'm sure Daddy probably thought that considering the shipping cost and the expense of getting it in shape, he would have come out better buying a secondhand piano in Kinston. But it was Mama's, it had sentimental value, and she wanted me to have it.

Mama had talked to Gladys Sitterson about being my teacher, and so for once a week for about a year and a half I went to her house to learn to play the piano. At my very first lesson, I greeted her as "Mrs. Sitterson" and she was quick to remind me that we were cousins and I was to call her "Cousin (pronounced 'Cudden') Gladys." She was Simon Sitterson's mother and was a gracious lady. Mama and I both had made it clear to her that I was not interested in being a virtuoso or concert pianist. I just wanted mainly to learn to play by ear and know some popular songs, not Beethoven and Bach. She had several books, which taught the chord method, so she started me off learning the basic chords of C, G, G7, F, etc. I caught on pretty quickly, and it wasn't long before I was able to progress from "Mary had a Little Lamb" to "Beautiful Dreamer," "My Irish Rose," "In the Good Old Summer Time," and other such tunes that Daddy liked. Just about everything I learned to play by ear was in the key of C, in the white keys, because that was the simplest way for me to learn. Daddy's favorites were easy to play and suited my style of playing perfectly. "Drink to Me Only with Thine Eyes," "Let me Call You Sweetheart," "Carolina Moon," and "Sweet Sixteen" were some of his as well as my favorites. After I got the feel for playing by ear, Cousin Gladys wanted me to branch out to learn more about reading music. "Ah, Sweet Mystery of Life," "Viennese Melody," and "Indian Love Call" were some of the more complicated pieces I learned. Although I learned the notes well enough to stumble my way through some of the easier sheets of music, I never did get too good at sight-reading. I had to spend a lot of time practicing. Finally, if I spent enough time on a piece and played it over and over again, I could make my way through it reasonably well, but nothing to brag about. Cousin Gladys knew that Daddy was a Sigma Chi and enjoyed the good ol' songs of his youth, so she made me learn "The Sweetheart of Sigma Chi." After I struggled with it a bit, I finally learned it and had a good time playing it for him.

One memorable day as I was riding my bicycle on Vernon Avenue on the way to a piano lesson, I saw Jack Blevins suddenly come running out of his house yelling and waving his arms. Then I heard him exclaim at the top of his voice, "Dan, President Roosevelt is dead! The President is dead!" I screeched to a halt, and them he told me he had just heard on the radio that President Roosevelt had just died. That was on April 12, 1945. Cousin Gladys had also heard the news and after a few appropriate comments my piano lesson went on as usual.

Daddy's Little Girl

One of my all time favorite piano memories was at Gordon Street Christian Church many years later. My baby girl, Radford, was about four or five at the time, just the right age for this special song. I had always wanted to be able to play and sing "Daddy's Little Girl." I found the sheet music and practiced it over and over again until I had the words and music memorized well enough to feel comfortable performing. It must have taken about a year to get ready. Finally, my time arrived. Someone suggested I entertain the Forever Young Group at one of their monthly meetings. That would be perfect! There was a piano in the Fellowship Hall at the church. That was all I needed. For the program, I started out by playing several old favorites on my ukulele, such as "By the Light of the Silvery Moon" and "Shine on Harvest Moon." Then I played several guitar numbers, ending up with "Sweet Caroline" and "Country Boy." Then I played several more oldies on the piano, such as "Sweet Sixteen," "Down by the Old Mill Stream," and "Moonlight Bay." I sang some of them myself and had the crowd sing along with the rest of them. Boy, was I having fun! Then came the time I had been waiting for—the grand finale! Margaret and Radford were in the audience. I had prepared Radford beforehand to come up and stand by the piano and look at me as I sang the special number just for her. She didn't hesitate as I called her forward. I remember thinking, "Don't mess up, Dan. This is what you've been waiting for"—a chance to accompany myself on the piano and sing "Daddy's Little Girl" to my baby girl. How touching, as well as thrilling, that would be for me—and something Radford would always remember. I said something like, "Now I want to play a special song for a special little girl; come on up here, Radford." She came forward just as we had planned. I managed to get through it without too many mistakes and the audience (mostly women of senior citizen age) clapped politely and seemed to enjoy it. I'm sure it thrilled me more than it did them. Anyway, my mission was accomplished.

That was in about 1978. When Radford was married in the year 2000, I surprised her at the rehearsal dinner by singing to her without accompaniment, those same words: "You're the end of the rainbow, my pot o' gold;

you're Daddy's little girl to have and hold; a precious gem is what you are; you're Mommy's bright and shining star; you're the spirit if Christmas, my star on the tree; you're the Easter Bunny to Mommy and me; you're sugar, you're spice, you're everything nice, and you're Daddy's little girl." We've got a video of that one and I'll always treasure it.

Chapter V

FAMILY TRIPS

The Lost Colony

We enjoyed taking trips together as a family. One of the earliest trips of any distance I can remember (other than to Morehead) was our trip to Manteo to see the "Lost Colony." This famous, nighttime, and yearly outdoor production of Paul Green began in 1937. I'm not sure if we attended the play in 1937 or 1938, but I do know it was one of the first, so I must have been six or seven years old. Daddy had heard about it from all the publicity and wanted us to see it. I remember it was a long journey (it seemed like it took forever), and we were all tired when we got there. One memory that stands out was that we spent the night in some lady's house where we slept on feather beds with feather pillows. We thought that was the greatest sleep experience you could have. I don't remember if I got much sleep, but I can still remember the softness of those feather beds. As to the play itself, I remember hearing the names Pocahontas, Virginia Dare, and John Smith. As the 1587 story was relived before our very eyes, Mama had explained a little bit about the play itself, but no one warned me about the sudden burst of the cannon fire. I spent a lot of the time with my fingers in my ears, sitting on that hard bench, all crunched over and cuddled next to Mama. I was scared to death! I remember praying, "Oh, please don't shoot those cannons again."

I relived my frightful experience some forty years later when Margaret and I took our children to Manteo and "The Lost Colony." Radford was probably six or seven years old. With my own fearful experience in my mind, I was careful to caution each of our children to be prepared for the noisy cannon fire. She, being the youngest of our three, lived up to my anxious expectations. As you can imagine, when the shot was fired, she started bawling, and the only way I could console her was to take her from the theater, which I did hurriedly. We managed to slip back into our seats when I assured her I "thought" the cannon noise was all over. Luckily, I guessed right and although there were some more anxious moments, we were both spared the fright of another cannon blast.

As with my first trip to Manteo years before, we spent some quality time in nearby Kitty Hawk and relived the Wright Brothers' first flight. We checked out those unforgettably high sand dunes. Daniel was especially impressed with the thought of flying "through the air with the greatest of ease."

Florida

We took several other trips in my early years as a family of five, mostly in the summertime, and all without air conditioning. On our trip to Florida, I remember keeping up with all our incidentals expenses. Every time we would stop for gas or get a coke and a snack, I would write it in a small ledger book. Daddy had given me a little training for that particular job. When I first started getting an allowance at age six (I believe it was thirty-five cents a week), I would write my entries in a ledger book Daddy gave me. He showed me how to write at the top of each page the words "income," "expenditures," "brought forward," etc. I also kept a diary from time to time for some of the trips.

The 1939 World's Fair

When I was eight years old Daddy told us we were going to the 1939 World's Fair in New York City. I had been to a couple of Lenoir County fairs and a circus or two, and so I got real excited when we talked about going to a world fair. Time was getting short and Mama was beginning to get our clothes lined up for the trip up north. Our plan was to stop in Towson, Maryland, for a night or two with Grandmother Seipp and the family members that we didn't get to see very often. Anyway, Mama and Daddy had it all planned out, and we were getting excited as the time grew nearer. But then it happened! I remember walking back from downtown with Z. A. one hot afternoon after seeing a movie at the Carolina Theater. We were walking along on the north side of Vernon Avenue. A couple of blocks away, we were to make our turn up West Road for the final few blocks home. All of a sudden, I began getting extremely hot. My face felt flushed, and I found no relief when I unbuttoned the front of my shirt. I was ready to get home, so we walked a little faster. When I finally got to Mama, she was quick to discover my face, neck, and chest were covered with some sort of rash. The only thing to do was to take me to see Dr. West. It didn't take him long to give us the bad news. I had a case of German measles! I later learned that German measles is not as bad as red measles, but still what I had would take a period of recuperation before I got back to normal. The bottom line was that I was going to miss seeing the World's Fair. I remember how disappointing it was because I had looked forward to it so much. But what about the family? Were they all going to stay home because of me? It all ended on a happy note. Dr. West said I would be well enough to go as far as Towson, Maryland, to stay with Grandmother Seipp while the other family members went on to New York for an exciting trip to the World's Fair. In the meantime, I had to be satisfied to spend time with Grandmother Seipp, Uncle Warren, and Aunt Eva and her husband, Mr. Corbin. I was honored one evening when a little three-piece pick-up band played "Carolina in the Morning" especially for me.

Buffalo, Hershey, Niagara Falls, Gettysburg

I think it was 1943 when we all went to Buffalo, New York, for the National Convention of the Christian Church. Our church at Gordon Street celebrated its 100th anniversary that year, and so Daddy thought it was fitting that we go to the convention. It also gave him a good excuse to take his family on another trip, all five of us. About the only thing I remember about the convention was the gathering of all those in attendance for a picture taking. How it was done I'll never know, because there were probably a couple thousand people or more, and we all seemed to be looking at the camera. The amazing thing was we could all be identified because it was a wide-angle camera, and the picture itself seemed like it was two-feet long. I had never seen such a big picture!

We also visited Hershey, Pennsylvania, on our way to Buffalo. Two things I remember about Hershey: First was the chocolate smell that permeated the whole town. Everything was centered on the Hershey Bar, Hershey Kisses, and the assortment of chocolate candies made there. We took a tour of the factory, and it was fascinating actually to see them make the candy. Second was the Hershey Country Club Golf Course. The amazing thing about it was the perfect condition of the fairways and roughs. There were absolutely no weeds, and not a blade of grass was out of place. Of course, the greens were cut to perfection, just like a billiard table—and they were a beautiful deep green, too. We were used to seeing brown spots on our greens and weeds poking up everywhere in the fairways as well as the roughs. Oh, how we wished we had our clubs! We all (not Mama) vicariously played several holes as we surveyed the course, hole by hole as far as we could see. We had a good time letting our imaginations run wild.

We also took time to tour the Niagara Falls area. The vastness of the falls itself was mind-boggling. The guide told us all about the people who had gone over the falls in a barrel. Some died, but some lived to tell the tale. The width and height of the falls and the tremendous force of the water, along with the misty conditions, are still etched in my mind.

We also came back through the Pennsylvania Dutch country and marveled at the beautiful network of roads and fields of corn, beans, and other crops. Everything was green and lush—a beautiful sight. Yes, we saw the Mennonite horse and carriages and barns and silos. It was all there for us to enjoy.

We visited the battlefields at Gettysburg and Vicksburg. I remember the words of our guide as he commented several times, "It was mighty, mighty severe fighting." We visited the cemetery where Abraham Lincoln delivered his famous Gettysburg Address in 1863. I was particularly interested in his "Four score and seven years ago" speech since I was in the process of memorizing it. Our trip made it easy for me to complete my goal.

We took a number of other trips as a family, but these are the ones that seem to stick out the most in my mind as of this writing.

Chapter VI

FIVE UNFORGETTABLE SPEED RIDES

Young people will tell you from time to time about a friend taking them for a fast car ride with a load of friends—all in the interest of having a good time and being reckless without having a wreck. We all knew this kind of thing was dangerous and childish, and we should have known better. There were five times I can remember in my youthful days of going fast, or what appeared to be fast, four in a speeding car and one in a boat.

- The first time I remember meeting George Bell was at his cottage in Morehead. He had a hamburger cookout with several friends. Z. A. and Lewis Bryan (of Goldsboro) were there and three or four others—no girls that I can remember. Sometime after that, I was at George's house. I'm not sure if Z. A. was there or not, but it was late in the afternoon and approaching dark. George's older brother, Carl, tempted us with, "Come on and I'll take you boys for a ride!" Carl must have turned sixteen and just gotten his license. George, Z. A., and I were probably fourteen. Anyway, we all hopped into Carl's Chevy, and boy did he take us for a ride! I don't remember any of the details—only that we were going east on Evans Street. We were going through intersections, and Carl was bouncing and joking and stomping—we must have been going at least sixty or seventy! I was scared to death! I don't remember seeing any other cars. All I remember is hiding in the back seat hoping and praying we would come out of the experience all in one piece. We must have made it back safely because here I am to tell about it.

I do remember the great sense of relief when we finally crawled out of the car! I, for one, was determined never to get in a car with Carl again—and I never did.

- My second speeding event was also down at Morehead but much less harrowing. Peter DuBose had just gotten a new Oldsmobile. I believe it was a two-door "Rocket Engine" beauty, and he was telling all about it. He bragged that it could get to sixty from zero in ten seconds. Several of us were in disbelief. That's really fast! We were not used to anything like that, so we took him up on his challenge. We were out on the Fort Macon Road going east, and no other cars were around. Pete stopped and paused a few seconds. He took off his watch and gave it to somebody; I don't remember to whom. Then he proudly and confidently said, "Watch this!" We were all looking at the speedometer. Well, with that I remember Pete stomping the accelerator to the floor! That ol' Rocket Engine really took off! All eyes were glued on the speedometer and the watch. With a tremendous roar of the engine, ten seconds later it was all over! He did it! We actually got to sixty in exactly ten seconds by his watch's second hand. We all yelled our congratulatory remarks almost in unison! What an amazing accomplishment! It almost felt like we were witnessing history in the making—an unforgettable thrill of a lifetime! That was in about 1947 when we were sixteen. I guess the modern cars of the twenty-first century can do it in four or five seconds, and race cars even faster. But back then when Peter DuBose's Rocket Engine Oldsmobile got to sixty in ten seconds, that was as fast as it gets—and I was there to witness it!

- My third unforgettable speed ride was also at Morehead, but this time it was on the water, in Bogue Sound. I was probably sixteen or seventeen. Fred I. Sutton Jr., who was quite a bit older than I, was a racing enthusiastic all his life—both in cars and in boats. I later understood he did a lot of competing in professional races both on land and water, and was often a winner.

One day I was with Fred down at Morehead, and he got to talking about his speedboat. Finally, he invited me to go for a ride. Although I had seen an inboard speedboat before, I had never been in one, so I was excited! I was used to putting along in a 85 h.p. boat at maybe thirty or thirty-five mph. Fred and I were cruising along at a relatively slow speed on the east side of the Atlantic Beach Bridge when all of a sudden, and without his saying a word, I felt this tremendous surge of power. I remember my head was thrown back and the wind was blowing against my face and cheeks with such G-force that I was immediately reminded of seeing pictures of an astronaut in training. It looked like his nose and whole face was almost flattening out. I was holding on for dear life! Fred was saying, "Hang on now!" Well, with that I experienced a second burst of speed! WOW! Thank goodness the top speed didn't last long. I was thankful he began easing off. The water was not what you might call "rough," but there were a few choppy waves here and there. I guess if it had been smoother or like a lake, ole Fred would have really let it go and pulled out all the stops. I didn't know if I would have survived at a faster speed. When we finally returned to his dock, I ventured to ask him how fast we were going. "Oh, about 65 or so," he casually commented. We may have been only going "65 or so," but it seemed to me like we were going "165 or so!" I don't remember if he said miles per hour or knots, but whichever it was, to me we were flying!

- My fourth unforgettable speed ride took place in Lenoir County on some dirt roads out beyond Hull Road, north of Highway 70, somewhere in that area. Guy Elliott Jr. was my patrol leader in Boy Scout Troop 43. We were winding up a patrol meeting in the log cabin behind my house. I don't specifically remember who was there. It was probably Z. A. and four or five others who made up the patrol. Guy was two or three years older than the rest of us. At least he was old enough to drive a car, so I was probably thirteen or fourteen. I remember his saying something like, "Come on, and I'll take you boys for a ride." I don't know how many were in the car, but we innocently accepted his kind invitation. We didn't know what to expect, but we ended up on a dirt road with ditches on either side. Guy was purposely swerving from side to side, making ruts and gunning the car from time to time, just for the thrill of it. I don't remember being afraid at any time, because he seemed to be in control. Guy was always soft spoken and low key, and we all respected him as a person and as our patrol leader. I guess I was a little surprised to see this "other personality" come to the forefront. I remember thinking; even ol' Guy can have a good time. Later he went into the ministry, serving in various capacities.

As I write light heartedly of these speed experiences, I am reminded, on a much more serious note, of a conversation I had just yesterday (at the time of this writing) while waiting to get a haircut from P.H. Pigford at his Model Art Barber Shop in the Plaza Shopping Center. When I came in, Horace Cox was in the chair. I hadn't seen him at Rotary in a long time, and so I struck up a conversation. He talked about his heart attack over a year ago, and, more recently, of his granddaughter. She was sixteen and apparently driving at a high rate of speed with several other young people in the car. There was an accident, and she was killed. The others were seriously injured. As he related the sadness of the tragedy, I was reminded that when we get in an automobile, whether we go fast or slow—anytime we are traveling—there is always the danger of a mishap. All of us have experienced at least one time in a car when we were spared only by the grace of God.

- With that word of caution, I'll tell you about my fifth unforgettable speed ride. I was going to the beach on Highway 70, when it was only a two-lane road. This was long before the present super highway came into being with a speed limit 70 miles per hour. I had never told anyone about this before last night when I shared with Margaret what I had been writing.

    Well, here it is. I was alone, driving the new family car on my way to the beach. It was a black Mercury, probably a 1951 or 1952 model. I think I was about twenty or twenty-one (old enough to know better). I believe the speed limit had recently been raised from 55 to 60 miles per hour, on one of those straight stretches of road. I had been cruising along at a so-called normal speed between Kinston and Dover when I realized the speedometer was showing a little over 70 miles per hour. The car was handling beautifully, and it felt like I was hardly going 50 of 55 miles per hour. Before I knew it, I was going over 75 and approaching 80 miles per hour. Being the "innocent" young fellow that I was, I didn't know if I had ever gone that fast before. I remember thinking to myself, "I wonder what it would feel like to go a little faster? Nobody is around." No cars were approaching, and certainly no one was behind me threatening to pass.

Besides that, no patrolman was in sight. Why don't I just ease it on up to 85? What could be the harm in that? I don't think I had ever gone much, if any, over 70 miles per hour before. But what if the car started shaking or a wheel came off or I ran into a bird or something? I never thought of the much more likely danger of a deer darting out in front of me from the nearby woods. Anyway, I made it to 85 miles per hour. So far so good! Well, if I can go 85, why not 90? It was one of those dare devil things I simply could not resist. I remember holding the steering wheel a little tighter and focusing on the road in front of me with quite a bit more concentration. I think I remember feeling the car vibrating a little as I hit 90 miles per hour. I was beginning to get somewhat anxious—but at the same time I was feeling the mounting pleasure of venturing into new territory that was totally unfamiliar to me. "Hold on now, Dan, don't be foolish. What would Daddy think if he knew I was going this fast? But why would he ever know? I sure would never tell him. I'll probably never do this again (that's one thing I was right about)." At this point my thought process was, I'm in a new car, clear weather, straight stretch of road, nobody around to give me a hard time—why not go on up to 100 miles per hour? I don't believe the car will fall apart. Surely someone has probably gone that fast before on this road! The only problem was the width of the road. The faster I went the narrower the road got. I decided to straddle the centerline and that helped a little. But it was still mighty narrow. Anyway, I thought to myself, "Why not go for it? You can do it!" I offered a little prayer for safety and slowly pushed down on the accelerator—up to 95 miles per hour! So far so good! At that point I told myself, "Go ahead and do it. Push it on up to your goal of 100 and then just coast on in!" And that's exactly what I did. I remember the feeling of seeing the speedometer go to 96, 97, 98, 99, and finally to 100. I had done it! I had reached the pinnacle, my goal of going 100 miles per hour! I didn't dare go *over* 100 miles per hour, and had no desire to. As I was gazing at the speedometer coasting back down to 95, 90, 85, and 80 miles per hour, I realized it was something I probably shouldn't have done. But, I did it, and it was quite a sense of relief to realize it was all over. By the time I got back down to 70, I felt like I was going no more than 35 or 40. I was hardly moving. It's amazing how your sense of speed is a relative thing. It depends on what you are comparing it to. The rest of the trip to Morehead was driven pretty much within the speed limit.

That 100-mph ride has been a secret I have kept to myself for over fifty years. I was afraid to tell anyone, especially my parents or my wife and children. They'd probably think I was crazy, as well as stupid and immature (which I was). Margaret was asking me last night about how I was coming along with my book. I told her I was writing about my five unforgettable speed experiences. As of last night, I had written only about the first three, but I proceeded to tell her about all five, saving the black Mercury trip to Morehead for the last.

As I was about to relate my experience of speeding on Highway 70 over fifty-five years ago, she innocently said, "How fast did you go, 80 or 85 miles per hour?" If I told the whole truth in the book, I figured I'd better go ahead and tell her the whole truth now. When I finally did tell her I went 100 miles per hour, she was in shock! She couldn't believe it! Her basic comment to me was, "I just can't believe it! And I thought you were perfect! What will the children think?" I'm certainly not proud of my "accomplishment," and I certainly don't recommend it or approve of it in any way. I'll be terribly disappointed if any of my children or grandchildren ever do that. In fact, I'd better not hear of any of them doing such a stupid, foolish thing. In that instance, "Do as I say and not as I do (did)."

Chapter VII

CAMP MOREHEAD—A GREAT EXPERIENCE

Camp Morehead will always hold a place close to my heart. C.R. "Pat" Crawford started it in about 1936 or 1937 and Ely Jr. was among the first campers to attend. I remember Mama and Daddy taking Warren and me down to see Ely Jr. after he had been there for a week or so. We explored the camp facilities, and it looked like lots of fun. I just knew it was something I wanted to do when I was old enough. I ended up going there for three years as a camper and one year as a counselor. Those four summers were among my happiest memories.

I think I was about ten years old (1941) when Z. A. and I took that train ride on the old Mullet Line, which came through Kinston and ended, I believe, in Beaufort. Mama had packed all my belongings in a trunk, and I remember her sewing nametags on the important items. I had never been on a "choo choo" train, and so I was real excited about taking that ride with Z. A. We were told not to poke our heads out the window because "you might get a cinder or some bit of trash in your eye." I remember Zollie warning us about that, but somehow I must have forgotten—and you guessed it. I poked my head out the window, only for just a few seconds—just to see what it felt like—but that was long enough to get a speck of something in my eye. I was fortunate in that it didn't hurt much, yet I knew it was there. Anyway, I got over it in a few minutes and everything was fine. The rest of the trip was great, full of excitement, riding on a real "choo choo" train.

When we arrived at the train station in Morehead, we were met by a couple of counselors in a big open truck with "Camp Morehead" labeled on the sides. There had been several other campers on the train with us, and all of us had trunks. We all were excited! We were finally on our way for six weeks of Camp Morehead. Eight of us boys were in our cabin along with our counselor and junior counselor. Along with Z. A. and me, there was Buddy Storm and Howard Farley from Kinston. I don't remember very many other names at this point, but I do recall "Scrap" Green from Tarboro. He was a left-handed baseball pitcher and was pretty good. Donald Chance told me his family had a connection with B. C. Headache Powder, a company founded by Mr. Bernard and Mr. Chance. Ashton Griffin from Goldsboro was another name that rings a bell. I believe he is a doctor now. Then there was Bill Hand from Belmont. He was good at horseshoes, and when throwing he would always use his favorite expression, "oo-daa; make-a-ringa!" He was hard to beat. Bill Trotman was from Winston-Salem. He was talented in theatrics and ended up being in the theater in New York City in some capacity. One of the plays he put on at camp was entitled, "The Monkey's Claw." One night Bill played a trick on us as we came back to our cabin after being at some event. When we turned on the cabin light, we were shocked to see Bill all sprawled out on his lower bunk in an awkward position. He was on his back—one leg on and one leg off his bed. One arm was dangling one way and the other arm was at some other crazy angle. His mouth was wide open, tongue sagging out to one side; his eyes were glassy and staring straight up in a fixed position. Oh, my gosh! Was he dead? What really made the shocking scene so authentic (just like in the movies) was he had poured a bunch of ketchup all over his shirt and had a pair of scissors sticking out of his chest, or at first glance it looked like it was his chest. For a split second, we thought our friend Bill had been murdered and was gone from this world! Actually, one blade of the scissors was stuck in his armpit, but it sure looked real to us!

During those three years as campers, we did all kinds of activities: swimming, water skiing, sailing, knuckle ball, basketball, softball, baseball, tennis, ping pong, archery, and the list goes on and on. "Pop" Cordova taught us some woodworking skills. We were kept busy all the time without being too busy.

Yes, there was plenty of time to goof around if we wanted to. A lot of people would describe Camp Morehead as being too "laid back." We weren't pushed to do anything. We never felt any real pressure to be busy, busy, busy doing something all the time. Yet our counselors were there not only to give us a good time, but to jump on us and hold us in line if we needed straightening up.

The first year I got "short-sheeted," which was standard for first-year boys. Snow Holding from Smithfield was one of my counselors. He sent me on a "wild goose chase" shortly after I arrived. He said, "Dan, I want you to find me a 'sky hook.' There is something special I want to do in the cabin, and I need a sky hook. Go up to the main building and ask Cap'm Pat if he will let you have one." Well, I proceeded like a good little boy to find Cap'm Pat so as to fulfill my mission. I never will forget Cap'm Pat's response when I told him, "Cap'm Snow needs a sky hook for the cabin and he thought you might have one." Cap'm Pat seemed a little slow to answer, and I could even see a twinkle in his eye and a slight smile on his face. I didn't understand why he didn't speak up and give me the sky hook, for I fully expected him to reach up on the shelf, open the tool box, and pull out a big sky hook for me to take to Cap'm Snow. I had actually never seen a sky hook before, but I pictured it as being something like a giant fishhook, something that could hold a heavy weight. I didn't know what Cap'm Snow was going to do with it, but I was sure he had a special project in mind.

After a few minutes of holding me in suspense, Cap'm Pat very softly said something like, "Cap'm Snow is just playing with you." At first I didn't quite understand what he meant by that. He sent me back empty handed without the sky hook I desperately wanted to bring back to Cap'm Snow. After all, many times Mama, Daddy, Warren or Ely Jr. would ask me to get something for them, and I was always anxious to be the good little boy that I was, and do as I was told. On my way back to the cabin, I had time to ponder the matter—and it finally dawned on me that I had been set up. It was all a trick, and I fell for it "hook, line, and sinker." It was all in fun, and I had learned my lesson—or had I?

A day or so after that, another counselor told several of us he was going to take us "snipe hunting." I couldn't ever remember seeing a snipe before but

I pictured it as being something like a sand piper or small swamp bird that would run along the ground and was hard to catch. Each of us was given a small paper bag and told to follow our leader down to the shoreline to hunt for some snipe. There may have been some down there, but our efforts were futile. We even learned how to call 'um: "Here—snipe, snipe, snipe. Here—snipe, snipe, snipe." After a period of frustration, somehow we got the message. We had been sent on another "wild goose chase."

"Headless Hattie" was among our favorite scary nighttime ghost stories. Hattie was the wife of the infamous Black Beard, and during one of his skirmishes, she was decapitated near channel marker 13, just down the way from where we were at Camp Morehead. At certain times when the moon was full, she could be seen roaming near channel marker 13 looking for her lost head. Some of the older counselors could really set our imaginations going with all kinds of wild stories. I remember Buddy Storm being especially scared of Headless Hattie and other such ghost stories. For that matter, we were all scared.

Cap'm Pat— the Spirit of Camp Morehead

Most every night we would all gather for some type of program, either in the gym or at the end of the pier. Cap'm Pat would generally be in charge, but lots of time counselors and others would put on a show or play or tell ghost stories. They were always interesting and captivated our attention. We had regular vespers, and I remember Claude Barrett of Kinston leading us in a devotion or two.

One of the most memorable talks Cap'm Pat gave us was the night he told us about the camp motto: "The Other Fellow." He explained to us that whatever we were participating in or whatever situation we were involved in, we should always be aware of the other fellow's needs. That didn't mean we shouldn't do our best to win against him when in competition, for that is the essence of being a competitor. The message Cap'm Pat was trying to convey to us was that we can be a sympathizer and an encourager to the loser as we celebrate our victory. Just be aware of the feelings of the other fellow. Don't put him down; lift him up. Be a good winner as well as a good loser.

Cap'm Pat always set a good example for us. I remember him as being patient and kind, never too busy to spend time with "his boys." He loved the idea of having a camp for boys (which, at times, was also a camp for girls). "Camp Morehead by the Sea" was his passion. He loved being in a position to develop character and good sportsmanship in young people. He could see the potential in every boy who came to camp, and he seemed to take a special interest in each and everyone of his boys. He didn't want to leave out anyone. He was an encourager, and we all felt good when we were around him. Cap'm Pat was Camp Morehead, and he made Camp Morehead a blessing as well as a memorable experience for all.

I don't remember ever getting home sick at camp; although I'm sure there were those who were from time to time. Camp Morehead may not have been for everyone, but it sure was for me.

One night out on the pier, Cap'm Pat had a group of boys around him, telling them some interesting stories. He told about a particular basketball game in which one player intercepted the ball and fed another as he dribbled the length of the court and scored the winning basket. Then he identified the team and two referenced players as being the "Blue Imps" and Z. A. Collins and Dan Perry. "And they're sitting right over there." How proud we were of having Cap'm Pat mention our names in front of all those other boys. That was Cap'm Pat's way of building up a couple of his boys and encouraging them on to greater heights. Cap'm Pat had been refereeing the game in Kinston, and I think the final score was something like 12 to 10. We were only about 8 or 9 at the time.

Cap'm Pat Crawford was an amazing man. He had been a professional baseball player, making his name with the old "Gas House Gang" of the St. Louis Cardinals back in the 1920s. He had told us about his baseball days and about the other players on the team, but I can't remember them now. I do remember him telling us in his own modest way that he had three home runs in one game. His career was cut short by a leg injury, causing him to walk with a noticeable limp. It was soon after his retirement from baseball that he returned to Kinston and became involved with the Recreation Department as well as furthering his longtime dream of one day owning a camp for boys down at Morehead.

Although Cap'm Pat was not a native Kinstonian, he came to our area through his marriage to Sarah Edwards who was from a prominent Kinston family. Sarah had two sisters, Eleanor (Mrs. Marvin Whitaker) and Virginia (Mrs. Thomas J. White), and they were all active supporters of Camp Morehead. I remember them as well as their children being at camp during the summer. Ellen Whitaker, Virginia Turley, and Sarah Ellen White were each a part of my Camp Morehead memories.

The food at Camp Morehead was not only very adequate but also quite enjoyable. After a good night's rest, after having been busy playing all day, we were always hungry and ready to eat. Sometimes Cap'm Pat or Cap'm Purcell would give a blessing for the whole camp, but most of the time I recall the counselors at each table saying a blessing. I remember apple butter being a standard at each meal, and there was always plenty of milk and ice cream. We never left the table hungry.

The Milky Glass Episode

There was one strange thing I learned at the meal table. It seems we only had one glass per place setting, and it was to be used for both milk and water. If you drank a glass of milk and later wanted a glass of water, you would fill up your empty milk glass with water. The only problem was it left the glass milky white or cloudy in appearance. It wasn't until about midway through my third year that I was able to get up enough courage to drink the stuff. It reminded me of old dirty dishwater. I remember seeing some of the counselors just drink it right on down as if there was nothing to it, no problem at all. It looked too unappetizing for me to even consider such a thing. On several occasions I remember telling myself, "Go ahead and do it, Dan. Some of the others are doing it, and you can too! Just do it and get it over with!" Several times I would put the cloudy glass to my lips, but that was as far as I could go. I just didn't have the nerve to even get started, and I wasn't by myself. There were a lot of boys in the same boat as I.

Then one day it happened—it wasn't prearranged or anything like that. I just decided I was going to do it, and believe it or not, I did. I saw somebody drinking it without making a big deal of it. He had filled up his empty milk glass with water and proceeded routinely to drink it on down without batting an eye. If he could do it, I could do it, too! After all, I never heard of anybody ever dying or even getting sick from it just because it looked like dish water. So I very boldly, and without wasting any time, filled up my empty milk glass, raised it to my lips, closed my eyes, and without hesitation started drinking. Much to my amazement, it tasted just like water—just like it was supposed to. It didn't turn my stomach and didn't make me sick. I had won the battle! From that time forth, it was a natural part of my routine at mealtime. It was so easy after that. Now it was my turn to be the leader. Now some of the younger campers could be envious of me.

Sailing to Swansboro

I enjoyed sailing, but I certainly never bragged about being very good at it. I learned the basics about letting the center board down when the water was deep enough, and raising it up when too close to a sand bar or coming into shore. I learned all about the mainsail, the jib sail and the boom; and how to tack and how *not* to jibe. One of the best sailors at camp was Howard Farley of Kinston. We use to call him "Chubby" in his younger days, but by the time he experienced Camp Morehead, two or three years later, he had slimmed down considerably and, therefore, lost his nickname.

The "Patty J" was the "big" motorized sailboat at the camp. It was named for Cap'm Pat's daughter, Patty, and son, Judge. Everybody seemed to respect it as the "Signature Ship" at Camp Morehead.

We all enjoyed the overnight sailing trips to Swansboro, in which an "Armada" of about six or eight sailboats would make the three-hour or so trek down Bogue Sound. It seemed like an all-day trip. Everybody would end up getting too much sun, but it didn't seem to bother us at the time (we probably paid for it later in life). Some got blistered, others a beet red which eventually turned brown or a deep bronze. The browner we got, the better we liked it. I don't remember being cautioned about the danger of getting too much sun and the wise use of sun lotion. I remember some of the counselors using some kind of oil all over their bodies and most of them were really brown. We would dock all the boats at some of the piers upon arriving in Swansboro. We would then stake out our territory by spreading our blankets on the hard timber of the dock. I don't think we got much sleep, but it was fun just making the trip and being together.

One year there had been some talk about polio epidemic, and I remember Dr. West telling us to stay away from being cooped up in crowded areas. He had said something about staying away from movie houses, but that didn't seem to bother Z. A. and me. We were on one of our trips to Swansboro and decided to check things out in town. "Hey, there's a movie theater. 'Tarzan' is playing. Why don't we go?" The title evidently was intriguing enough to tempt us to at least consider going on in. After all, we each had the ten or fifteen cents for the cost of admission. But what about the warning not to go to the movies? What if we caught polio? Z. A. and I had it all figured out how we could keep from getting polio. We decided to cup one hand over our nose and practice shallow breathing. Just don't breathe very deeply. If we didn't take in much air, we could probably keep the germs out of our nostrils. That seemed like a good plan, and besides we had learned in school something about cilia, which was the hair in the nose. Those hairs would probably keep at least some of the germs out. We both felt it was worth taking a chance. We hadn't seen a Tarzan movie lately—so we were ready to go. I remember paying our money and taking our seats. The first thing we did was slump down with our hands over our noses and peering up to see Tarzan swing among the trees. We tried not to breathe any more than we had to, because we sure didn't want to get any of that polio stuff. After the movie was over, I remember how exhilarating it was to get out in the open air and take deep breaths; we kept right on exclaiming what a great feeling it was. Z. A. and I both agreed we felt confident we would be OK. I never got polio—but years later when Z. A. was in the Air Force, he contracted the dreaded disease in one of his legs, which left him with a slight limp. I hope one movie escapade at Swansboro that summer night had nothing to do with it.

Being a Counselor Was Fun

With three years as a camper under my belt, I was now ready to be a counselor. We had completed our third year at Carolina when the time and schedule was right. In looking back, I many times wished I had had enough sense to have taken the time to be a counselor for more than just one year, because that summer was one of the most memorable experiences of my early life.

Both boys and girls were allowed to come to pre-camp. I can't recall if it was for one or two weeks, but I remember how exciting it was to have girl counselors to mingle with each day. Cap'm Toddy Smith from Bethel seemed to attract my attention more than any other, although I had reached the age in my life when just being around girls was rather exciting. Z. A. took a liking to Cap'm Dawson Thompson. There was always something to do around the camp after we put the campers down and left the junior counselors in charge. Several times Cap'm Pat would let us take the camp truck and go into town to see what was going on. Cap'm Pat trusted us, and we were always back within a reasonable time. It was a fun time in our lives, and I frankly don't recall the conduct of any of the counselors ever being out of line. It was just good clean fun! Howard Farley, Alan Drash, and Dallas Foscue of Kinston; Cooper Taylor of Raleigh; and Julian Vainwright of Greenville were also among the counselors at that time.

An Unusual Talent

One of my most unusual memories during the regular session was preparing my boys for talent night. Each cabin was expected to have something that displayed some sort of talent, whether it was a short skit or something that could amuse the crowd in at least some small way. I had been into poetry since early childhood, and so the only thing I could think of was to have one of the boys recite a poem. I had never heard of that being done at talent night before, but anyway I decided to give it a try. None of the boys knew any poetry so I pulled out my "101 Famous Poems" book my father had given me some years before. After leafing through it a few times, I finally decided on "The Daffodils" by William Wordsworth. I can't remember which of my cabin campers "volunteered" to learn that four-verse (six lines each) poem, but after quoting it to him and giving him a little encouragement, he decided he could do it. He only had about three days before curtain time, so time was of the essence. I was pleasantly surprised to find that within a couple of days, and with a lot of practice during rest period, he completed his assignment and was ready for the task. It turned out he gave a flawless performance! Even the audience was somewhat surprised at our talent selection; we heard several favorable comments, which led us to believe that maybe it wasn't too bad after all. Cap'm Pat came to me afterward and in a serious tone of voice said something like, "Dan, that was most unusual for you to be able to get that boy (he called his name, but I can't remember it now) to recite a poem that he just learned at camp. Maybe it will spark an interest that will go with him the rest of his life."

The Day I Collected My Thousand Dollars

During that summer in 1952, Mother and Daddy dropped by to see me on two occasions. The first was on July 2nd on my twenty-first birthday. They had called me at camp saying they wanted to take me out to supper, if I could take the time off. I was glad that they called because I wanted to talk to them anyway. I had a debt to collect!

As we were leaving camp, the conversation went something like this: "Daddy, do you remember some years ago when Warren was about twelve and Ely Jr. was ten, we were all together in the living room and you had been talking to Warren and Ely about life and the future? And then you made this statement to both of them: 'If you don't smoke or drink (any alcoholic beverage) until you are twenty-one, I'll give you a thousand dollars.' I was playing on the floor, but was listening to the conversation. Mother was also listening. Then you turned to me and said, 'And Dan, I'll do the same for you. If you don't smoke or drink 'til you are twenty-one, I'll give you a thousand dollars'."

As Daddy was slowly driving down that dirt road leaving camp, I remember pausing a moment and then saying, "Well, I want you to know that I am twenty-one years old today, and I've never smoked or drunk any alcoholic beverage. I've done what you said, and so I want to collect my money!" Daddy was obviously elated and replied with excitement in his voice, "Congratulations, son. I'm proud of you, and I'll certainly write you a check when I get back to the office!" We continued to talk about my "accomplishment" as we drove to their hotel. I told them of some challenges I had at Carolina, especially during "Hell Week" before joining the Kappa Sigma Fraternity. Each of the pledges had to get in the phone booth at the Fraternity House and smoke a cigar. The obvious purpose was to make us sick, but somehow I was able to avoid that fate. I told the fraternity president of my commitment not to smoke until I was twenty-one, and I would appreciate it if he would allow me not to participate in that activity. Surprisingly enough, he was very understanding of my pledge. In fact, I could tell from his response that he respected me for my stand. That same respect carried over throughout my fraternity days at Carolina, and I ended up being elected president of Kappa Sigma my senior year.

Daddy had some bourbon in his hotel room. He poured a little bit in a glass, added a little water in with it, and offered me my first taste of whiskey. His words were, "Here, I want you to see what it tastes like." Then he said, "I'll give you another thousand dollars if you don't drink or smoke 'til you are twenty-five." I never got that thousand dollars. Although I've never abused alcohol, I figured I went for twenty-one years, and I'm not going to be legalistic about it any more. I didn't have any trouble avoiding cigarettes, even to this day. They never appealed to me, although I did try a few cigars from time to time, just to see what they were like. I remember smoking one when my first daughter, Elizabeth, was born. Oh, and I passed out a whole box at our next Rotary meeting in celebration of my first-born.

While I was living at home, I never saw Mother or Daddy drink any alcohol or smoke a cigarette. Having grown up without it in the home made it a lot easier for me to win that thousand dollars. Their witness and example played a big part in making me who I am today.

I'm An Uncle!

The second visit from Mother and Daddy during that summer came as a surprise and without warning. It was July 13, 1952, only eleven days after my birthday visit. I was taking a lunch break from camp activities and noticed their car had pulled up in front of the dining room. As I approached them, I could tell there was something exciting going on! Their first words were, "We've got some good news!" They told me all about it. "We've got a grandson, born this morning, and you're an uncle!" Barbara and Warren were the proud parents of a nice, healthy, red-headed boy. Red-headed? I didn't know we had any red heads in the family. Then they told me that Barbara's grandmother on her mother's side had red hair. We all agreed it was nice to welcome to the family a little red-headed boy. We were all on cloud nine! His name was Warren Seipp Perry Jr., and they were calling him Wes. That was a special day and my first of many experiences at being an uncle.

Ghost Story Time

One night before bedtime, I was asked (or maybe told) to tell a ghost story at the camp gathering. It was a spur of the minute thing, and I couldn't think of anything that resembled a ghost story so I started talking about a scary fraternity initiation we had at Carolina. I made most of it up as I went along—something about this boy being blindfolded in a car and being let out in some desolate wooded area in the country, far from any known road—and then challenged to get home as best he could. That much was true about my own experience. I picked a fraternity brother of mine by the name of Frank Davenport of Timmonsville, South Carolina, as the main character and told how he came to this haunted house and had all these weird experiences. I picked the name "Frank Davenport" because nobody would know him, being that he was from far away South Carolina. Well, would you believe that when I got through, one little boy came up to me and said, "Cap'm Dan, I'm from Timmonsville and I know Frank Davenport." My first thought was, "Great Scott, I hope he doesn't go home and try to verify my story with him!" So much for my true ghost story.

Camp Activities

Cap'm Pat gave me the assignment of being camp photographer in addition to my other duties around the waterfront of sailing, swimming, waterskiing, etc.

I made it a point to have my little Brownie camera available for both candid as well as posed shots of the campers and their activities.

I remember teaching tennis to some of the boys. I was only a fair tennis player myself and had never had an official lesson on the fine points of position, stance, backhand, and forehand, etc. Ely Jr. had taught me how to keep score when we played together growing up at the Kinston Country Club, so I guess I at least knew some of the basics. After spending a time of instruction with one of the young campers, Cap'm Pat happened to be watching (unbeknown to me) and afterward complemented me on helping the youngster get a feel for the forearm shot. After listening to Cap'm Pat's calm words of encouragement, you would have thought I was a seasoned teacher. He was just that kind of person.

Roger Kingsberry, from Washington, DC, area was considered the best tennis player at camp. He won the camp tennis tournament rather handily. He was about six feet six inches tall and was a good basketball player, too. I believed he played on the freshman team at Carolina. I got beat by a red-headed Jewish boy named P. Sugar, I believe in the semifinals, so I was spared the embarrassment of facing Roger in the finals.

Cap'm Purcell Takes Over

As Cap'm Pat got older, he apparently was grooming Cap'm Purcell to buy him out after retirement. Cap'm Purcell had the good fortune of working under Cap'm Pat as a counselor for many years and learned a lot about camp administration as well as working with the boys. He followed right in line with carrying on Cap'm Pat's tradition of excellence in keeping Camp Morehead by the Sea the envy of every young boy. After Purcell Jones retired and closed the camp in the late 1990s, he set about subdividing the land into beautiful waterfront lots and residential sites. It was a sad day for all Camp Morehead boys when the camp ceased to exist. The many pleasant experiences will continue to bring thrills and pleasure during the lifetime of all who attended.

One Last Time

The last time I saw Cap'm Pat was shortly before his death. He was bedridden in the high-rise nursing facility in Morehead City, which was located appropriately by the waterfront. His health had declined to the point where he was almost totally blind and deaf. I had visited him several previous times. I had to lean over his bed and shout in his ear, "Cap'm Pat, this is Dan Perry. I've come to see you!" I think the last time was in the mid 1990s. We had a very pleasant (but loud) conversation recalling old times and interesting Camp Morehead experiences. When I finally said my goodbyes, I walked out the door and had gone probably 30 or 40 steps when I suddenly remembered I had left my umbrella in Cap'm Pat's room. As I turned around and started back down the hall, I could hear him saying in a loud voice, "Bless him, Lord! Bless Dan Perry! Bless him, Lord!" As I appeared in his open doorway, he was still calling upon the Lord to bless me, as if to be sure he was heard. I decided not to speak to him again, for it would be anticlimactic to break the spell of the emotional experience I was having. I could only think to myself, "Here is Cap'm Pat in the condition he is in, thinking not of himself, but giving his total attention to one of his camp boys, and asking the Lord to bless him." He was truly exemplifying the Camp Morehead motto, "The Other Fellow."

I silently picked up my umbrella, took one last glimpse at my esteemed mentor, and silently strolled back down the hall. It was a time I will always hold dear. The final chapter of Camp Morehead had been written.

Chapter VIII

MY INTEREST IN SPORTS

From early childhood, I had an interest in all kinds of sports. Warren spent a lot of time with me in our front yard at 908 West Road teaching me about baseball and football. As my big brother, he would brag about the way I could catch a football and a baseball. I would center the football to him and "run out for a pass." We had set plays where I would take five steps off to the right and then cut sharply up the middle. He would lead me just right and the ball would be there every time (or most of the time) for an easy catch. I loved to catch those long ones, too. It was such fun. One day he told me, "Dan I predict that one day you'll be playing left end for the Green Bay Packers." Then he paused and figured, "Let's see, that'll be in about 1956!" That would give me enough time to play four years at Carolina. In my imagination, I could see it all coming true. Warren was an encourager. Oh, what fun!

In baseball he would throw me long flies where I had to run back and snag one on the run. But pitching was my thing—or at least that's what he would tell me. I would pitch and he would catch and call balls and strikes. After a while, I was good enough for Warren to make another prediction: "Dan, one day you'll be pitching for the New York Yankees." Oh, what a thrill that was to think about pitching for the New York Yankees and playing left end for the Green Bay Packers. Well, as you can imagine, my dream never really got off the ground, but that didn't stop my imagination from soaring to the clouds, at least for a brief moment in history. At the tender young age of six, or seven, I didn't know any better and nobody told me any different.

As time went on, Z. A. and I played a lot of ball together—baseball, football, and basketball. Z. A. was the catcher, and I was the pitcher. We started with pick up games at school and Emma Webb Park, and then we joined organized teams in all three sports. Jimmy Byrd and Joe Whaley stood out as natural athletes in those sports.

I Enjoyed Basketball

It wasn't until the seventh grade that basketball became a priority, because there had been no basketball goals in the neighborhood. When we got to the seventh grade at Grainger High, we started going to basketball games, and on Saturday mornings we would go to the high school gym for pick-up games. As our interest grew, Z. A.'s daddy put up a basketball goal in his backyard. It soon became a popular place and we named it "Collins Square Garden." Z. A. and I spent a lot of time shooting baskets, and we actually got pretty good at it. Soon after, Zollie put up another goal, and we had a full-fledged basketball court right in his backyard. John Langley and Sterling Gates were two of the stars on the high school team, and they even joined us from time to time in pick-up games.

Z. A. and I played junior varsity basketball in the seventh and eighth grades along with Cecil Roberts and some other friends. I was fortunate enough to make the varsity team in the ninth grade but played very little in the games—only when we were so far ahead there was no danger of losing. Herbert Whitfield and John Langley were co-captains while Paul Bennett, Gene Leigh, and Sterling Gates rounded out the starting five. Vincent Jones and R. A. Phillips were probably the sixth and seventh men on that team, with Bill Fay as coach. We were runner-up to Greenville as the Northeastern Conference champions. Games were fairly low scoring because the pace was quite a bit slower than it is today.

Boy, Was I Wrong About Bobby!

One of the first times I remember seeing Bobby Hodges was at Emma Webb Park. Several of us were shooting baskets and up came this big guy who started shooting with us. I remember him as being big, lanky, clumsy, and uncoordinated. There was nothing positive about him as an athlete other than his height. He towered over all the rest of us even though he was a year or so younger. Occasionally, he would make a goal, but only because somebody would throw him the ball under the basket. If the throw was high enough we couldn't guard him, so all he had to do was toss it in while standing flatfooted. Most of the time, he would miss several times before scoring. I remember thinking to myself, "This guy may be tall, but he sure doesn't know much about basketball. He'll never amount to anything on the basketball court." That was the only time I ever played basketball with him. It also must have been one of the first times he ever played, because as time went on, he sure proved me wrong. I went off to school after the ninth grade and was never around personally to follow his athletic career, except through the wide spread publicity he received in high school and college. He turned out to be one of the greatest athletes in both basketball and football ever to come out of Grainger or Kinston High School and East Carolina University. He received All-State honors in high school and All-American honors at East Carolina in basketball and football, a rare accomplishment for any athlete. In fact, to my knowledge, he is East Carolina's only athlete to be a two-sport All-American. He was later inducted into the Kinston High School Hall of Fame and also the North Carolina Sports Hall of Fame. He is truly one of the all time greats. Boy, was I ever wrong in my first impression and assessment of Bobby Hodges.

What Happened to Baseball?

My baseball career was short lived. As a ninth grader and freshman at Grainger High, I decided to go out for the team. I was playing a lot of golf and basketball at the time and had not been playing much baseball for the past two years. But what about Warren's prediction that I would one day pitch for the New York Yankees? I didn't want to let him down. After all, I had pitched a little down at Camp Morehead as well as in the Midget League in grammar school and seventh grade. Even though I was not in very good shape, I just had to give it a try. Frank Mock was the coach, and the first thing he did on that first day was to gather us all around him and give us a little pep talk. I don't remember anything he said specifically, except for what he said at the end: "Boys, you've got to be in shape to play baseball." Then he said, "All right, I want you to jog around the ballpark, to get warmed up and then we'll get started." My first thought was, "You mean you want us to go all around the entire ballpark?" As he pointed down the first base line to get us started, off we went. He had gathered us along the first base line about midway between home plate and first base. I happened to be standing near the tail end of the group closer to home plate. Then we took off along the first base line on into right field toward the right field fence. This is where the Kinston Eagles played their games, and I had been in the stands many times, even as a six- and seven-year-old to watch the Eagles play. To me it looked like a mile to that right field fence; nevertheless, I would give it a try. I had hardly gotten past first base and into the outfield when I began to think, "I didn't know we would be doing this. Is this what I really want?" Soon, I began to really huff and puff, and by the time we got to right field fence, I was beginning to wonder if I was going to make it or not. I was barely able to keep up with the tail end. I surely didn't want to be the last one, so I managed to plod along. Somehow the Lord gave me the strength and endurance to finish the course. I remember coming down the left field line and on back to home plate; I was completely worn out and ready to flake out. But Mr. Mock had no pity. The next thing I knew, we were out there catching and throwing and going through the next phase of our workout.

 I think Mr. Mock did put me on the mound for a few practice throws to the catcher, but I didn't make a good showing. My timing was off, and I could hardly get it to the plate. I'm sure Mr. Mock was not impressed at all. Besides, he already had two stars in Gene Leigh and Vincent Jones. They were both outstanding pitchers, and I knew they could both fire the ball in there pretty good. I didn't show up for the next day's practice, and my baseball career was over just like that. I still had an interest in baseball, just not as a player.

Daddy loved the Kinston Eagles and would take us to the games. For quiet a few years, I knew the names of all the players and the batting averages of most of them. One of the games, in about 1940, was interrupted with an announcement over the loud speaker that a tornado had just touched down in west Kinston. The game itself had not been delayed because of rain or high winds, so I don't remember Daddy being all that concerned. The next day we found out a tornado had cut a path about 50 yards wide in a southwest to northeasterly direction crossing over Perry Park Drive, just east of its intersection with Carolina Avenue. There weren't any houses in the area so apparently the only damage was to the trees and underbrush. The destructive path was right about the area where Cousin Tony Carey and I later built our houses at 1307 and 1305 Perry Park Drive; and also where Cousin Lillian (John) Burton and Cousin Lillian (Marion) Parrott built on Sweetbriar Circle. I think it went just east of where Brother Warren later built on Sweetbriar Circle. We were all blessed by the tornado coming before our family started building our homes. It could have been disastrous for all of us had the timing been 35 years later.

Daddy's Most Memorable Baseball Game

Daddy got his undergraduate degree in 1917 from UNC, had one year in the Navy, and then went to one year of law school at Harvard in 1919 before finishing his last two years at Carolina. He told us the story of how "the boys took me to a ballgame on my birthday" on June 7, 1919. The Boston Red Sox were playing the Detroit Tigers and the big drawing card was to see Babe Ruth and Ty Cobb play in the same game. What a treat that would be! Both players were legends in their own time. "The Babe" had started his career as a pitcher, and in the 1916 and 1918 World Series, he pitched 29 consecutive scoreless innings. But he had even greater talent as a hitter, and in about 1919 he began to play regularly as an outfielder. Ty Cobb, "The Georgia Peach," was quickly developing into one of the greatest baseball players in history. He was known not only as an excellent hitter but also as an exceptional base stealer and brilliant strategist. It was a game Daddy never forgot, for when it was over he had seen Babe Ruth hit three home runs and Ty Cobb hit five singles with five stolen bases. What a game that was! Babe Ruth went on to hit 60 home runs in 1927, a season record which stood until Roger Maris hit 62 in 1961. Ruth hit 714 career home runs, a record which stood until Hank Aaron hit his 715th home run in 1974. Ty Cobb ended up with a record lifetime batting average of .367 and 892 stolen bases, which was also a record of long standing. Daddy saw both players at their best in one game on his birthday. What a memorable experience that must have been!

Golf Was My Game

My golf career started at the early age of six. Warren was thirteen at the time and was beginning to play the game at the country club. One Saturday morning, he was talking about how much he was enjoying golf and convinced me to go with him. He had a few clubs and a bag and told me he would even give me a club to help get me started. It was a short chipper he had outgrown, known as a "33" club. He showed me how to grip it and swing it, and it didn't take me long to get so I could hit it pretty well, at least for a six-year-old. With that one club, I played my first round of golf, and would you believe I made a 12 on the first hole and shot an 86. When I tell that story today, people are amazed that a six-year-old could have shot an 86 on his first round. How could that be? I doubt if even Tiger Woods did that well the first time he played. Well, you haven't heard the rest of the story. Two things you need to know: one, I didn't count any of the ones I missed, and two, I only played nine holes. "Now you know the rest of the story." It didn't take me long to catch on to the game. I really enjoyed it and looked forward to Warren showing me more. Soon I had a bag and a set of clubs of my own, and I was off and running for a lifetime of golfing fun.

Between the golf course, swimming pool, and tennis courts at the Kinston Country Club, my summers were pretty well taken up during those grammar school years. Z. A. and I took time to play a little baseball when we could get a group together. During some of those years, I remember walking to the country club in the morning, playing 27 holes of golf by myself, taking a quick swim to cool off, and walking back home for lunch. After a brief rest, the whole process started all over with 27 more holes in the afternoon. It was just a 9-hole course at the time, so I got to know every inch of each hole. It was 54 holes a day, time and time again. By taking the short cut from home, it didn't take long to get there. It wasn't much more that a mile, and I had plenty of energy and didn't seem to get tired. I remember many times when I got home in the afternoon I would pour almost a whole box of Wheaties in a big mixing bowl. With a quart of milk and a big spoon, I would polish it off in pretty quick order. There were hardly any young people my age playing golf back then. Z. A., John Montgomery, and Herbert Whitfield (two years older than I) were the three I remember most. There weren't many ladies that played, but Doris Whitfield was the best. Later, Marie Croom and Bet Long were also excellent. The men would play on Wednesday afternoon and weekends. Among Daddy's group were "Slim" Montgomery, Julian "Snide" McCullen, British Long, Jesse Jones, Buck Wooten, and Boots Jeffress.

When I was old enough to carry a big bag, I would caddy for Daddy. That's where I learned the golf lingo. Daddy didn't pay me to caddy for him, and I never thought of getting paid. Actually, the first time I got paid was when I caddied for Jesse Jones, the lawyer. The caddy fee at the time was 25 cents for each nine holes. When my foursome finished the last hole, Mr. Jones thanked me and said, "Dan, I want to give you a present." It was a 50-cent piece. I thanked him and took his bag back to the clubhouse and was about to go home when someone stopped me and said I forgot to get my money. At first I didn't understand, because Mr. Jones had already paid me my 50 cents. Then I was told that the policy was for the player to pay the caddy fee in the clubhouse where the caddies would pick it up. It wasn't until I got my second 50 cents that I realized Mr. Jones had given me a 100% tip for my service. That was most generous, and I never forgot it.

The 9-hole country club golf course was built in the late 1920s or maybe around 1930. The first clubhouse (or caddie house) was just a small one-room shack and was located in the same spot as the present pro shop. It was big enough to keep the player's bags and have a counter to transact business. I started playing in 1937, and I think I remember the first pro as being Mr. McLawhorn. Everybody called him "Mr. Mac." Gamel Cotton came about 1940 followed by Al Johnson. Although I never had an official lesson from Al, he gave me some helpful tips from time to time. I would watch him hit practice balls and try to copy (at least to some extent) his swing. We played together a number of times, and we became pretty good friends. I even took him home to lunch one day, and Mother fed him a good ol' country meal including corn on the cob and corn bread. I still use a couple of expressions I heard him use is a lighthearted moment. Sometimes when someone is talking in a low voice or saying something I don't understand I might say, "Shot who?" or "Preaching where?"

Our Family Foursome

Every chance we got, mainly Sunday afternoons, Daddy, Warren, Ely Jr., and I would play 18 holes together. We had a great time as a family foursome, and played for some 25 years until shortly before Daddy's death in 1968. He was so proud of his three boys and the fact that we all could be seen playing together as a family. I count those family times as a special blessing that enriched my life and played a vital part in the growth and development of each of us boys. Mother supported our golf togetherness and would drive out to the club to see her four boys coming in on the 18th hole. After we finished, she was frequently there to greet us and find out who won. Daddy picked the teams, and it was always "the oldest and the youngest against the middle two." One of the most memorial remarks I ever heard Daddy make was when he said, in the presence of all of us, "You may think that people look at me as a lawyer and businessman—but you know how I'm really known?" And then he answered his own question and said, "They think of me as a father with a beautiful wife and three fine boys." He looked at that as the ultimate compliment, and I always treasured the fact that I was his baby boy. In fact he always introduced me as his "baby boy," even up to the time of his death. Warren was his "big boy," and Ely Jr. was his "middle-size boy." I often heard him say that Warren was "the best big boy in the world" and Ely Jr. was "the best middle size boy in the world", and I was "the best baby boy in the world."

His encouraging and loving assessment of his three boys carried over after his death when I had the privilege of introducing Warren and Barbara at a Rotary meeting. They were to give a report on a trip they had taken to Russia. I referred to him as "the best big brother in the world." One of my Rotary friends knew that Ely Jr. was in the audience and jokingly said to me after the meeting, "You said Warren was the best brother in the world. Where does that leave Ely? What kind of brother is he?" I told him. "You misunderstood what I said. I didn't say Warren was 'the best brother in the world.' I said he was 'the best big brother in the world'." My friend laughed a little and then I said, "Ely is the best middle brother in the world." He caught the message and we both had a big laugh!

My Shining Hour of Glory

The first time I played in any kind of golf tournament was when I was fourteen years old and in the ninth grade. I had been playing pretty well at the time and was shooting in the 70s and low 80s. Daddy had been playing in the East Carolina Golf Association tournaments on Wednesdays. They would play in different towns each week. I was playing better than a lot of the men so Daddy arranged for me to play on the Kinston team against Goldsboro. Apparently, I had no trouble skipping a couple of classes after lunch for I showed up at the country club for the match. I was paired against a Mr. Allen Vinson. My playing partner was Mr. Tom Harvey of Kinston. He was a member of Daddy's regular foursome. I remember being excited—not particularly nervous, because I had played with men before and was somewhat used to the competition. I guess I was too young to know the difference. Mr. Vinson was really nice to me and made me feel comfortable and at ease. He was definitely encouraging me on each shot. About the only specific hole I remember was when I made a good chip shot to the 4th green which landed fairly close to the pin. When we all got to the green, Mr. Vinson said, "Dan, I'm going to give you that one. I know you'd never miss one like that." I'm sure it was a little longer than the "gimme" range, and I sure was relieved that I didn't have to putt. As he knocked it back to me I said a polite "thank you," but inwardly I was saying, over and over again to myself "Thank you, thank you, thank you!" It turned out that I won my match and Kinston won the team play. The next day the headline of the Free Press account was "DAN PERRY SHINES AS KINSTON SCORES 39–32 WEDNESDAY." The article went on to describe how I, a fourteen year old, playing my first match, shot an 81 and took two points from "veteran golfer Allen Vinson who came in with an 82." It also mentioned that Johnny Farabow and Jim Parrott shot 74s and compiled the best scores. Tom Harvey shot a 74. It was interesting to note that Mr. Vinson didn't appear at all disappointed that a fourteen-year-old had beaten him. To the contrary, he was bragging about my play and seemed just excited as the Kinston group in celebrating my victory. His gracious and encouraging attitude in defeat was obviously exemplary and served as a pattern, which I have tried to follow. I always try to win, but when defeat comes (and it often did, and still does), I learned from Allen Vinson the need to be a gracious loser.

Back in those days and for many years to come, Johnny Farabow, Jim Parrott, Rosco Baker, and Dr, Cecil Wooten were all top-notch golfers. All were club champions in their day. Johnny was the smallest of the group, but his natural inside-out swing was the envy of us all. He just had that pro look about him. Distance-wise, he could keep up with the best of 'um.

I Was Wrong About Horace, Too

Horace Ervin didn't start playing golf until 1954 when he was 30 years old. My first memory of him was seeing him hit practice balls at the Kinston Country Club. He was new to the game, but he had a natural-looking swing. The best one-word description of Horace at that time was "wild". Another word would be "erratic". On the practice tee one ball would go way left and the next would go way right. He hit it long, but there was no consistency at all. He was just plain wild, and I remember thinking to myself, "That man will never do much in golf." It wasn't long before I found out that he may be wild, but he sure had a passion for the game. Every time I'd go to the course, there was Horace hitting balls, spraying 'um right and left. But the most interesting thing about it was the "width of the spraying of his shots" became less and less until in only a matter of weeks he was hitting 'um straight and long. It was simply amazing how quickly he learned to play a great game of golf. My main claim to fame is that I beat Horace the first time I played him. But the rest of the story is he had only been playing a few weeks and I caught him when he was still in his wild, erratic stage. After that there was no stopping him. He went on to have an amazing, though short-lived, golfing career.

When I first started writing this account about Horace I called his son, Curt, to be sure I had my facts straight. Curt said that within four months after his Daddy first picked up a club he shot a 69 at Kinston Country Club. Within six months he shot a 64. In 1959 at the age of 35, after only five years of playing golf, he won the Carolina's Amateur Championship by beating Billy Joe Patton in the finals. Billy Joe had been in the national headlines for being rated as the number one amateur in the United States. The main thing I remember about Horace was the air of confidence he displayed with the golf club in his hands. It was not a boastful confidence, but rather more of a humble regard for the game and the God given talent he displayed. Curt said that when most of us are faced with a 30-foot putt we are surprised if we make it. But with his Dad, he was disappointed if he missed a 30 or more foot putt. He wanted to make 'em all and he had the confidence to know he could (or would) do it. He was an exceptionally good putter as well as ball striker. Curt said he had only one putter throughout his golfing career. He turned pro in 1962 and went on to win many other tournaments, including the West Virginia Open. He beat the local pro, Bruce Crampton in the Azalea Festival Tournament in Wilmington, NC. He even beat "Slammin' Sammy" Snead out of $50 in a friendly match on his own course. When it was over, Snead signed a $50 bill and gave it to him. Amazingly enough, Horace spent that same $50 bill in the Club House after the match. Horace was that kind of guy. Keeping such memorabilia was not in his nature. Horace died at the young age of 48 in 1972. By the way, Curt inherited his father's swing and turned out to be an excellent golfer in his own right.

Two Confessions: I was not only wrong in my initial assessment of Bobby Hodges in basketball, but I was also wrong about Horace Ervin in my initial assessment of him as a golfer.

A Lesson Learned: Ever since those two experiences I have tried not to judge people too quickly, especially upon first impression. I have learned to "evaluate" a person in terms of his potential for success rather than his apparent destiny toward failure. Another way of putting it is to always look for the good in a person, no matter how low his circumstances. You never know how he will turn out. Such an attitude will stimulate positive words of encouragement rather than negative words of doom, gloom and failure. It's amazing how a positive attitude can change the direction of one's life.

Chapter IX

WOODBERRY FOREST SCHOOL FOR BOYS

Woodberry Forest is a Preparatory School located just outside of Orange, Virginia, northwest of Richmond, about fifteen miles south of Culpepper. Warren graduated in 1942 after attending two years. My cousin, Clifton West, graduated a year ahead of Warren in 1941 and Oscar Greene was also a graduate about that same time. Oscar made an outstanding record as Senior Prefect, which is the equivalent of President of the Student Body. Jim Parrott, Bud Wooten and (I think) Haywood Weeks were also Woodberry boys. Ely was there three years, graduating in 1944. With all those preceding me I was at least aware of the good reputation of Woodberry.

After Woodberry Warren entered the R.O.T.C. program at UNC Chapel Hill and upon receiving his Commission in 1943 he reported to the Battleship USS Alabama in the Pacific. Mother would describe Ely Jr.'s experience as, "He graduated from Woodberry on June 3rd, was 18 the next day, and three days later he was in boot camp in the Navy at Bainbridge, Maryland." After his training he was assigned to the Aircraft Carrier USS Lexington, also in the Pacific, to fight against the Japanese. Warren and Ely both saw plenty of action but came out unhurt and in good shape. Warren was even able to visit Ely on board the Lexington during the Campaign. I remember the little banner with two stars hanging in our front living room window in honor of our two family members who were serving in the Armed Forces. I also remember how thrilled Mother and Daddy were to receive letters from them.

They both received their discharge shortly after the war ended in 1945 and returned to Chapel Hill to further their college education.

Now it was My Turn

I remember attending Ely's graduation from Woodberry in 1944, so at least I knew a little something about the campus. It was a beautiful campus located in the foothills of the Blue Ridge Mountains. As my ninth grade year was drawing to an end, Daddy started talking more about my going to Woodberry. I would need to take an entrance exam to see where I placed. About the only thing I remember about the exam was that the math portion was very difficult because they were asking questions and giving problems, which I had never had or seen before. Maybe I should say I don't remember ever studying them before. Anyway I knew I didn't do well at all on the exam. The results came back fairly soon and showed I was very weak in math—and probably some of the other courses too.

In the meantime I broke my right little toe while playing tennis barefooted at the Country Club. Regarding the incident it is interesting to note that as I was running to my right I heard a popping sound. My first thought was that somebody had thrown a steel marble that had hit my right little toe. I stopped immediately in my tracks and looked around to see who had done such a thing. No one was in sight. When I took my next step I crumbled to the ground. As I got up and hobbled off the court I realized my toe was broken.

At that point I don't remember thinking much about Woodberry one way or the other, for in my mind Woodberry was "on hold". Our family's attention was directed toward traveling to Philadelphia to attend the wedding of my Cousin Clifton West and Joan Darby. He had finished medical school in Philadelphia where they had met, and we were all going up for the big celebration, including "me and my crutches", with a broken toe. Warren was already in Philadelphia, so Ely made the trip with us. By the way, the rehearsal dinner was at the Book Binders Restaurant there in Philadelphia. That was the first time I ever had lobster and I remember being impressed by not only the delicious meal itself, but also having to wear a bib.

Daddy Put Me on the Spot

The trip back home was quite interesting. Daddy "decided to drop by Woodberry" to check things out. He had evidently called Mr. J. Carter Walker, the Head Master, for an appointment, because the next thing I knew, Mother and Daddy and I were in his office for a conference. I remember Mr. Walker as being a very serious, elderly gentleman. His mouth was turned down and I saw no hint of a smile or any light-hearted conversation. Frankly, I was scared to death! Mr. Walker went on to explain to Daddy that with the way I showed up on the entrance exam it was very doubtful if I could make it through Woodberry. We all knew the school's high standards for academic excellence. Daddy was being a good lawyer and advocate as he tried to defend his son's position. He told Mr. Walker that a lot of the material I had been tested on was not familiar to me and I just didn't do well on the test. He was doing his best to justify why I did so poorly. Then he said, "And besides that he broke his foot." (If the truth were known I probably broke my toe after taking the test, so what difference would a broken toe (foot) make?) I never will forget Mr. Walker's response: "Well, he doesn't write with his foot, does he?" As comical as that was I don't remember anyone laughing, although I'm sure Mr. Walker must have at least cracked a slight smile.

At that point Daddy, seeing his case appeared hopeless, made one last valiant effort to convince Mr. Walker. He looked him straight in the eye and said, "Mr. Walker, I know my boy. I know he can do the work. Both his brothers did well at Woodberry and Dan can do well too. He's just as smart as Warren and Ely. I know my boy." (Daddy may have stretched the truth when he said I was as smart as Warren and Ely). Anyway, Daddy kept expressing his confidence in me and was really becoming impassioned as he pleaded with Mr. Walker to just give me a chance. Then he came in with the final blow and said in no uncertain terms, "I'll tell you what I'll do. If you'll let him in, I'll give you a thousand dollars if he doesn't graduate in the upper 20% of his class. Just give him a chance and I'll prove it to you. I know Dan and I know he can do it! He'll do as well if not better than my other two boys. And besides that, he's a better athlete. He's an excellent golfer and a good basketball player." There I sat, listening to Daddy talk about what a great guy I was. I was both humbled and "scared to death" at the same time. He really put me on the spot. But way down deep I was thinking to myself, "If Daddy thinks I can do it, if he has that much confidence in me, maybe I can do it. I knew a thousand dollars was a lot of money back then (60 years ago)—probably worth ten or fifteen thousand dollars in today's money. I could tell Mr. Walker was greatly impressed with the intensity of Daddy's passion and zeal. After a brief pause to reflect on Daddy's comments he said, "Well, if he had his bags packed, maybe he could finish out the summer session to see what he could do." Daddy's instant response was, "He's all packed and ready to go!" Unbeknown to me, Mother had packed a suitcase full of clothes and other essentials for summer school at Woodberry. I remember being assigned to Mr. R.W.D. Taylor to show me around for a brief orientation, etc. Ely was there too, which helped. He showed me the dining room and tried to boost my morale by saying, "You'll have a good time once you get used to it." As he observed the boys coming and going he also offered another word of encouragement by saying, "In one way, I sorta' wish I was back here in school."

A Sad Goodbye

It was time now for Mother and Daddy and Ely to head home. It's a long drive back to Kinston and we needed to say goodbye. There I was, watching them pull away and go slowly down the road leading away from the main building. It was not a good feeling as I watched their car make the final turn and disappear from view. I felt all alone. I didn't know a soul at Woodberry. Daddy had stuck his neck out for me, so I definitely had an incentive to give it my best shot. I couldn't let him down.

A Quick Adjustment

One of my major problems was I had to play catch-up. It so happened that I was in the middle of a six-week term of summer school. I was three weeks late in arriving, so there were only three weeks left to do the work and prove myself. I think I had only three courses, but they kept me busy literally night and day. I was fortunate to have Blair Gammon teach me Spanish one on one.

Having never taken Spanish before, it was all new to me. "Mr. Gammon" was in Ely's class of '44 and at graduation I remember him as being constantly called forward to receive award after award. He led the class as Senior Prefect. Not only did he excel in academics, but also in athletics as well as character and service. He was an excellent teacher and was very patient as he led me day after day. Mr. Sipp was my math teacher and I was in a class with ten or twelve others. I took to him because his last name was pronounced the same as my Mother's maiden name, Seipp. My English teacher was Mr. Jack Chapman, and the class assignment had been to read Dickens' *Oliver Twist*. Being a slow reader with not the best comprehension, I really had to burn the midnight oil to plow through it and catch up. Somehow I managed to finish the book, but when I was told to do a character sketch on one of the characters, I was at a total loss. What was a character sketch? I'd never even heard of a character sketch, so I had to ask questions. Again, the teacher was patient and somehow I managed to write something about Oliver Twist himself. I think there must have been about eight or ten in the class, and as far as I knew they seemed to know what they were doing. I didn't get much sleep, so I guess I was going on pure adrenalin. It seems it was study, study, study all the time. I was slow but persistent in my efforts. When summer session was over I ended up with a 98 in Spanish, a 92 in math, and something like an 88 in English. I don't know how I did it. I guess it was another example of God's grace and mercy.

My real salvation in that summer school (next to God's grace and mercy) was that I was able to take the time to play a little golf. Some form of athletics was required each day to allow us to get some exercise and clear out the cobwebs. A few days before the end of the session they had the "Woodberry Open Golf Tournament." Teachers (or Masters, as they were called) as well as students could participate. I don't remember what I shot but somehow I managed to win the tournament. I played with Mr. Barnette, who was one of the better golfing Masters. Being the summer school golf champion didn't hurt my cause in getting in Woodberry, for when Mother and Daddy came back to pick me up Mr. Walker seemed satisfied enough to let me return in the fall to begin the 10th grade, which was my Fourth Form year.

My First Year at Woodberry

The rest of the summer of 1946 was spent relaxing, playing golf and getting ready for the fall and my first full year at Woodberry. I remember that feeling of excitement, but also one of anxiety and apprehension. At least I had a taste of boarding school and knew a little something of what to expect.

When the time finally came to make the long trip to Orange, Virginia, Mother had packed all my clothes in a big trunk. I think it was the same one I used at Camp Morehead. Ely and Warren were both enrolled at Carolina, so it was just Mother and Daddy and I who made the trip. Of course we had to make room for my golf clubs and other incidentals. It was a packed car, but somehow we made it. Saying goodbye to Mother and Daddy was always hard, but down deep I knew I was going to be all right. I knew the Lord was going to look after me, even though I still had the anxiety that goes with new surroundings. I was able to settle in "House E" with Charlie Richardson as my roommate. He was from Memphis, Tennessee and also a "New Boy". Time would prove him to be one of the smartest boys in the class. Tommy Cover from Gaston, Maryland and I ended up palling around together. Although small in stature, he was a wrestler and we nicknamed him, "The Crusher."

It didn't take long to get in the swing of things. By staying busy all the time we didn't have much time to be homesick. I went out for JV football. After the first two or three weeks of getting in shape we had intra squad games, which was fun up to a point. I was rather skinny and never really pursued going any further with football. My most thrilling moment came when playing right end on defense; I somehow anticipated a long lateral pass and intercepted it, running 40 yards for a touchdown. I still remember the smile that lingered on my face long after the play was over. I continued to play as much golf as I could, looking forward to the spring and trying out for the team. I had heard about having Saturday classes, every Saturday, but I was somewhat shocked to learn that we also had classes on *Thanksgiving Day.* Back home Thanksgiving Day and Friday were vacation days, making for a long weekend from Wednesday through Sunday. Not so at Woodberry! We went to classes six days a week every week from the first day of school in

September until Christmas holidays began in mid-December. Saturday night they usually showed a movie in the auditorium. My first movie was the old version of "Les Misérables" with Charles Lawton as Jean Valjean. I remember how impressed I was with the story and its message of encouragement. We had no weekends off and no chance to see family all during that time. But we got used to it. Sunday was our only day of rest. We would sleep late, catch up on our studies and play golf or basketball in the afternoon. Our church service was held in early evening in Saint Andrews Chapel on campus. It was based on the Episcopal services of worship and was always a meaningful time for me. We had a school Chaplain who usually conducted the services and delivered the sermon, although at times one of the Masters or a Senior would give the inspirational talk. That was one of my first experiences of kneeling for prayer in church, and I remember how impressed I was of the effectiveness of being in a kneeling position while praying. Kneeling with eyes closed tends to humble one before the Lord. Even today, with morning devotions and prayers, my usual habit is to kneel beside my bed.

Adjusting to Woodberry Life

The fall of 1946 was spent mainly getting adjusted to being away from home and concentrating on my studies. I don't remember the exact hourly time schedule, but we got up in time for an early breakfast. The whole student body of about 250 or so ate all our meals in the big dining room. Mr. Walker gave the blessing after ringing a bell at 7:30 A.M. (I believe) sharp. I don't remember anyone ever being late for any of the meals. Most of the time, his blessing was always the same. I can still hear him now, speaking clearly and with authority: "Bless we beseech Thee this food to our use and us to thy faithful and loving service; help us to bear in mind the needs and wants of others. Amen." The food was generally very good. We were always hungry and had plenty to eat. We wore coats and ties to all meals as well as classes. "New Boys" could easily be spotted with black ties. At the end of the year we were allowed to snip a portion of our tie after each exam.

The Honor Code

At least once a week we would meet in the assembly hall after supper where Mr. Walker would speak to us about Woodberry or some topic of interest. He talked about values and the need to be honest in all of our dealings. He emphasized the Honor Code, which has always been the essence and backbone of what a Woodberry boy is expected to be. Since the school's founding in 1889 by Mr. Walker's father, the Honor Code has been the most cherished of all Woodberry's traditions. He made it clear to us that without honesty and integrity, academic excellence meant absolutely nothing in the overall development of a boy's character and success in life. He emphasized the need for hard work and fair play in everything we did. Even though these same values had been a vital part of our family life at home, it was refreshing to hear them continually being brought to our attention. Mother and Daddy set a wonderful example for Warren, Ely, and me and we were fully aware of the value of having the Honor Code a natural part of our character. He also emphasized that we were among a privileged few to be able to attend Woodberry. Not every boy could afford to come. We were to display a natural sense of humility and not think that just because we were Woodberry boys we were any better than anyone else.

At the end of every test and exam we always wrote and signed the same statement setting forth the examination pledge: "I hereby pledge my word of honor that I have neither given nor received assistance on this examination (or test)." As a part of our training we were also told that any sign we saw entitled "WHITE FLAG" meant that we were not to touch it, whether it was a door, a piece of machinery or whatever. White Flag was strictly a "NO-NO."

The Honor Code in Action

In one assembly meeting Mr. Walker told of one Woodberry boy who was playing in a golf match with another school. It seems that while he was addressing his ball in the rough (or wooded area) his ball moved slightly from its original position. No one saw it and he could have easily kept going without being noticed. But he knew that such a movement called for a two-stroke penalty. He immediately called the penalty against himself, resulting in his losing the hole as well as the match. No one else would have ever known, but the boy himself knew. His conscience and sense of honest and fair play led him to abide by the Honor Code he had learned to value at Woodberry.

It's interesting to note that some years later while Warren, Ely, Tom Griffin and I were playing for the "Perry Family Birthday Trophy", I applied that lesson on the 18th green at the Morehead City Country Club. It was my birthday and son Daniel couldn't play, so I got Tom to take his place. We came to the 18th green and all I needed to beat Warren by a stroke was to make a four foot putt. Well, I made the putt and they all congratulated me. No one said anything about what appeared to be an incidental happening in the process of my stroking the ball. I said, "Oh, I hit the ball two times and that's a penalty." Warren said, "What do you mean? I didn't see anything." Tom and Ely both agreed that they saw nothing wrong or out of order. I told them I must have had too much follow through, for I definitely hit it twice. That is somewhat of a phenomenon, but it does happen from time to time. Normally in everyday friendly matches we don't worry about this sort of thing. We overlook it and move on. Of course this was a friendly match, but at the same time it was something special. We all knew we were playing for the trophy. Anyway, I knew I would "feel funny" if I didn't assess myself a penalty. A day or so later, Warren brought up the matter again saying that I had really won instead of resulting in a tie. It was then that I told him the story of the Woodberry boy Mr. Walker told us over 50 years ago. If my memory serves me correctly, that boy was Mr. Walker's own son.

The School Prayer

Every time we met in the assembly hall with Mr. Walker he would always have us pray what he referred to a "A Boy's Prayer." In my first assembly when he led us in prayer I had to just listen along with all the other new boys while the others prayed along with Mr. Walker. It didn't take but two or three times before the words became second nature to all of us. It was so ingrained in me that I have remembered it throughout the years and even to this day I still use it from time to time.

Here's the prayer as we learned it:
>Dear Heavenly Father,
>Give me clean hands, clean words, and clean thoughts;
>Help me to stand for the hard right
>Against the easy wrong;
>Save me from habits that harm;
>Teach me to work as hard,
>And play as fair in thy sight alone,
>As if the whole world saw;
>Forgive me when I am unkind,
>And help me to forgive those who are unkind to me;
>Keep me ready to help others at some cost to myself,
>Send me chances to do a little good every day
>And so grow more like Christ.
>Amen.

Back then no one thought of questioning the political correctness of Mr. Walker expecting us all to join in.

How Much Time do we Have?

One of the funniest things I heard Mr. Walker say was at one of the assemblies when we had a guest speaker. I don't remember his name but his subject had to do with the Communist threat throughout the world and especially to and in America. He was making the point that time was short and our country needed to be prepared and on guard. After a moment of silence he emphatically posed the question to his attentive audience, "How much time do we have?" Mr. Walker cleared his throat and with assurance answered back, "I think about twelve minutes." With that, the whole assembly burst forth in laughter and giggles. We all knew he had misunderstood the context of the question, but it sure afforded us a minute of relief from the seriousness of the occasion. At the time, Mr. Walker was not in good health and was only a few months away from retirement. Although his mind was generally clear there were times when he showed lapses in concentration. This apparently was one of them.

Counting the Curves

Before I went to Woodberry, Ely had told me the story about Mr. Walker's "tunnel vision." His particular eye disease restricted his peripheral vision to seeing only that which was directly in front of him. The traditional story was that when driving the two-mile long winding road through the wooded area leading to the school he would use the counting system. He knew every curve, every turn. He had all of them memorized. He couldn't see to the right or to the left—only straight ahead. His only recourse was from the onset to establish his predetermined speed and start counting. He knew each degree and angle of each curve. It was straight for a count of five, then a 30° left curve for a count of seven, then a 20° turn back to the right for thirteen, straight for four, 35° left for nine, 25° right for 12; on and on until he was home free going up the final straight stretch to the main building. That was the way I understood the story and I never questioned its veracity.

My First Report Card

Schoolwork was not easy for me. I had to work for what I got. For some of the boys, it was a snap. They seemed to sail right through. In fact, some were brilliant. I remember "Shady" Eller from Winston Salem as being one of the leaders in class-ranking. In a straw vote at the end of my senior year, we voted Gus McCommell of Frankfort, Kentucky, Walter Ramberg of Chevy Chase, Maryland, and Ned Slaughter of Charlottesville, Virginia as "Best Students." I haven't kept up with Gus and Walter, but Ned turned out to be an outstanding attorney in Charlottesville. By the way, I was voted "Most Optimistic." It was not common knowledge for each of us to know how everyone else was doing. Class-rankings weren't posted after each reporting period, but word would get around from time to time as to who was at or near the top. The grading system went something like this:

90 to 100 A-Excellent
80 to 89 B-Good
70 to 79 C-Average

60 to 69 D-Poor
0 to 59 F-Fail

I don't remember that we were given a class-ranking for each reporting period, and I frankly can't remember how many reporting periods we had. I believe there was a midterm report, and then a final report for each quarter or semester. I never thought of myself as being any better than an average student; compared with all those smart Woodberry boys, I knew I was not in the same ballpark. Therefore, I was pleasantly surprised that my first report showed my grade average was 86 with a class ranking of 16 (or was it 14?) out of a class of about 85. Anyway, when Daddy got the report, Mr. Walker had written at the bottom, "Commendable Report. I don't think I'll get that $1,000!" That tickled Daddy pink! Of course, I was thrilled too, but somehow I didn't understand the real meaning of the word, "Commendable." My first thought was it denoted average or maybe good, but nothing to get excited about. Knowing my own limitations, I thought Mr. Walker should have said EXCELLENT report. Not until I checked the dictionary did I understand he was saying, "Worthy of praise and recommendation." That made me feel better, even though I knew I lacked the acumen and mental sharpness of many of the others. In class, I didn't feel comfortable expressing myself and conveying my thoughts. I was afraid to speak up at certain times, even though I thought I knew the answer.

During my "new boy" year as a fourth former (sophomore), I think I did rank as high as 12th one time, but most of the time I recall being in the 20s. I seem to recall there were two or three times I ranked in the 30s and 40s. Out of an original class of 85 or 86, I think we ended up with a graduating class of about 65 or so. Quite a few had dropped out for various reasons. Some flunked out; some just didn't like it and had a hard time making the adjustment to boarding school life; and I think one or two were dismissed for honor code violations.

Mother and Daddy became fairly close acquaintances of both Mr. and Mrs. Walker. Mrs. Walker was known to be the "Grand Old Lady" type. Having known her since Warren and Ely were at Woodberry from 1940–1942 and 1941–1944, respectively, Mother often took her flowers and Magnolia leaves from our yard. She died sometime during my time at Woodberry, I think in 1947. Mr. Walker retired in 1948 at the end of my junior year and died shortly thereafter.

My First Speech

You would think that by this time in my educational career, I would be able to stand before a group and make a short speech without being scared to death. Actually, my first speech at Woodberry was not really a speech at all. It was a poem. The assignment was to memorize "The Concord Hymn" by Ralph Waldo Emerson and then to recite it before the class. That sounded simple enough, for it happened to be published in "101 Famous Poems" which Mother and Daddy gave me when I was younger. I had memorized quite a few of the poems in the book, but not the "The Concord Hymn." I was accustomed to reciting poems in front of Mother and Daddy but not in a classroom setting. To my best recollection, I don't believe we ever had to quote a poem or make a speech anytime during my nine years of school in Kinston. For some reason, I felt intimidated and self-conscious even thinking about having to do it in front of the class. Mr. Chapman called on several to recite each day until all the class had participated. When my time finally came, I remember standing there and saying the first line, "By the rude bridge that arched the flood." That was about the last thing I remember. I had memorized those four verses, sixteen lines, so well that after I started, the rest was automatic. I remember standing in front of a sea of people saying something—I don't know what. I must have gotten through it without any flaws or hesitation, because no one said anything, and Mr. Chapman didn't have to correct me.

Many years later, Margaret and I visited that arched bridge in Concord, Massachusetts. We were on a trip to the New England and made a special point of viewing the bridge that Emerson immortalized in his famous poem. It took me back to the day I was "scared to death" to talk about it. It was actually a hymn that was sung at the completion of the Battle Monument on April 19, 1886, four years after Emerson's death. Standing at the bridge, I was able to recall and recite to Margaret the first verse, totally unafraid and fully aware of its historical meaning:

By the rude bridge that arched the flood,
Their flag to April's breeze unfurled;
Here once the embattled farmers stood;
And fired the shot heard round the world.

My Love for Poetry

As I write about "The Concord Hymn," my thoughts go back to the beginning of my love for poetry. As a three-, four-, and five-year-old, I had to rest in the afternoons. Rest meant sleep, for I had no trouble sleeping during my rest period. It was a part of my development and "went with the territory." But as I got older, Mother noticed that I was just lying there with my eyes open, restless, and wanting to go outside and play. It was then she laid down the law. She gave me a choice. I can hear her saying even now, "Dan, you need your rest. You can't go outside and play during your rest period. You'll either have to go to sleep—or if you can't go to sleep, you'll have to learn poetry." Well, I just couldn't go to sleep, and so I became familiar with "101 Famous Poems." Mother and Daddy had given a copy to Warren and Ely, so now I guess it was my turn.

Daddy would challenge me to learn as many poems as I could by paying me money. I got 25 cents for the longer ones: "If" and "L'Envoi" by Rudyard Kipling; "The Builders," "The Day is Done," and "A Psalm of Life" by Henry Wadsworth Longfellow; "The Daffodils" by William Wordsworth; and "Abou Ben Adhem" by James Leigh Hunt. The book also included several prose selections, and I got 25 cents for learning The Ten Commandments and Lincoln's Gettysburg Address. He paid me 10 cents for the shorter ones such as "Trees" by Sergeant Joyce Kilmer. Learning such poems as a young child really gave me a special appreciation for poetry. I was later inspired to learn several lengthy well-known epics, such as "Casey at the Bat"; and "The Shooting of Dan McGrew," and "The Cremation of Sam McGee" by Robert W. Service. Warren was big on epics, and it must have rubbed off on me.

I had known all along how both Mother and Daddy loved poetry. During their courting days, Daddy would bet Mother a kiss that he could quote more poetry than she could. He would quote a poem, and then she would quote one. Sometimes, he would quote the first line of a poem they both knew, and she would quote the second; they would alternate line by line until they got to the end. He said he knew a lot of poems, but she knew even more—so I guess she won the kiss. (Sounds to me like there were no losers in that bet.) On family car trips, we spent a lot of time quoting poems. Daddy would start, and from there, we'd all follow along.

Music—Clarinet, Piano, and Singing

I was able to keep up my interest in the clarinet and piano all through my three years at Woodberry. We had a little eight-man band we "messed around with." My senior year, Billy Keiter of Kinston (third former) played the trumpet with us. He became a doctor and still lives in Kinston. Frank Maloney of Hopewell, Virginia, played the trumpet. He practiced law in Richmond before his death a few years ago. Bill Pittman of Sanford played the trumpet. He's a lawyer with a title insurance company in Raleigh. Before home football games, we would go marching down the hill toward the football field, playing fight songs and marches, setting the stage for the big game. That was a lot of fun! I also had a good time being one of several cheerleaders at the football games.

Vernon Purdue-Davis was in charge of the musical program at Woodberry. We had an eleven-man choral group, which performed in white coats, bow ties, and straw hats. George Ives from New Bern, George Irvin (doctor) from Winston-Salem, Brad Harris (roommate) from Lynchburg, Frank Davenport (doctor) from Timmonsville, South Carolina (of ghost-story fame at Camp Morehead), Ned Slaughter (brilliant student and later a lawyer) from Charlottesville, Virginia, and Bill Pittman (lawyer) from Sanford were among that group. One of the best times I had as a member of the "Woodberry Octet" was when we went to St. Catherine's School for Girls in Richmond and sang some of the old Gay Nineties and Roaring Twenties favorites. "Daisy" ("A Bicycle Built for Two") was my favorite. We had a great time strutting around, tipping our straw hats, and cutting up. The girls seemed to like it, too.

In May of 1947, the music club of Woodberry and the Glee Club of Saint Anne's School presented the comic opera, "The Headless Horseman." I also played Tchaikovsky's "Chanson Triste" as a clarinet soloist. Our Woodberry choir of St. Andrews Chapel also performed at graduation in June 1947, and I noticed the bulletin listed us as having 42 members. As a clarinet soloist, I played Dvorak's *Largo* from the "New World Symphony." As I was about to play the last notes, I wondered whether they would be clear and mellow. Relieved, I managed to get through it without a blemish. Mother and Daddy were on hand for that one.

George Ives from New Bern, Brad Harris (roommate my second year), and I were among the tenors in the chapel choir. George and Brad were both better singers than I, but I learned a lot and eventually was able to keep up pretty well. At least we all had a good time, and it was a great experience. My first year, seniors Neal Howard from Farmville and Noell Carr of Durham were very good baritone soloists.

Al Jolson, My Hero

Sometime in the early 1940s, I was captivated by "The Al Jolson Story," the movie about Al Jolson, the popular vaudeville and minstrel-show singer. I just loved his style of singing "Mammy," "California, Here I Come," "Rosie," "April Showers," "Danny Boy," and many other hit songs of the 1920s and 1930s. I got records (78 rpm) of all his songs and memorized the words. I also could imitate his moves and mouth his words so perfectly that in my own imagination I became Al Jolson himself, prancing around and having a good time. I spent hours and hours practicing and hamming it up, just like ol' Al (at least I thought so). I guess that is why I liked singing all the vaudeville oldies with the Woodberry Octet. That was great fun, and I'm sure it was through my love of Al Jolson that I developed the reputation for being a "ham at heart."

During my senior year at Woodberry, I lived in House B with George Bell as my roommate. One Saturday night, a bunch of us were listening to Al Jolson. I was hamming it up singing "Mammy," complete with straw hat and bow tie. A younger boy named Dan Moore from Huntington, West Virginia, took some pictures, and later, to my surprise, he presented me with an oil painting portrait. There I was with straw hat in hand and mouth wide open, singing "Mammy"! He actually did a pretty good job, and I still have the portrait somewhere in the attic.

During one of my exams, I was stumped on a math problem and my mind started wandering. Before I knew it, I was picturing Al Jolson singing "California, Here I Come." As I was struggling to figure out the answer to the problem, I had a hard time getting him out of my mind. All I could see was Al Jolson singing, with straw hat and out-stretched arms. It was an anxious time, but somehow I managed to pass the exam in spite of ol' Al.

One time, shortly after becoming hooked on Al Jolson, I was telling Ely at the breakfast table how I loved to sing Jolson's songs and imitate his voice. I was telling him I never got tired of him—in fact, the more I listened to his records, the more I wanted to listen. Ely jokingly said, "Well at that rate, after a while that's all you'll be doing—singing and listening to Al Jolson." That was before I went to Woodberry. The memory of Ely's remark came back to me during that exam when the ghost of Al Jolson kept popping in and out of my mind.

It wasn't until I got to Carolina that I bought a 45-rpm record of Eddie Canter singing some of Jolson's signature songs. My roommate, Cooper Taylor of Raleigh, and I had a good time learning the words and singing, "How 'Ya Gonna Keep 'Em Down on the Farm after They've Seen Paree?" We would dance around the room with the record player turned up—acting just like Eddie Canter. In many respects, Eddie Canter and Al Jolson had the same style as entertainers. They were "right up my alley"; even to this day, I still get a thrill listening to them. "Ida" was another one of my Eddie Canter favorites. I still love to sing, "I-da, sweet as ap-ple ci-a-a-da." Many of those oldies I can play on the piano—and I get a thrill every time I play them. From time to time, people used to tell me, "Dan, you were born too late. You should have been born before the turn of the century, so you would be in your prime singing with Al Jolson and Eddie Canter." That would have been fun back then, but in retrospect I have come to understand that the Lord has me exactly where he wants me. He meant for me to be born July 2, 1931, and living today at the ripe old age of 76 (and counting)—doing exactly what I am doing.

Chapter X

SPORTS AT WOODBERRY

Golfing was fun at Woodberry. The nine-hole course was right there on campus. The first tee was only a few steps from the gym, and the ninth green was only a short walk from the main building. Those of us who were on the golf team played at least a few holes most every day—even when it rained. Golf was in our blood. That first year we were undefeated, winning all nine matches. Apparently, we had some good competition, for two of our victories were over the freshman teams at the University of Virginia and Hampton-Sydney College. Based on our perfect record, we were invited to participate in the Eastern Interscholastic Tournament in Greenwich, Connecticut, on June 10th 1947. That was the first time a Woodberry golf team had been invited to this tournament, comprised of the top prep school teams from the eastern part of the country.

All eight members of our team made the trip, but only the top four scorers for each team would count for the medal play. Our coach, Sam McLaughlin, was unable to go with us, so Paul Brightman, another master, became our official chaperon. Mother and Daddy also made the trip. We were fortunate enough to stay in New York City at an apartment owned by the parents of one of our classmates. Mr. Brightman got us tickets to see "Kiss Me Kate" on Broadway, which was a real treat. Because it was my first trip to the big city, it was quite an exciting time. Television was just beginning to be developed commercially, and I remember the fascination we all had with this newfangled picture box. The reception was not the best, by any means. Snow and wavy streaks seemed to be more prevalent than the pictures themselves, but, nevertheless, the general idea of TV was made known to us for the first time.

After a day of practice and getting used to the course, the tournament got under way. It was an exciting time together as a team, representing Woodberry and competing in such a prestigious tournament. The other five schools were Choate, Taft, Hill, Peddie, and Andover. Since this was in 1947, almost 60 years ago at the time of this writing, I don't remember all the details. Mother had kept a scrapbook, which helped me recall the excitement. The headlines of a *Daily Free Press* article, Monday, June 16, 1947, read, "DAN PERRY IS ONLY FRESHMAN MEMBER OF WINNING PREP GOLFERS." The article explained that "Woodberry Forest, famous Virginia prep-school, alma mater of many young men in this section won the eastern prep-school tournament played last week at Greenwich, Connecticut." It further stated that, as a member of the winning team, I was, "the only freshman on any of the six teams." Of course, that was incorrect, for I was a sophomore, fifteen years old at the time. It also said, "The medal play gave Woodberry an eleven stroke victory over runner-up Choate"; It also said our four-member team average was 82 strokes. Craig Wright, from Lima, Ohio, our number-one player, was medalist with a 78. Other team members were Bob Agee of Huntington, West Virginia and Joe Fiveash of Norfolk, Virginia. By today's standards a team average of 82 is not all that good. In fact, the junior golfers I know and read about today would outshine us in every way. The best of them can break par on a regular basis.

The Carolinas Junior Golf Tournament

The Sunday after returning from Greenwich, I left for Greensboro to compete in the Carolinas Junior Golf Tournament. I stayed in the home of Mr. and Mrs. Shahane Taylor who were friends of Mother and Daddy. We must not have had a practice round because the tournament began on Monday morning, but I was fortunate enough to have a good day. I managed to shoot a 74 and tie Henry Clark of Reidsville for medalist honors. The *Greensboro Daily News* put me in the headlines accompanied with pictures. I was really flying high! The write-up said, "The old and the new got together on the Carolinas Junior Golf Tournament medalists honors here yesterday. Henry Clark, Jr. of Reidsville getting to the top after eight years trying and Dan Perry of Kinston hitting the jackpot on his first endeavor." The second day began the match play and the following day's headlines in big bold letters read, "PERRY TAKES FIRST ROUND IN JUNIOR LINKS TOURNAMENT." The sub-headline read, "KINSTON YOUTH ALSO CAPTURES MEDAL HONORS." The write-up said, "He squeezed out a 2 and 1 victory over Tommy Langley of High Point…. By shooting a 79, Perry copped medalist honors." Henry Clark skied to an 85. In the interview, I was asked all sorts of questions. With full coverage, I told them everything from how Warren got me started at an early age, to Woodberry, to winning the tournament in Greenwich. The article even mentioned about a recent round in Kinston in an eight-hole span when I was five under, with an eagle and three birdies. The coverage was two, full pages. I was not accustomed to such attention. The next day, my bubble burst when Bill Delk of Greenville, South Carolina beat me in the second round 3 and 2. It was fun while it lasted, but it was over now. It was quite an experience for a fifteen-year-old. Henry Clark went on to reach the finals against Al Fitzgerald of Charlotte. I left Greensboro before the tournament was over and don't remember who won. By the way, Bill Williamson of Charlotte also played in the tournament. He went on to play at Carolina and win All-American honors.

I think it was a week or so later that Warren drove me to Pinehurst to play in another junior tournament. The main thing I remember was that Warren followed me around, and I started out with a double bogie on the first hole. I followed with a bogie on the second—that's three over par—on the first two holes with sixteen more to go. I distinctly remember the feeling of despair and discouragement I had as I walked off the second green. Had I driven that far to start off with such a poor showing? I was thinking, "Well, it's all over now. I'm hitting the ball poorly and I'll never be able to recover enough to do much in this tournament." I know Warren must have been disappointed, too, even though he didn't show it at all. He just said, "Don't worry about it. Just keep playing and you'll be all right." At that point, two things apparently happened.

First, I was encouraged by Warren's remarks, and second, I was relieved of the pressure of having to compete. From then on I played just to have fun. I didn't even think about what I was shooting. I parred the next hole and moved on to the fourth. I don't remember if I had any more bogies. If I did, I had a birdie to counteract each bogie, for I ended up shooting the last sixteen holes in even par. Even when I finished the eighteenth hole, I really had no thought of what I had done or how my score compared to that of the rest of the field. To my surprise, my 74 won the medalist honors. I couldn't believe it!

Lesson learned: Even to this day when I start off badly on the first hole or two, I remember that tournament of some 60 years ago. I still get disheartened, but at the same time, I just keep playing and don't give up just because of a slow start. In fact, even when playing today, as a word of encouragement to my playing partner who messes up the first few holes, many times I'll make the comment, "Don't worry. I've had some of my best scores when I start off with a double bogie." With the high scores I shoot today, I have plenty of opportunities to apply that lesson to my own game. In my younger days, it was somewhat of a rarity to be three over par on the first two holes. Now, it seems to be the rule rather that the exception. In fact, it's not unusual to start off four over on the first two holes and six over on the first three. When that happens, such starts set the stage for the rest of the round. But at least I can return to "yesteryear" and remember the "good ol' days" when Warren saw his baby brother win a golf tournament after a slow start.

June 1947—A Month to Remember

June of 1947 was the high light of my golfing career. That month I was the number-two man on the Woodberry team that won the Eastern Interscholastic Tournament in Greenwich, Connecticut, as well as winning medalist honors in both the Carolina Junior Tournament in Greensboro and another tournament in Pinehurst. After returning home from Pinehurst, I had two 68s in the span of a week, before turning sixteen on July 2nd. I still remember the elation I experienced when everyone at home was talking about what a fine golfer I was. It was exciting, and confidence in my game was beginning to show in my actions and talk. I honestly didn't think I was to the point of bragging about my accomplishments. It was more in the nature of feeling good about myself and looking forward to what the future held for me as a golfer. It wasn't until some time later that I began putting all the attention in perspective. I began to realize two things. First, I was not as good as I thought I was; nor was I as good as others may have perceived me to be. Second, any talent or degree of expertise I was displaying in golf was not of my own doing, but was a gift from God. I may have worked hard at it while enjoying the game, but there was nothing I could brag about myself. The credit should be given to the Creator and not the creature.

We continued to have an excellent golf team during my last two years at Woodberry. In fact, I don't believe we lost a single match, if my memory serves me right. Joe Fiveash and I had the distinction of beating the "Guatemala Open Champion" in successive years. Apparently, Guatemala was not very much into golf at the time. He was young and on one of the school teams we played, but I don't remember which one. My recollection is he was only a "pretty fair" player, which made the distinction of beating the "Guatemala Open Champion" not all that great an accomplishment.

I continued to enjoy playing golf at Woodberry and competing against other schools. I was elected captain of the team my senior year. My lowest score on Woodberry's 9 hole course was one 32 and a couple of 33s. I also had several 34s, but I don't remember my lowest 18 hole score on that par 35 course. In post-season play, Woodberry was also invited back in both my junior and senior years to compete in the Eastern Interscholastic Tournament in Greenwich, which we had won my first year in 1947. We came out second in 1948. I don't remember how we placed my senior year. I just know we didn't win.

Basketball at Woodberry

I was fortunate enough to be a starter on the varsity basketball team my last two years, and was elected alternate captain my senior year. Being more of a team sport than golf, basketball afforded me the opportunity to develop some rather close ties with several of the players. Ben Walden from Midway, Kentucky, was our center, captain, and leading scorer my senior year. "Big Red" could be counted on to pull us through when the going got rough. He was a good leader, and we became close friends. Although he was only 6' 2½" tall, we thought of him as being the big guy in the middle. I played forward at 6' 1½" and was also considered to be tall back in those days. By today's standards, we were a short team. Ballard Morton of Louisville, Kentucky, was the other forward at about 6'1". Bruce Glenn of Lexington, Kentucky, was our playmaker at one guard and Ferd ("Pete") Carter was the other guard. My one moment of glory in basketball was the first game in my senior year. We played Fredericksburg High School, and I scored 26 points on 13 of 15 shots, most of which were from the outside. It seems that every time I threw it up, it went in. I remember that feeling of being in control of my shots. We had all worked hard and were glad to start the season with a big win. The amazing thing was that I played less than half of that game. Everyone had visions of my being a big star and leading the team to a great year. We actually did have a good year, but I was not the overall leader. Ben Walden proved to be the man to count on. Also Ballard Morton, only a junior, also had a great year. By the way, Ballard and I were the only two on the team who wore glasses. We stuck a strip of adhesive tape to our temples across each stem to keep them in place. It worked pretty well most of the time. In fact our glasses fell off only a couple of times all season. My specialty shot was the "one-handed push shot" from out around the circle. One write up referred to me as "the one handed push shot artist." I wasn't much of an artist, but it was fun trying.

Woodberry's chief rival in all sports had always been Virginia's Episcopal High School. It was like the old Duke-Carolina rivalry. If we beat EHS, we had a good season. It was always the last game of the season, and the preparation was always emotional. In my junior year, we lost a close one at EHS. It was a long bus ride home with very little conversation. As I sat there in a seat by myself, Coach Mac Pitt asked me a question. My response was such that he knew I had been crying. He didn't pursue the conversation any further—he just left me there to mope in my own pity party. The next year, the game was at Woodberry, and we managed to come out on top. Blair Gammon was our coach. What a day of rejoicing that was!

Three Other Memorable Games

One day I got a message from Warren, at Carolina Law School, who said that he wanted to come watch me play a game. Shortly after he arrived, he came by my room and said he brought Bobby with him. At first I didn't know who "Bobby" was and was naturally expecting a boy. Evidently, he thought I was aware he had been dating Bobbie Stockton, a law classmate. After I inquired further, he told me, "No it's a girl." It was then I learned that his friend spelled her name with an "ie" and not a "y". I don't remember who we played, whether we won or lost, or how many points I scored; however, I do remember how thrilled I was at the thought of Warren and his girlfriend making the special effort to travel from Chapel Hill, North Carolina, to Woodberry Forest, Virginia, just to see me play. Bobbie Stockton turned out to be more than Warren's friend, for they were married on June 9, 1951, after their graduation from law school in 1950. Barbara S. Perry then became my friend and dear sister-in-law, a relationship that has been cherished throughout the years.

A second memorable game occurred when we traveled to Pennsylvania to play Mercersburg School. It was a long trip, which only the players and coach made. No Woodberry cheerleaders or supporters were in the stands. We were expecting a long and tough game, since Mercersburg was known to have a very good team. When Mercersburg scored the first basket on an easy lay up, I thought the roof was going to cave in, the noise was so loud. At that point, I knew we were in for a long day. But a strange thing happened! When we made our first basket, we heard some loud cheers, yelling, and applause coming from the stands. How could that be? We brought no cheering section, and the only cheers we were expecting would be from our own bench of eight or ten players. Well, would you believe that the cheers we were hearing came from supporters of the Mercersburg team? The first time it happened, I thought they might be ridiculing us and saying, "Congratulations! We didn't expect you to score at all!" Strangely, they continued to cheer every time we scored. Although it wasn't of the same magnitude as when our opponents scored, it was enough support for us to know they really meant it. It went beyond a little polite applause for a team so far from home. Their unusual expression of good sportsmanship had left a lasting impression on me. I still remember how shocked I was to hear them cheering for their opponents. I had never heard of it before—and I haven't heard of it since. By the way, we lost to a better team. My recollection is that Mercersburg's star player, Jack Wallace, ended up playing for the Tar Heels.

The third memorable game was in my junior year when we played St. Christopher's in Richmond. We were leading by five points with the clock ticking down. They had the ball. 10 – 9 – 8 – 7 – 6 – 5. Surely, we had this one in the bag! But they scored a basket and called a time out with only three seconds left. With a three-point lead, we still felt good about the outcome. We had the ball. Our strategy was for Ben Walden to throw a long pass to me down court. Easy enough, and the game would be over. But that was just not to be. As I was breaking down court for the pass, I looked back and saw that they had intercepted the ball and scored two quick points a split second before the buzzer. That still gave us a one-point lead. The only problem was the referee called a fowl against us. You guessed it. The player from St. Christopher's made the free throw, and the game went into overtime. The stands went wild in that little cracker box of a gym! They definitely had the momentum! We lost the game (I think it was by five points), and the journey back home was sad and full of regrets. How could we have lost a game with only three seconds to play and ahead by five points? Unbelievable! We had to wait 'til next year to get our revenge.

My Introduction To Soccer—Fall of 1948

Mr. Harold Donnerly came to Woodberry as a new master my senior year and is credited with introducing soccer to Woodberry. I was not necessarily looking forward to playing football my last year, so several of us basketball players decided to give soccer a try. Most of us were new to the game, although several had grown up with it and welcomed the change. One boy in particular who grew up in France was pretty good. I believe we elected Ballard Morton, a junior and a star basketball player, as captain of the first soccer team. Ballard was a good scholar and natural athlete and all around good guy. His father was

U.S. Senator Thruston Morton from Kentucky. The main thing I remember about playing soccer was that we were constantly running up and down the field. We spent most of the time learning the fundamentals, for most of us were totally inexperienced. It was a fairly big squad, so Mr. Donnerly divided us into two teams as equally as he could, which enabled us to scrimmage each other. I don't remember playing any outside games that first year; that came the following year. In the meantime, soccer practice served as a good tool to get us in shape for the coming basketball season.

Chapter XI

FRIENDS AND OTHER WOODBERRY ACTIVITIES

My First Airplane Ride

Tom Helm and I became close friends, which led to an invitation for a week's visit at his home in Louisville, Kentucky, the summer of 1947, after our first year at Woodberry. Piedmont Airlines had recently come to Kinston, and I was about to take my first plane ride. I was excited about visiting Tom, his family, and friends; however, at least for the moment, I was even more excited about flying. I remembered Ely telling me during the War that the most dangerous part about flying was the take off and landing—and we were about to take off. I can well remember as we taxied out to the runway how noisy that two-engine prop plane was. It was deafening! I could hardly hear myself think. Then we came to a stop. The engine revved up louder and louder, but we weren't going anywhere. The plane was beginning to shake more and more, but still no movement. I learned later that the pilot was testing the engines as he went through his checklist before take off. From my window seat, I could see the wing flaps moving up and down—then finally we slowly began to move. As we picked up speed, I remember how my eyes were glued to the scenery of buildings and trees racing by. We picked up more speed, but we were still on the ground. "We can't go much faster," I thought. "When would we be airborne? I wanted to fly, not race along the ground. How long was the runway? Would it give out while we were still on the ground?" Then I thought of Ely's comment about the take off being so dangerous. As I sat there, anxiously looking out the window with all those thoughts racing through my mind, I suddenly felt a different sensation. We were gradually leaving the ground! I never will forget the thrill of that lift off. The biggest smile came over my face—a smile that stayed with me as we slowly gained altitude. I was actually flying for the first time! I just couldn't get that big smile off my face. It lingered for what seemed like a half hour as we gradually climbed through the cluster of white clouds. Even though it was a bouncy flight, I wasn't really afraid, just a little anxious at times. I remember the landing as also being a little bouncy. The first time the wheels hit the runway, the engines revved up a little causing us to be airborne slightly, but then settled back down. I then knew we were OK. I wore that same broad smile as we taxied toward the terminal. It lingered just as before. My first plane ride was over, and I looked forward to a nice visit with Tom. Daddy had told me to call him after I arrived so he would know I had a safe trip. It totally slipped my mind until the next night—over a day late. When I telephoned him of my safe arrival, he said, "I know. I would have heard had anything happened."

Several things I remember about that visit to Louisville in 1947. Everybody welcomed me as if I was a long, lost brother. The Helm's home reminded me of a large two-story house in a country setting, something like "The Ponderosa" in the TV series. I don't specifically remember seeing horses, but I do remember the traditional type of white fence. Mrs. Helm was a great cook and gave us great meals. Tom had two younger sisters, Mary being the older of the two. I don't remember the younger one's name (something like Louise)—but I remember Ely dating her for a Kentucky Derby weekend several years later. I still haven't figured out how he got into the picture ahead of me. I just remember his telling us about what a great time he had.

One of my most vivid memories was when Tom and I were given the task of whitewashing the fence. I don't remember our finishing the whole job, but we spent several hours over a two-day period reliving my memories of Tom Sawyer's experience, lapping on buckets of whitewash with scrub brushes. With gloves on hands, we would dip our brushes in each of our buckets and slap it on. Tom took one section of the three-rail fence, and I took the next. At that rate, we moved along fairly quickly. That was fun type of work.

Tom had an army Jeep that he let me drive, mainly around the countryside. We played golf a couple of times and went to several parties. I sorta' took a liking to Cecy Norman, whom I met at a party, and ended up inviting her to the dance weekend at Woodberry the following fall. Tom and his family were great hosts and made me feel right at home. In fact, I had such a good time, I ended up staying a few extra days. (Actually, I think I invited myself. It wasn't until much later that I realized I should have had better sense.) Anyway, we made up for it by having Tom and his parents spend some time with us at Morehead the following year.

My First Debutant Ball

Frank Daniels of Raleigh was in my Woodberry class. In September 1947 (apparently before school started), he invited George Ives and me and several others to stay with him and attend the Debutant Ball festivities. I had heard about the Debutant Ball, but knew little about it. Mother took me to Stadiem's to buy my first tuxedo. When it came time to get dressed, Frank's father did the honors of teaching us all about cuff links, studs, bow ties, and cummerbunds. I had never been dressed up like that before. Mr. and Mrs. Daniels said we all looked handsome, so I guess we at least passed the test to get into the Memorial Auditorium for the big event. Pretty girls in long white evening dresses were everywhere. I didn't know any of them, but they sure looked nice as they were "presented to society." Each girl's name was called as she paused on stage, and then slowly made her way down the steps to gracefully take the arm of her poised and patiently waiting escort, who was dressed in tails. It was a picture to behold as they slowly strolled to take their places in the huge outer circle, then the inner circle, and finally the leader in the middle, making up the formal presentation. Each girl had a streamer, all ending in the middle. It was quite a sight and quite a night. The band played. Formal white dresses were all around. Couples were dancing and milling around, having a good time—and there I was in the midst of all of it—being introduced to a whole new lifestyle. Being a big city guy, Frank and the other boys from Raleigh were familiar with the festivities, but it was all new to me.

Frank Daniels and Julia Jones

For quite a few years, I attended each of the Debutant Ball weekends in Raleigh. There were dances and parties, and all of the boys looked forward to meeting the new debutants. Of course, the girls had to shop for the latest fashions in clothes so as to attract the boys. Everyone was "foot loose and fancy free," and, needless to say, a good time was had by all.

At one of the dances I remember seeing a real cute girl that I wanted to meet. There was something about her smile as she was twirling around the dance floor in her red evening dress. Even though I was still shy in many respects, I finally got up enough nerve to tap on her partner's shoulder to ask her to dance. I was not the best dancer in the world, by any means, but at least I had reached the stage where I was bold enough to give it a try. After all, I had had some pretty good training with the Simple Set back home before my Woodberry days. I had already found out her name was Julia Jones—so after our first few steps, I introduced myself and we were off to a good start. She was charming and smooth on her feet, and she made me feel quite comfortable as we strutted around the dance floor. Hey, I liked this girl, and she seemed to like me. I ended up dancing with her quite a few times and each time it was fun and enjoyable. I was thinking, "Maybe I've found a girlfriend. I'd like to see more of her." I ended up dating her a time or two and decided to ask her up for one of the Woodberry dance weekends.

On a particular weekend at school, I was dating Julia, George Ives was dating Catherine Maxwell from New Bern, and George Bell was dating Joanne Bell of Raleigh. I can't remember who Frank Daniels dated, but I think she was from Raleigh. Anyway, I remember all of us had a good time, but when it came time for the girls to go home, Julia needed a ride back to Raleigh, and she ended up going back with Frank. They must have hit it off mighty well; that was the last time I ever dated Julia. From then on it was Julia and Frank. As a matter of fact, he ended up marrying her, and they lived happily ever after in Raleigh, even to this day, over 50 years later. There never was anything other than a good friendship between Julia and me. She was, and is, a fine girl. Ol' Frank did a good day's work to get her.

Another Date at Woodberry

During my senior year, I was business manager of the Fir Tree (school annual) and was in charge of running the snack shop (also known as the Fir Tree) located in the basement of House B. George Bell and I had a good time serving the students drinks and snacks after the evening study period. One day, George Bell, George Ives, and I were talking about getting dates for the coming Germans weekend. It was then I thought of Katherine Armstead and Dot Smith. Both were beauty queens and members of the Simple Set at Kinston High. They would both be a real hit with the Woodberry boys and good dates to squire around during the weekend. I called; they accepted; and Mother and Daddy agreed to give them a ride to Woodberry. George Ives ended up with Katherine and I dated Dot. George Bell dated Joanne Bell from Raleigh. Back then, the boys and their dates were always in the company of others on campus. There was very little pairing off. We just had a good time being together. Yes, and I was right. George Ives and I were proud of our two good-looking Kinston girls who also made a big hit with the other boys. We all had a good time, and the weekend was a real success!

Songwriter and singer Johnny Mercer was a Woodberry boy. One weekend he came and sang some of his hits. "Accentuate the Positive" was one of our favorites.

My First Pair of Glasses

One day Mother and Daddy came up to take me back home for vacation, and before leaving, we got in 18 holes of golf. On the third hole, I hit a good ball on my second shot, thinking it should be in the green. "Where did it go?" I asked. Daddy said, "It's right there on the green, son. Can't you see it?" I strained and then I strained again—but I just couldn't see it. Daddy kept saying, "It's right there, about 20 feet to the right of the pin!" It was then that Daddy said, "We'd better get your eyes checked." I had never thought of my eyes being bad or that I couldn't see well at a distance. When we got home, Daddy talked to Dr. West about my eyes and got me an appointment with Dr. Banks Anderson at Duke Hospital. His eye examination revealed that I was near-sighted with a little astigmatism. He prescribed the necessary corrective glasses, and I've been wearing glasses ever since. At first it took some getting use to, but after a while I became adjusted to them, and now I can't imagine myself without them. I had to put all vanity aside and not worry about what others (especially girls) thought about my glasses. For the first time since I could remember, I could actually see leaves on trees and the many details I had been missing. The classroom chalkboard became more readable. It was like a whole new world was opening up, and it made me feel more confident about myself as my new surroundings became sharper and in focus. I could now see what I had been missing for several years (and didn't even know it).

Other Woodberry Activities

To be a prefect at Woodberry was quite an honor, and, needless to say, I was pleasantly surprised when I was told I had been named to join that elite group. The members are chosen each year by combined vote of the faculty and the prefect board of the preceding year. According to the school annual, "They [the prefects] are selected for their outstanding qualities of leadership, loyalty, and a general attitude of sincerity and cooperation towards their fellow students and the School as a whole." The information continued: "In its responsibility to both the faculty and the student body in upholding the School's democratic ideal of government, the Prefect Board assumes a task which is essential to the over-all success of the administration. Of leaders and the ideals such as these, Woodberry can be justly proud." The committee also named my good friend Chuck Haywood, from Statesville, as senior prefect to lead the eleven-member board.

I was also chosen junior warden of the Chapel Council, which was composed of eleven members and served as the representative of the student body in the religious activities at Woodberry. One of the group's main duties was conducting the weekly Thursday evening prayer services. Chuck Haywood was also senior warden as well as senior prefect. Serving as a prefect and a member of the Chapel Council was a real blessing by providing a unique opportunity to learn certain leadership skills, which otherwise I would not have experienced. Such service also helped me in relating to others. I was particularly pleased to be on the Chapel Council, for since my early days I had an inclination toward spiritual matters.

Mr. Walker Never Got His $1,000

As my senior year was drawing to a close, so was my three-year Woodberry experience. I can say with all honesty that I am thankful to have had the opportunity to attend such a prestigious preparatory school. If I wasn't ready for college, it wasn't the school's fault. I'm also thankful that my father had enough confidence in me to place his own reputation, as well as his $1,000, on the line. I'm sure I wouldn't have been accepted for admission had not Daddy been so dogmatic in insisting that Mr. Walker give me a chance. I can still picture the scene when Daddy made his impassioned plea: "If you'll let him in, I'll give you a thousand dollars if he doesn't graduate in the upper 20% of his class. Just give him a chance and I'll prove it. I know Dan, and I know he can do it!" Evidently, Mr. Walker told his staff of masters that story because shortly before graduation, one of the masters told me in a rather light-hearted conversation, "Yes, I know all about how you got in." Actually, class ranking was never discussed, and I had no idea where I ranked. I was pretty confident, however, that I was not in the top 20%. After Mr. Walker's comment on my first report card ("Commendable Report. I don't think I'll get that $1,000"), I don't remember it ever being discussed again. Actually, Mr. Walker retired in ill health in 1948 and died before I graduated on June 11, 1949. The new headmaster, Shaun Kelly, presented my diploma, and Mr. Walker never got his $1,000. If the truth were known, I think Daddy owed him the money. On the other hand, had Mr. Walker lived to give me my diploma, hopefully he would have considered the spirit and circumstances of the offer as well as my other record at Woodberry.

Retrospect

I can see where I missed a lot by not living at home during my last three years of high school. I missed those formative years living with my parents. I missed developing friendships with hometown classmates. I missed playing basketball in front of hometown fans. (Actually, I'm not sure I could even have made the team, for I think Kinston won the state championship at least one of those years.)

John Hines of Kinston was a Woodberry Boy, a few years younger than I. He did well at Woodberry and ended up as a brilliant lawyer in Kinston. I was a little surprised to hear him say some years ago that if he had to do it over, he would not have gone away to school. He feels he missed too much by not being home. Maybe he's got a point. A boarding school is not for everyone. There are pros and cons for each side. Since I went and there's no chance to do it over, I'm glad I'm a graduate of Woodberry Forest School.

My Most Amazing Fish Story

A couple of weeks after graduating from Woodberry, in late June 1949, I had a house party at Aunt Susie's beach cottage. Woodberry classmates who attended were George Bell and Frank Daniels from Raleigh; Ben Walden from Midway, Kentucky; Tom Helm from Louisville; and George Ives from New Bern. My Kinston buddy Z.A. and I rounded out the seven. The highlight of the house party was a fishing trip to the Gulf Stream on which Daddy took us. J. Worth McAlister from Chicago, a family friend, also joined us making nine in all.

Although I had been to the Gulf Stream a couple of previous times, Bill and Tom and one or two others had never experienced deep-sea fishing. After an early start, it was about a four-hour trip to our destination. Our boat was the "Bill 'n Jim" and the captain evidently knew what he was doing because we had some pretty good luck. We each took our turn manning the four chairs. We didn't have electric reels back then, so all the reeling was by hand and arm power. As I was sitting there patiently waiting for something to happen on the other end of my line, I suddenly felt a big surge and my rod bending with the weight and pull of something big. After struggling for a few minutes, I heard the captain exclaim, "He's got a big one!" We all were excited to find out what it was! I pulled back on the rod and then reeled in, and pulled back and reeled in several times more. Then the fish would run with it, and I'd have to start all over. I was about a week shy of my eighteenth birthday, so I was in pretty good shape, even though I was skinny and not very muscular in the arms and legs. The minutes ticked by. Before I knew it, I'd been struggling with that monster for over ten minutes. I'll have to admit I was beginning to get a little weary—but I still kept going. Another five minutes passed. I still couldn't get him in. Finally, after twenty minutes of straining and struggling, I got him to the surface (I guess the fish was tired, too), and the captain was able to land him. He identified it as a giant red snapper. When we returned to the dock that afternoon, the official weight was determined to be thirty-six pounds. My red snapper was reported to be "the largest taken this season off the North Carolina coast, and one of the largest ever caught there." George Ives also caught a seventeen pound black grouper, which is a Caribbean species and most unusual to be seen that far north. For George and me, as well as all of us, it was an unforgettable experience.

But wait, that's not the end of the story! Both of us got worldwide publicity from our catches. Newspapers throughout the country, as well as from far away as Europe and Asia, carried each of the fish stories, with pictures and captions. The Associated Press sent me clippings from New York, Kansas City, Minneapolis, San Francisco—and even London, Rome, Madrid, and Tokyo to name only a few. I had a whole stack of newspaper pictures with informative captions. They kept right on coming! George said he also received several such clippings regarding his catch.

But wait, I said this was my most amazing fish story. "You ain't heard nothing yet!"

The big fish, and the world-wide publicity, was one thing—but here's the amazing part of the story: Exactly twenty years later to the month, June 1969, Margaret and I were at Morehead. Our two children were back at the Perry Cottage at 1701 Shackleford Street with a babysitter. We had been to a movie and decided afterwards to drop by the Morehead City Newsstand to get a magazine for reading. We walked into the store, and I was waiting near the front while Margaret browsed around, tying to find the magazine of her choice. I had nothing in mind, not even thinking about buying anything for myself. But then my eyes happened to glimpse a *Police Gazette* magazine.

Out of curiosity, I decided to take one from the rack and see what it was all about. Almost immediately, I turned to a two-page spread with pictures. The headlines caught my attention: "How to Catch a Red Snapper." I thought to myself, "Ah, here's something that should interest me. After all, I caught a big one back in 1949." I noticed there were two or three rather big pictures with several smaller ones scattered about. And then my eyes drifted to the larger picture on the left page. There was something familiar about it. Looking more closely, I exclaimed to myself, "That looks exactly like me—twenty years ago!" And then I saw it! The caption read, "Dan Perry Catches Record Red Snapper off Morehead City, NC." The article told about my thirty-six pounder. There were other red snappers featured, but none as big as my record catch. I couldn't believe it! Here I was in June 1969, looking at a picture of me published in June 1949. I bought that issue of the *Police Gazette*; Margaret bought her *Home and Garden*, and we headed home in utter amazement. How could that be? How could I just happen to drop by that newsstand and out of curiosity—and among the countless magazines—just happen to pull out a magazine I had only heard of and just happen to turn to the page featuring a twenty-year-old picture of myself holding a thirty-six pound red snapper? Margaret and I figured the chance of that happening was 1 in 10 zillion. Utterly impossible!

After returning home to Kinston a few days later, I realized I should have purchased several other issues, just to be able to prove my story. I mistakenly clipped out the picture and stuck it in my Bible for safekeeping. I later realized I should have kept the entire two-page article as well as the magazine itself. I tried to order a couple more issues several years later, but my attempts were futile, for by that time *Police Gazette* was no longer in publication. The picture was temporarily misplaced, but then later found. The last time I saw it was in my study on Perry Park Drive, long before moving to 1902 Holding Place. Today, sadly, I don't know where it is. Maybe the children will find it one day after I'm gone—just so they can substantiate my amazing fish story.

An Announcement of Things to Come

I had completed my freshman year at Carolina when I received a call from Jimmy Thompson. He was a Woodberry classmate and wanted me to visit him in Louisville. I had a great time on my first visit several years earlier with Tom Helm, so I decided to accept with pleasure Jimmy's invitation. Although I was not as close to Jimmy as I was to Tom, we were good friends and I knew a lot of the Louisville people.

The visit was fun, but in retrospect here's the thing I remember most about the trip. It was June 25, 1950. We were at the country club swimming pool, milling around, having a good time with all the young people—boys and girls. A portable radio was playing popular music, loud enough for all in and around the pool area to hear. Suddenly, the program was interrupted by an important announcement—South Korea had been invaded by troops from North Korea. No one seemed to know much about Korea at the time, but the way the announcer was telling it, it sounded like a serious event. I didn't even know where it was on the map, and little did I realize at the time that in less than five years, I would be in an army uniform serving a sixteen-month tour of duty in South Korea. After the announcement, the music continued, and we resumed our good time around the pool, oblivious to the importance of the announcement and the unsettled future which lay ahead.

Chapter XII

MOREHEAD CITY—MY SECOND HOME

Morehead City and Atlantic Beach have always played a major role in the social life and overall development of all the Perry family, and me in particular. I remember Daddy telling me that when he was about a year old his mother took him to Atlantic Beach for a visit. I guess that was shortly after his father died in April of 1897, when Daddy was nine months old.

"Daddy, You're In the Ditch!"

My earliest recollection of Morehead was when Highway 70 was still a dirt road. I must have been only about three years old, about 1934. Daddy had driven all five of us in the family Chevrolet all the way to the beach for a swim in the ocean and a seafood dinner. The bridge over to the Atlantic beach was not very old. Although I don't remember too much about getting in the water, several things I do remember.

First of all, it took forever to get there, something like three hours. This was long before air conditioning. We had all the car windows open; not only was it hot outside, it was stifling inside the car, and all five of us were cooped up together, wringing wet with sweat. I remember having to go to the bathroom, like any young boy would do on a long trip. At times when we would go on trips, Daddy would take time to stop and let us go behind a bush or tree beside the road, but this time was different. He didn't want to take time to stop, so Mama gave me an empty Coke bottle in which to relieve myself. I remember kneeling on the floorboard. After I finished, Mama handed the bottle to Daddy. He didn't slow down one bit, but proceeded to extend the bottle out the window, in his left hand, to empty its contents while we were flying down the dusty road at 40 to 50 miles per hour! Certain parts of Highway 70 to Morehead were sandy and rutty, and it just wasn't safe to go the speed limit, which I think was 50 miles per hour at the time.

I don't remember, on this particular occasion, passing anybody or anybody passing us. In fact, I'm not so sure we even met anybody going in the opposite direction—maybe one or two cars. All I remember is that it was a lonely, dirt road back for most of the way. The road was narrow, and there were two main ruts—one going east and one going west. Sometimes the ruts were sandy and deep, other times they were fairly shallow, which allowed us to go faster. Sometimes the ruts were fairly straight and other times they zigzagged almost to the shallow ditch on the side of the road.

Anyway, Daddy must have been going a little fast for the condition of the road, and we ended up in the ditch on the right side. I remember Daddy going back and forth—forward and reverse —rocking that old Chevrolet, frantically trying his best to get out of the ditch. I was frustrated, too, even at my tender age, and all I could shout was, "Daddy, you're in the ditch! You're in the ditch, Daddy! You're in the ditch!" Well, with that Daddy let go of some unrepeatable words of angry irritation: "&%$#@?X# blankety-blank, I know I'm in the ditch, son! I know I'm in the ditch!" He obviously made the point clear that he knew he was in the ditch, and he didn't need me or anybody else to tell him he was in the ditch! I don't remember exactly how we got out—I guess we all pushed. That turned out to be one of Warren's favorite stories about my younger days, and I'm sure that's one of the reasons I remember it so well. (He would remind me every ten or fifteen years!)

Aunt Susie's Cottage

Another one of my favorite memories of Morehead was visiting Aunt Susie at her new cottage at 3211 Evans Street—a white two-storey house with a long backyard going right down to the water. It was more than a cottage. It was built about 1937, and Daddy drove us all down to see it. I would have been about six. Bogue Sound looked inviting, and my first impulse was to head for the water for a refreshing swim. Because somebody had to accompany me, Warren joined me. I don't remember if Bud was swimming with us or not. I hadn't been in the water but a very few minutes when my knee scraped a large pipe loaded with barnacles, and I knew immediately something was wrong. I yelled out to Warren for help! I remember him carrying me out of the water with blood streaming down my right leg. Mama and Daddy came running down toward the water to meet us! At first glance, it looked like I was really hurt bad because the blood was everywhere. As it turned out, the source of blood came from about an inch-and-a-half-long cut, along with a smaller cut on my right knee. The blood mixed with the salt water made it look a lot worse than it really was.

After discovering I was going to live—and with a little tender loving care from Mama—we hopped in the car, and Daddy took me to the local hospital on the waterfront in Morehead. Dr. Kenneth Royal (whom Daddy knew) took good care of me. He was really patient and encouraging. He made me feel that going to the hospital was not so bad after all. He put three stitches in the large cut without doing anything to the smaller one. After wrapping it with a nice tight bandage and giving me some crutches, I was ready to go home. It seems like we stayed a day or two with Aunt Susie because I remember walking out on the pier with my crutches and receiving the sympathy of several people as well as the fishermen who inquired about my crutches. Of course, I built up the story of my accident to be a little worse than it really was.

Aunt Susie and Her Hospitality

Aunt Susie was always very generous in sharing her cottage at the beach with all of us Perrys. On a number of occasions during the summer, she would invite me, or a buddy and me, to spend a few days with her in Morehead. I was always ready to go.

She had a little blue floating-board about half the size of a surfboard on which Z. A. and I messed around in the sound for hours at a time. We called it "Blue Baby," and it was fun just splashing around and doing our own thing, without a care in the world.

A lot of times, I didn't always have a big appetite for food that was good for you, especially if the food was green or yellow—but I was always ready for some ice cream. After every meal and as well as between meals, I looked forward to several scoops of vanilla ice cream in a glass with ginger ale or 7-Up poured up to the brim. Aunt Susie always seemed to have plenty in the refrigerator, and she apparently didn't mind us helping ourselves—so we did!

Aunt Susie loved Morehead, and sunning and swimming at the beach were her favorite activities. She was a member of the old Dunes Club, and part of her daily routine was to drive across the bridge to the beach about 10:30 or 11:00 A.M., get out on the beach, have a lifeguard stake an umbrella for her, sit a while, go for a swim, speak to all her friends, and then go back for a light lunch. Most times she would go back for a second encounter in the afternoon. Aunt Susie was our ticket to the beach. I remember her filling up her car with kids—Clifton and Lillian (her children), Warren, Bud and me—and anyone else who was around—and off to the beach we would go. I loved to jump the waves and ride the big ones in.

Back in the late 1930s and into the 1940s, the Dunes Club had several slot machines. I seldom had money to put in them but I enjoyed seeing all the men and ladies stand around and pull those "one armed bandits". Occasionally, somebody would win a bunch of nickels, dimes or quarters, but I don't remember seeing anyone win a Jack Pot.

Z.A.'s Almost Big Catch

Z.A. and I enjoyed fishing on one of the piers down from Aunt Susie's. One day we were fishing with our hand lines and weren't having much luck when Z.A.'s line got real heavy. In fact, he was having a hard time pulling it in. It didn't feel like a fish because it wasn't moving around and didn't have that "nibble" feeling like a pinfish or hogfish. It was just dead weight. We thought it might be an old tire or piece of seaweed or something like that. He kept pulling and finally he got it to the top of the water. Z.A. casually said, "Look, it's an old newspaper." It was big and gray and looked about the size of an open newspaper; then it began to sink below the surface. It was about that time that an old fisherman on the pier identified it as a big "skate.". We were only eight or nine years old and "skate" was not in our everyday fishing vocabulary. He battled him for what seemed like several minutes—at least long enough for us to get a good look at him. Z. A. never did pull him in, for our monster fish eventually managed to get off the line—but he sure did give us some excitement that I've never forgotten.

Two More Skate Stories

When I told Daddy about our "skate story," he related his own skate story to me. He said that a number of years ago he and another man were fishing in a rowboat on the north side of the Beaufort Bridge. They were not having much luck, but all of a sudden he saw two big skates coming directly toward them. He said they looked like monsters coming straight at them! The next thing he knew, one of them jumped over the boat and the other one zoomed under the boat. He said the one that jumped over the boat looked like a "big black umbrella"—it was so big! He ended up telling that story several times over the years, so I guess it was true, or at least we never doubted it. He always used the same descriptive words: "big black umbrella."

The only other skate story I know is when my son Daniel and I were fishing just off the shore in the sound north of Fort Macon. Daniel must have been about fifteen or so, and we were in the "Perry Winkle." We had caught several nice croakers and hogfish, and I believe a gray trout or two, and we were having a good time. All of a sudden, Daniel hooked something big! I first thought it was a big skate as it jumped straight up out of the water. But there was something different about it. It was a strange sighting, because I can still see those two big eyes—they looked like they were protruding from its head. Anyway, they were funny looking. That was the only time it jumped out of the water. Daniel fought it for a few minutes, and I think it even pulled the boat a little bit. Eventually, the line broke. It was all over. We were both really excited, and I recalled Daddy Ely's story. I told Daniel all about Daddy and the big skate that jumped over the boat that looked like a big black umbrella. We both agreed that we could well understand that description because Daniel's big fish reminded us both of a "big black umbrella." After checking the World Book, we determined it was a manta ray, and that they generally got to be much larger than skates. Whatever it was, it was a whopper of a fish and looked like a big black umbrella with two protruding eyes!

Meeting Two Friendly Girls

I remember our family being down at Aunt Susie's when Mother told me I was invited to a party down the street at a girl's house. I must have been about ten or eleven, and I wasn't interested in going to a girl's house. I didn't know any girls in Morehead. Why would I want to go somewhere I didn't know anybody? It just wasn't appealing to me at all, and I was reluctant to say the least. Anyway, Daddy got in the picture and they somehow convinced me to go. Mother suggested that Daddy walk me down to the girl's house and sorta' help me break the ice. Maybe I could stand it if Daddy came along, too. Anyway, off we went a couple of blocks on Evans Street to Anna Frank Strosnider's house. The main thing I remember was meeting Anna Frank, who was known as Frankie, and her good friend Millie Cobb. They were both from Goldsboro and turned out to be my life-long friends, even to this day. I think George Bell and Pete DuBose were there along with six or eight others. They both had cottages several blocks in the opposite direction from Aunt Susie, and they both turned out to be life-time friends. Pete was from Durham and ended up marrying Frankie. George was from Raleigh and later moved to Kinston, and as we grew up we became close friends, especially as our interest in girls grew, and in looking around as to who to date.

But the main thing I remember about meeting Frankie and Millie was how cordial and friendly they were. They made me feel right at home, and I actually enjoyed being with two girls, even at that age. When Aunt Susie would take me to the Dunes Club to go swimming, I was always on the lookout for Frankie and Millie. I couldn't believe I was actually beginning to like being with girls! I guess they were the ones that gave me a "jump start" in developing my interest in the opposite sex.

Chapter XIII

UNDERGRADUATE YEARS AT CAROLINA

The Day I Left for School

In the fall of 1949, I entered my freshman year at Carolina. It never entered my mind that I would go to any other college. The entire Perry families were Tar Heel fans through and through. I don't remember exactly how I got to Chapel Hill for my first day of orientation, but I do remember right before leaving, Warren said, "Come on, Dan, I want to make a movie of you singing like Al Jolson." He had just gotten a new 8mm movie camera and wanted to try it out on me. We went in the backyard where there was plenty of light. I placed my portable Victrola on the steps, turned it up full blast, and started playing my 78-rpm, Al Jolson record. With the camera rolling and my old straw hat in place, I started mimicking my all-time favorite entertainer. Of course, the camera was not sophisticated enough to record the music—but there I was going through the motions of mouthing the words to "Mammy": "Rock-a-bye your bab-y with a Dix-ie mel-o-dy…." It was the next best thing to being on Broadway. Well, I never saw the movie, and I don't remember Warren ever telling me if it even turned out. I do remember while the camera was rolling, wondering whether any cars were passing by—what would they think seeing such a sight? I didn't particularly care, because I was having a good time and was just before leaving for Chapel Hill to be a full fledged Tar Heel.

A Freshman in Stacy Dorm

Z.A. and I both were assigned to the first floor in Stacy Dorm. We decided against rooming together, so as to allow us to meet and develop new friendships. I had two good roommates from High Point, Heywood Washburn and Bob Neil. We got along great together, with no problems at all. It didn't take me long to realize the sense of freedom that was mine as a freshman at Carolina. It was totally different from my Woodberry experience. At Woodberry we lived somewhat of a sheltered life—everything was structured—we had time schedules to meet. We got up at the same time—ate together at the same time—classes and break times—athletics in the afternoon—study halls (or periods) when everyone was expected to be hitting the books—and lights out for bedtime. After a period of adjustment, we all grew accustomed to it and mostly had no problem in abiding by the rules and keeping up with the rigid schedule. At Carolina we were in an entirely different atmosphere. We were totally free to come and go as we please— no rules, no curfew at all. Get up when you wanted to; go to bed when you wanted to; you didn't even have to go to classes, although some of the professors limited you to three unexcused cuts. You were pretty much on your own to live and go as you pleased. Of course, when grade time came, you would have to deal with it accordingly. I guess the administration felt that by college age you should be old enough to make your own decisions and bear the consequences of your own actions. I often said in looking back, "Carolina can either make or break you. It's up to you."

A Most Unusual Survey

Shortly after getting settled in Stacy Dorm, word got around there was a survey being taken. I didn't know who was in charge, but the word among the boys was that it would tell you how you fare with the ladies—whether you are a real ladies man who's had a lot of experience, or a prude, or mama's boy with no experience. Being new to all this, I went along with the crowd and started circling the answers. My best recollection is it was a "yes-no-sometimes-seldom-never" type of survey of a couple of pages. It started out with something like, "Have you ever had a date with a girl?; Have you ever been alone with a girl?; Have you ever been in a car with a girl?; Have you ever held hands with a girl?" Well, it went on from there, and you can guess where it was going. Everybody was supposed to be honest with their answers, so as to get a true evaluation. Somebody took up the papers and came back shortly with the results. I don't remember what the specific categories were (except mine), but I do remember several boys bragging about their high rating, they must have been real ladies men—like Rudolph Valentino or Don Juan. I also remember when they called out my name, I was rated as, "Pure as the driven snow." I guess that meant I didn't have much experience with the ladies. They all laughed, and I probably laughed, too—but at least, they knew where I stood.

Being a Freshman—A Lot of Fun

Although I enjoyed all four years of my undergraduate work, I think my freshman year was probably the most fun. I really enjoyed the freedom of being "foot loose and fancy free." It was a time of checking out the girls, developing friendships, and being under very little pressure. Going to football games was always a thrill, mainly because Charlie Justice, Art Weiner, and Walt Puppa were all stars. Justice was already a legend in his own time. By the way, the first time I ever laid eyes on him was in the 1948 UNC at Virginia game in Charlottesville. I was a senior at Woodberry, and a busload of us went to the game. I can still remember coming into the stadium late. As I got my first glimpse of the field, I saw Charlie Justice running through a big hole in the left of the Carolina line. It looked at least twenty-feet wide as he skirted his way into the defensive secondary for a long gain. He made a number of long runs and completed a bunch of passes to his favorite target, Art Weiner. We scored seven touchdowns and Bob Cox kicked seven extra points for a 49-0 victory! At Carolina I saw them play every home game, and it was a thrill each time.

When suppertime came several of us would get together and walk to the Monogram Club for a sandwich, or walk down town to the Porthole or Ratskeller for a chicken cacciatore dinner or a hot roast beef sandwich with hot apple pie. Classes were not too hard. Except for our class schedules we were on our own—free to go anywhere and do anything we wanted. Everyone enjoyed the life of freedom.

My First Quarter Grades

As part of the orientation process, we took placement exams to determine our beginning classes. Having already had most of the first year college work in math, English, and Spanish, I was able to place out of the first quarter courses and move on to the next level. Woodberry gave me a solid foundation on which to build, and I had no problem with the work. My first grading period showed two As and one B, which was good enough to qualify for Phi Eta Sigma, the top freshman academic fraternity. Ely had made "Phi Bet" at Carolina, so I felt pretty good about my start. At the initial ceremony, I met Edgar Love from Lincolnton. He continued his scholastic achievements and ended up being president of Phi Beta Kappa and an outstanding lawyer in Charlotte. My scholastic career was much less distinguished: I got two Bs and a C my second quarter and even a D in biology the third quarter. Somehow, biology was rather hard, because I didn't put my heart into it. It just didn't interest me that much, and I didn't spend the necessary time to memorize a lot of the material. Most of my grades throughout my remaining four years were Bs and Cs with very few As, and I think a D or two along the way. So you might say I was just an average student, nothing to brag about. I'm sure my extra curricular activities probably had something to do with it.

An Unforgettable Breakfast

Chuck Haywood, my old Woodberry classmate and now Carolina classmate, invited several of us for an overnight at his house in Statesville. His father had recently died, and his mother was gone for the weekend, so it was just Chuck's manservant and four or five of us boys. The main attraction was for us to spend Friday night, sleep late the next morning, eat a big breakfast, and then see the Carolina—Notre Dame football game on television. I think it was the first time Carolina had ever played Notre Dame, and we were excited because they were nationally ranked (#1 as I recall) and we had Charlie Justice. I remember the game, but even more I remember the humongous breakfast. The servant was quite a cook. He made everything you could think of: bacon, country ham, sausage, scrambled eggs, grits, stewed apples, cantaloupe, orange juice, milk, etc., etc. We piled our plates high. The more we ate, the more he brought to the table. Each of us boys not only had an extra helping—we had three or four extra helpings of everything. I'd never had such a breakfast! I didn't realize I was so hungry. It goes without saying that during the life time of most everyone there are certain meals that stand out as being really special. As for me, that breakfast at Chuck Haywood's was truly unforgettable. By the way, Carolina was able to keep up with Notre Dame for most of the first half, which gave us hope of pulling off an upset. But they were just too strong for us. They wore us down and ended up handing us a resounding defeat. Although our spirits were low after the game, there was one big redeeming feature about our visit to Chuck's house: we had a monstrous breakfast that I've never forgotten.

I Can't Believe I Was That Stupid!

I'm now about to tell you something that I've never told anyone—not even Margaret, and certainly not the children. The reason I'm telling it now is simply because I don't want to have gone through this life leaving the false impression that I always had pretty good sense. Back then I might have been thought of as being immature at times, yes, but certainly not stupid, at least I was not aware of it. A graduate of Woodberry Forest and a Carolina boy is not supposed to be outright stupid. But, that's exactly what I was in this instance.

Although I've never forgotten the incident, Chuck Haywood reminded me of it at our 50th class reunion at Woodberry back in May 1999. After graduating from Carolina in 1953, I sort of lost track of Chuck, and we simply didn't keep up with each other as we should have. He was the one who mentioned it to me at the reunion, and we both had a big embarrassing laugh together. I told him then that was the first time it had been brought up since it happened.

My memory is vague on the details, but here's what happened, the best I can recall. I believe it was during the winter of out freshman year at Carolina, and it was a cold, dark, moonless night. We were driving through a wooded area when we ran out of gas (mistake #1). I don't remember how we got it, but we ended up with a five-gallon can of gas, so as to give temporary relief until we could get to a station to fill up. So far, so good. The problem was it was so dark we couldn't see how to put the gasoline in the tank. I don't know if the spout of the container was too short to reach the gas tank opening, or whether the location of the tank itself was the problem. But for whatever reason, we couldn't see where to pour the gas. We were totally in the dark. We could feel the tank, but we couldn't put the gas in. We needed a flashlight. After looking in every nook and cranny in the car, Chuck determined he just didn't have one. We racked our brains as to what to do—then it came to us. The only thing left to do was to light a match. I guess we could have walked back to the main road to the country store and borrow a flashlight, but that would take too long. I'm not sure whose idea it was to use a match (probably mine), but we both agreed that if we were careful not to get too close to the tank we would be O. K. All we needed was a little light to get us started. We decided to give it a try. Chuck found a book of safety matches, and I think I must have been the one to light the match (I'll take infamous credit for it anyway). When I struck the first match, we still couldn't see what we were doing. I didn't want to get too close. After all, we both had enough sense to know not to play with matches around gasoline. It wasn't doing us any good because we still couldn't see. The first match went out, so I lit a second one. If I could ease it just a little closer, maybe Chuck could at least see well enough to pour a little gas in the tank to get us to the station for a fill up. Then we could be on our way. I needed to get close enough without getting too close. My thought was to try just one more time. Get just a little closer—just a little. Well, at least I was right about one thing. It only took one more time—but "that was all she wrote." We had not even considered that an empty gas tank could have fumes. The next thing we knew a big flame was shooting out from the mouth of the gas tank. Chuck and I both let out a big holler, "The car's on fire!" We both screamed (as well as making a few other choice comments). My first thought was, it's going to explode at any time! I had seen cars on fire in the movies and most of them resulted in a big explosion. We both moved back, far enough away hopefully to avoid being hurt too badly in such a disaster. I don't believe I ever told Chuck, but I even had thoughts of rolling his car down the embankment to the nearby lake to put out the fire so as to avoid the expected explosion. The flames kept pouring out. In a few seconds we could tell they were beginning to subside. As we watched in utter amazement, and utter embarrassment, we silently stood there as the flame died down and finally petered out. We couldn't believe what we had done!

I don't remember exactly how we finally got enough gas in the tank to get home. The car was undamaged and we did make it home—embarrassed but unhurt—and thankful to be alive. It was another example of God's grace and mercy. Chuck and I both agreed we would tell no one about our stupidity. I don't know about Chuck, but I had kept my end of the bargain. Although I thought about it from time to time, my lips were sealed for almost 50 years—until Chuck mentioned it to me at our big reunion. I jokingly told him that as a Woodberry senior prefect and senior warden of the Chapel Council he was supposed to have better sense. He also made appropriate remarks about my own stupidity. I guess the lesson to be learned from that experience is that even the best of us can at times be led astray by a dumb bunny.

Chuck and I Were Not the Only Stupid Ones

Telling that embarrassing tale after more than 55 years was made a little easier when I was reminded of a somewhat similar embarrassment Allan Heath experienced when he was scout master of Troop 41 in Kinston. Actually, the incident was humorously related by Allan's preacher, Mark Benson, from the pulpit at his funeral in July 2006, so I guess it's all right for me to mention it here. A member of Allan's troop, Billy Hood, who was a witness to the incident, emailed the story to Mark before the funeral.

All of us who knew Allan Heath knew him to be a highly seasoned and respected scout master and mentor to the youth, not only at Gordon Street Christian Church but also young people throughout Lenoir County. He was a DuPonter and was considered to be a solid, knowledgeable man of good judgment in working with his boys.

Allan and his scout troop were at the Cliffs of the Neuse for an overnight camping trip. It was suppertime, and for some reason Allan was having trouble getting his charcoal lit. Apparently, all his efforts were in vain. There just wasn't enough starter fire generated to sustain a charcoal fire— or if there was, Allan didn't know it. Everybody was getting hungry. Something had to be done. As scout master, Allan's job was to come up with the answer. Easy enough. Gasoline would do it, but he knew he had to be careful, so he advised his boys accordingly. "Never, never, never, do this—what I'm about to do," he cautioned. "It could be dangerous." He was just going to pour a little gasoline on the coals, just to give them a good start. That was innocent enough—but still he had to make it clear to his boys that they were "never, never, never" to do something like that. Apparently, the coals were hotter that he realized, for when he splashed on the gasoline, the resulting sudden flames flashed back to haunt him. He suffered rather severe burns on his arms, serious enough to warrant being rushed to the hospital for treatment. Eventually, he healed, but the embarrassment before his boys lingered his lifetime. The difference in Allan's experience and mine was that he had a bunch of witnesses who never let him forget it. I had only one, and we kept it a secret for almost 50 years—at least until now.

Me? A Politician?

I can't remember if it was my first or second quarter, but I do remember I was still living in Stacy Dorm. One of the older boys on campus asked me to run for the Student Legislature. After telling me what it would involve, I told him I would think about it and let him know in a couple days. I talked to Ely about it and he said, "Yeah, go ahead, it'll do you good." I actually was pretty much in the dark about the legislature. I knew it was one of the three branches of government, and it was charged with the responsibility of making laws; other than that I knew very little. Government and politics were not one of my interests. Anyway, I said "yes." The election was coming up in a few weeks, and we had to get ready. I would run with three others on the University Party ticket, representing the freshman class. I learned that fraternity boys usually represented the University Party and nonfraternity boys usually were in the Student Party. I was not in a fraternity yet, but that didn't matter. I remember going with the others to the printer to have the advertisement posters and pictures made. I had entered the political arena, green as a gourd. I don't remember too much about the campaign, but our party made a clean sweep and I was now in the Student Legislature.

I think we met once a week, and I became exposed to the legislative process for the first time. As a novice, I sat there while motions were made, followed by speeches, and more motions—ending with votes usually taken by a show of hands. I don't remember anyone approaching me to vote a certain way or any kind of strategy session being held to push a bill through. Of course, most of the issues were about university and campus matters.

Back then, I was basically very shy when it came time to give a talk or say anything with a lot of people looking on. I felt reasonably comfortable in small groups and with people I knew well, but in big groups, especially with strangers, it was another story. My most embarrassing memory of my service in the Student Legislature was when Bunny Davis asked me to second a certain motion someone else was to make. Bunny was a senior from Greensboro (I think) and was presiding over the session. He had a deep, mellow voice and was well respected by all. Up until this time, I never said anything or opened my mouth at any of the sessions. All he wanted me to do was say, "second" or "second the motion" after the motion was made—that's all, no speech, no comment, no nothing. Just one word: "Second." I don't know why it would be any big deal. Anybody could holler out, "Second." But for some reason, when the big moment came and the motion was made, I just sat there. I didn't open my mouth. I was "scared to death." There may have been a lot of commotion going around and someone else probably seconded it. All I know is I didn't do it. I just sat there. I think what probably happened was that in the normal course of the process, someone else seconded the motion, thereby getting me off the hook. Hopefully, that was the case, for Bunny never let on he knew I had "frozen in my tracks" when it came time to speak up.

Addendum: I have never told anyone about that before, and I don't know why I even mentioned it now, other than to let the reader know that I was far from being a polished speaker or communicator. I'm just trying to be honest and tell it like it was. How could any freshman at Carolina be so shy?—especially when he, at least at times, gave the impression he had it all together and was a leader.

Continuing on in Politics

Even though I didn't feel like a leader and didn't think of myself as one, I continued on in the political arena. I attended the regular meetings of the University Party and eventually felt better about sharing my ideas and thoughts. Apparently, the party thought enough of me to ask me to head the slate of class officers by running for president of the junior class. By that time, I had developed enough friends so that I felt comfortable running. I didn't really seek the office—but they asked me to be their candidate, and I said "yes." Our whole slate won. The following year, the same thing happened. Nobody else seemed to want it, so I ran and was elected president of the senior class. There weren't any particular issues to debate or worry about, so I guess it was more or less a popularity contest. Anyway, it made me feel good to think that my fellow classmates thought enough of me to elect me as their leader.

Chapter XIV

FRATERNITY LIFE AT UNC

Pledging Kappa Sigma

During the latter part of my freshman year fraternity rush took place. I had thought all along I wanted to join a fraternity. Warren and Ely, along with a lot of Kinston boys through the years, were Kappa Sigs, so that would likely be my natural choice also. All of the interested freshmen developed a list of invitations from fraternities and schedules for visits to the various houses during rush week. Then we would narrow our choices down to the ones in which we had the most interest. Z. A. and I both narrowed our choices between Kappa Sigma and Sigma Chi. Kappa Sigma was generally thought of as having boys mostly from eastern North Carolina, while Sigma Chi was more of a western North Carolina fraternity. Both were strong in many ways. The Sigma Chis I met were all nice, clean-cut fellows, and they had a fine looking fraternity house. Daddy was a Sigma Chi at Carolina, and Cousin Gladys had taught me to play "The Sweetheart of Sigma Chi" on the piano. I was really impressed by the Sigma Chi Quartet and their singing in beautiful harmony their fraternity song. Z. A. hit it off real well with the Sigma Chis, and he, along with my two roommates (Haywood Washburn and Bob Neil), decided to go Sigma Chi. Neither Warren nor Ely pressured me into pledging Kappa Sigma—but I finally decided that's where I should be. At the time, Warren was in his last year of law school, and Ely was in his second year of med school. Can you imagine, Daddy having to support all three of his boys at Carolina at the same time?

Hell Week

Soon after pledging Kappa Sigma, I went through *Hell Week* with the other fourteen or so pledges. We were all a little uptight and anxious about the hazing that we had heard so much about. If I was going to be in a fraternity, I had to go through it. We had to do all sorts of things, some of them embarrassing, some painful. I will tell you only of four.

One: We were each given a wooden paddle to be signed by each of the brothers, after we "assumed the position" of bending over so they could express their privilege of giving us three healthy whacks! I finally discarded that paddle in 2002, just before moving to Holding Place. Interestingly enough, I only kept two-thirds of it, for the right side was split off when a "mighty whack" was taken while I had assumed the position. I wrote the brother's name on the remaining two-thirds of the paddle, but I frankly can't remember, 56 years after the fact, who it was who delivered the blow. After getting used to it, I remember all of the blows hurting a little, but not too badly. It was more like a stinging sensation. Of course, our butts were red, but none of the pledges let on it even hurt at all. We had to prove ourselves worthy of becoming a brother of Kappa Sigma.

Two: One night one of the brothers said, "Come on, we're going to take a little ride." I knew something was about to happen, but I didn't know what. He and another brother blindfolded Dick Griswald of Goldsboro and me and put us in the back seat of a car. It was a pitch-black night, and we didn't know where we were going or what they were going to do to us. After a few miles, they told us the plan. They were taking us to a secluded wooded area in the country and drop us off with no flash light and no idea of where we were. Our job was to find our way back to the Kappa Sig House as best we could. After hearing of the plans, I was trying to remember the roads and general direction we were going so as to have at least some idea as to where they might leave us. Even though blindfolded, I could tell we left Cameron Avenue and took a right on to Columbia Street. So far, so good. But then he pulled in a driveway, backed up, started in the opposite direction, went a little ways further; stopped, turned around, made a circle, backed up again, turned left, turned right. Needless to say, it wasn't long before Dick and I were thoroughly confused. We didn't know which way we were going. We were at a complete loss as to where we were or in which direction we were traveling. We must have been in the car for an hour or so. They drove us over bumps and ditches and everything else. All this time, everyone was basically silent. Finally, the car gradually slowed down and came to a stop. Then our blindfolds were removed and we got out. About all they said was, "O. K., boys, you're on your own. You can find your way back the best way you can." Dick and I just stood there in the pitch dark as we watched the tail lights of the car disappear around the curve 20 or 30 yards away. We were all alone with a real challenge on our hands. At least we had a starting point. We both agreed to follow the dirt road as best we could and see where it led us. We were surrounded by woods, in total silence— no noise of any kind. Even though we were in total darkness, somehow we were able to follow that lonely, narrow dirt road. We must have walked for 20 or 30 minutes before we could finally detect in the distance a car traveling as if on a paved road. As we continued to walk, we gradually began to hear another car or two. Maybe we were making some headway. It was another 15 or 20 minutes before we reached a rural, paved road. We didn't know if we needed to go north, east, south or west—or which way town was—or anything. We were totally lost. Finally, we were able to flag down a car. It was easy for the driver to tell we were lost and needed help. Anyway, he decided to take a chance and give two lost pledges a ride back to their fraternity house. During the ride back, we found that we had been dropped off on a lonely country road on the other side of Pittsboro, some 30 miles or so from our house. It was about midnight when we got back to the Kappa Sig house, weary but unscathed. We had passed the test!

Three: They made us do a really crazy thing: two pledges at a time had to get into a telephone booth and each smoke a cigar. That must have been real tough. I can't remember how that test came out for my fellow pledges for I was able to escape that one. When I learned of the scheme, I had a serious conversation with Dan Taft, my assigned big brother. I told him how my father had offered me a thousand dollars if I didn't smoke or drink until I was 21 years old. I told him I didn't want to be treated any differently from the rest of the pledges, but, at the same time, I really wanted to get that thousand dollars. Dan said he understood completely and agreed I would not be required to participate in the event. By the way, Dan Taft was from Wadesboro, and ended up living in South Carolina where he became president of the South Carolina Jaycees.

Four: Warning: The following story is restricted to mature readers only. This is, by far, the most embarrassing thing I had to do, not only as a pledge, but also during my entire career at Carolina.

My memory is somewhat vague on some aspects of this one, but this is how it happened, the best I can recollect. One of the brothers told me one night at the Kappa Sig House, "Dan, I've got something I want you to do that may seem hard, but you can do it. Here is a paper bag. I want you to bring me the panties of a particular girl." He went on to give me her name and where she would probably be. I honestly can't remember her name. All I can remember is she was the beauty-queen type. I had never met her, although I did know she was popular. He said she usually studied on the second floor of the library at a particular table or section. "I want you to bring me back her under panties," he said in a low but emphatic voice. My first thought was, "How in the world am I going to do that? I just can't go up to a girl I've never met and ask her to give me her panties!" The brother—I can't remember who—I think it may have been Dan Taft, my assigned "big brother", who is now deceased. Anyway, upon seeing that I was both baffled and embarrassed, he went on to make a suggestion. He said something like, "All you've got to do is go up to her, introduce yourself, tell her you are a Kappa Sigma pledge, and you have been given an embarrassing task. Then you can explain it all to her." He kept telling me, "You can do it. Don't worry about it. Just do it!" I kept telling myself, "I can't do that! I can't. I just can't do it. I can't go up to a strange girl or any girl for that matter, and ask her to give me her panties!" He could see I was hesitating and bewildered. I had heard about Hell Week and hazing, but this was going too far. I didn't dare tell him, "I ain't gonna' do it!" What would he think? What would the other Kappa Sig brothers think when he told them? Warren was at the law school, and Ely was at the med school, probably studying. I couldn't go whining and complaining like a baby to them. What was I to do? I certainly couldn't let the pledges know there was a baby in the pledge class who wasn't man enough to be their fraternity brother. I thought to myself, "I would never live this down. After all, I had already made it clear I was not going to smoke a cigar in a phone booth." I kept talking to myself, "You've got to do it. You don't want to, but you've got to do it." Then I rationalized, "I guess there's nothing immoral about it. It's just embarrassing." Then I thought of the survey and my designation as being "Pure as the driven snow." Up until this time, I had never done anything out of line that anybody could point to and make me feel guilty. Would this stain my reputation? Only time would tell.

My mind was made up. I just had to go through with it! So with paper bag in hand (folded in as a small bundle as possible), I sheepishly walked out of the Kappa Sig House with the brother looking on. I don't remember anybody else being around to witness our conversation or my starting my "mission impossible." The Wilson Library was on the other side of the campus from the fraternity house. I was thankful for the additional time to contemplate my speech and was in no hurry as I strolled to my destination. Finally, I reached the library steps and then up to the second floor. Maybe, she wouldn't be there. That would be the best scenario—then I wouldn't have to go through all this humiliation. Maybe, just maybe she wouldn't be there. No such luck! There were a lot of tables, but only a scattered few students doing their homework that particular night. The object of my search was at a table all by herself. At least that was something good in my favor. I took a seat several tables away from hers, sat for a minute or so and then got up to get a book (just any book would do) from the closest bookshelf. Maybe she wouldn't notice me "studying" along with all the others. At any rate, she never looked up from her writing and looking at the book before her. She looked like she might be doing a book report. I sat there a few more minutes, convincing myself that she was the one I was to approach. She was the one all right, no doubt about it. My memory of the occasion won't let me give you her name or what she looked like. All I remember is she was pretty, and I had a mission to fulfill. I had practiced my speech enough to know exactly what I wanted to say. At this point, I was just hoping I could say it.

After several false starts, I finally got up the nerve to take the long stroll to her table. I don't remember sitting down beside her, although an empty chair was reasonably nearby. I remember leaning over and in a low voice—a very low voice—whispering something like, "Excuse me, could I talk to you a minute?" I don't specifically remember if she said "yes" or "no" or what. In fact, I don't remember anything she said as I introduced myself. I think I said something like, "My name is Dan Perry and I'm a Kappa Sig pledge—and as a part of Hell Week, I've been sent on a scavenger hunt." At least she didn't turn me off. In fact, my recollection is that she seemed interested in what I had to say. At that point, I must have been sweating beads of perspiration. I don't recall my exact words, but I remember getting up enough nerve to show her the paper bag and say, "I'm supposed to bring back a pair of your panties." As I timidly made my request known, I also remember wondering what her response would be. Would she scream and call for a security guard? Would she make a scene and tell me to jump in the lake? Would she tell me to go back and tell those Kappa Sig boys, "That's none of your business!?" I just didn't know how she would react to this young upstart of a freshman fraternity pledge asking her such a personal question.

Well, would you believe that everything worked out beautifully and without a hitch? I am thinking she must have been a senior with a baby brother having to go through a similar experience as mine. I don't remember her being embarrassed in the least. She seemed to understand exactly what I was going through. I frankly don't remember her exact words, but she was calm and polite. Much to my amazement, I remember her taking the bag from my hands, excusing herself, and telling me to, "Wait right there." As I saw her leaving the table, I kept telling myself, "I can't believe I did that. I just can't believe I did that! But, so far so good." Her books were still on the table so I figured she wasn't just going to leave me there all alone, not knowing what to do next. She had to return to get her books. The one redeeming feature was she didn't seem upset or mad at me. I anxiously waited with head down and with an uncomfortable, unsettled feeling in the pit of my stomach.

Finally, I spied her emerging from around the corner from the direction of the ladies room. She had the brown bag in her hand, with a slight smile on her face. She sat down beside me. As she slyly handed the bag to me, she merely said in a soft voice, "Well, here it is." I don't remember what I said or how I thanked her. All I remember is getting out of there as quickly as possible. I knew there was something in the bag, but I never looked to see what it was. The walk back to the fraternity house seemed a lot shorter than the walk to the library. As I handed the bag and its contents over to the brother in charge, my uneasy feeling about the whole assignment was tempered by a prideful awareness of mission accomplished.

Addendum: The above is another one of those first-time-telling stories. I never thought I'd be writing about it in a book.

Fraternity Life Was Fun

After being initiated into Kappa Sigma, life was fun and fairly smooth. There were plenty of parties and sorority girls. We went to all the home football games and even some of the away games, especially, Duke, State, and Wake Forest. One time we traveled to the Georgia game. Many times we, as UNC Kappa Sigs, would bet on the outcome of the game with Kappa Sigs from the opposing schools. The loser would send the winner a "skin" showing the final score, date, etc. The skin was a piece of cowhide approximately two by three feet and was to be hung in the fraternity house for a memento of the weekend.

The Wilmington Azalea Festival was always a fun-filled weekend toward the end of March when all the azaleas were in full bloom. It seemed like all of Carolina as well as other schools were partying and having a good time. For most of us, it was just good clean fun, although at times we would hear of some of the boys getting in some minor trouble with the law. I don't believe the spring break mass exodus to the Florida beaches had become popularized during my stay at Carolina—at least it never crossed my mind to participate. Debutant balls and related parties were the focus of our attention during the early part of September. We had a Kappa Sig basketball team, which played several out of town games arranged by "Tab" Scott, one of the older brothers. Bill Sanders of Raleigh was our center, and I played my usual position of forward. We enjoyed playing intramural basketball and softball against the other fraternities. My most embarrassing moment in an intramural game was hearing the crowd yelling and screaming as I dribbled the entire length of the court only to discover I had scored at the wrong basket. I actually scored two points for the opposing team! I must have had a mental lapse and headed the wrong way. As I was dribbling at full speed, all along I thought I was being cheered on. Actually they were trying to get my attention to warn of the obvious mishap. Oh, well, so much for that major mess-up!

That story reminds me of another incident involving the father of Tom Zachery, one of my fraternity brothers. Tom's father was credited with throwing the pitch in 1927 which allowed Babe Ruth to hit his 60th home run, a season record which stood until 1961 when Roger Maris of the Yankees set another record by hitting 61 home runs in a 162 game season. Ruth's 60 home runs came at a time when the season consisted of 154 games.

Freshman Basketball

Somebody suggested I ought to go out for the freshman basketball team. I came to Carolina with absolutely no intention of trying out for the basketball team. Even though I was a two-year starter at Woodberry in basketball and a three-year member of the golf team, I never even considered I would be good enough to play at the university level. But you never know. At least maybe I ought to give it a try. So when the first day of freshman basketball practice came, I showed up with four scholarship boys and a whole host of others, just to see what it would be like. Back in those days, Carolina was not known as a basketball school as it is today. The Carolina basketball team had been known as the White Phantoms (according to Cooper Taylor) up until shortly after World War II, when it acquired the name "Tar Heels." Tom Scott was the varsity coach. I believe we had been having losing seasons for several years. On that first day of freshman practice, we spent most of the time shooting. We lined up to shoot crip shots so the freshman coach could take a look at us. Then we shot short shots, long shots, and all kinds of shots. With my "skin and bones" frame, I was beginning to see that most of those boys were way out of my class. I lasted two days. The next day freshman coach, Jim Hamilton, picked a team to play a scrimmage game with the scholarship boys. It was then I realized that I need not come back the third day. They were fast and they were husky (compared to me). A lot of them were taller and seemed to know what they were doing. I was not in good enough shape to keep up with them. I remember Bud Maddie and Vince Grimali from New Jersey as being two of the scholarship boys and Cooper Taylor reminded me that Ernie Swartz and Jack Wallace were the other two. You will remember that when I was at Woodberry I played against Jack, who was the star for Mercerberg Academy in Pennsylvania. Although Cooper was not on scholarship, he was one of the better players on the freshman team. He went on to play the next year for Tom Scott and then two years for Frank McGuire who was brought in to bring Carolina basketball to a new level. I think he came in 1953, and by 1957 we had won the national championship, which really put Carolina on the basketball map. He was followed by the legendary Dean Smith. "All the world" knows that Dean Smith became the most successful coach in history, having won two national championships and setting all sorts of conference and national records.

Freshman Golf

I never really tried out for the golf team. The only exposure I had to the freshman team was when one day in the spring of 1950 two members of the team, Lou Brown and Bob Black, asked me to play in a match against the Marine team from Cherry Point. One of our team members couldn't play that day, and they needed a fill-in. They were going to Cherry Point the next day and they needed to know if I would join them. My first thought was, "Who me? Play on the freshman golf team at Carolina? WOW! That'd be great." Then I came to my senses and realized they weren't asking me to join the team as a permanent member. They were just asking me to play as a fill-in for just that one match. Of course, if I could shoot a sub-par round and beat all the others, maybe the coach would be so impressed he might even offer me a scholarship right there on the 18th green! At the very least, he would probably invite me to join the squad as a walk-on. I may be exaggerating my thought process there a little bit, but I'll admit I was thinking about some possibilities which might lie ahead. To cut the story short, I did play with Lou Brown as my playing partner. I don't remember the details, but I do remember Lou had a great swing—smooth and deliberate. I think he was about one or two under par. I think I had something like a 78 or so. I don't remember if I personally won or lost, but at least we won the team match with the Marines, and I had the distinction of playing with the UNC freshman golf team that one and only time. I think most all the players on the freshman team were Sigma Chi's. I remember that Bob Black had beaten me 3 and 2 in one of the Eastern interscholastic tournaments in Greenwich Connecticut. Also, Bill Williamson, another member of the freshman team, from Charlotte had played in the Carolina Junior Tournament in Greensboro in which I was medalist. It so happened that Lou Brown's brother, Wes, married Hontas Whitaker of Kinston a few years later. Carolina and Wake Forrest were two of the best teams in the country. Those were the days when the famous Harvey Ward was at Carolina and Arnold Palmer and Art Wall were at Wake Forest. In rationalizing my one freshman match, I concluded that even to try to make the team I would have to play every day and travel for the out of town matches. Too much was against me. First, I was too busy doing other things; second, it would take time away from my studies; and third, and most important, I simply was not good enough! Those boys were out of my league!

Addendum: Cooper Taylor was not only on the basketball team, but he was also on the freshman golf team. I called him at his home in Georgia to confirm all those names. He reminded me that Jim Ferree from Winston Salem was also on the team. Jim, along with Lou Brown, Bob Black, and Bill Williamson went on to play varsity golf at Carolina. Jim later turned pro and played on the P.G.A. tour for a number of years. I'm not sure if he won any tournaments on the regular tour, but he did win a couple of tournaments on the Senior Tour.

Social Life and Special Girls

Since I was in a fraternity and in various other activities, I naturally was into the dating scene. Even though I was still very shy in many respects, I enjoyed dating and being with girls. Something was going on all the time. The big band era was still going strong. I was on the Inter-fraternity Council and the Executive Committee of the German Club, so I was in the middle of the social scene. Big weekends required dates. Some of the big bands that came to Carolina included: Ray Anthony, Tommy Dorsey, Benny Goodman, Gene Kruper, Al Hurt, Louie "Satchmo" Armstrong, and the Glen Miller band. Glenn Miller himself had been killed in an air plane crash during the war, but his special sound continued on. Home football weekends were also big occasions. One of my first "import" dates was Paula Whitaker of Kinston. I was a freshman (or sophomore) when she was still in high school. I got her a room at some lady's house, which was the custom. It was not hard to find a widow or some older couple to open up their home for such occasions. By the way, a year or so later Paula asked me to be her chief marshal when she made her debut at the Debutant Ball in Raleigh. Shortly after that, she became engaged and married Jack Calhoun, after her first year at Women's College in Greensboro.

Martha Erwin, from Durham and Duke, was also a special girl. I had known her during the summers at Morehead. She was cute, with a great personality, but I was too shy to make much headway. One afternoon I drove over to her house in Durham for what I thought was a date. I was looking forward to seeing her, but evidently I had misunderstood the arrangements. When I went to the door to pick her up, she said I must be mistaken, for she already had a date inside. She had a date with Dan, but it was not with Dan Perry. It was with Dan Uzzell of Durham. She ended up marrying that Dan a few years later.

Another special girl was Bobbie Love from Lincolnton. She was Edgar Love's younger sister; she had a twin named "Libby." The first time I saw Bobbie, she was with several other girls walking down Franklin Street in Chapel Hill. All of the girls were cute, but one stood out above all the others. I was with several boys. As we approached and casually passed the girls, I kept thinking, "Who in the world is that? She is so cute! I'd sure like to meet and date her!" A week or so later, I happened to meet her and found out who she was. She had dark hair and a beautiful, attractive smile. I always did like a smiling girl. I could see the resemblance with her brother Edgar whom everyone respected as a true gentleman and scholar. I must have been about a senior, and she was a freshman when we first met. Anyway, I managed to get up enough courage to ask her for a date. I remember liking her enough to want to go out with her again. But, it was about that time that I developed the policy of not dating the same girl more than three times in a row. I had to keep up the appearance that I was not getting too serious with any one particular girl. Although I liked Bobbie a lot, I was not ready to get serious with anyone. Needless to say, I am sure it probably never entered her mind to get serious with me because I knew she was popular and dated others, too. On second thought, I may have been more interested than I admitted at the time, because I remember how much I looked forward to taking her out. If we had a 5:00 P.M. date, I had to force myself not to get there too early. That would not be good, no matter how anxious I was to see her. So I would time it perfectly to go strolling up the pathway to the Chi O House at exactly 5:00 P.M.—not 4:59 or 5:01, but exactly 5:00 P.M. on the dot. Although we dated off and on for several years, nothing ever developed between us, and she ended up getting married some years later. Shortly afterwards, she was tragically killed in an automobile accident.

Another one of my special girl friends was Bish Fox from Roanoke, Virginia. She appeared in the 1953 *Yackety Yack* as a member of the queen's court. She was another one of those pretty-smiling girls that attracted my attention. Before we even started dating, on at least one occasion (maybe two), I saw her walking eastwardly toward my Old West Dorm where I was rooming with Heywood Washburn. I happened to spy her from my third-storey window as she approached 25 or so yards away. I thought to myself, "If I'm fast enough, I can run down the stairs, go out the back east side door, and casually walk around the corner just in time to say hello." Well, that's exactly what happened. My plan worked perfectly! I hoped she didn't hear the racket

I made racing down the stairs from the third to the first floor. Even if she did hear the commotion, I didn't care. I just wanted to be able to say hello. My recollection is we did say hello, but that was about all. I guess I was too bashful to start up a conversation. Can you believe that? Going to all that trouble just to say hello or some such simple greeting—not having enough nerve to pause and start up a conversation. If we could just have talked a little while, maybe she would have shown some interest, then I might have been able to call her for a date. But no, I just said hello or something like that, and kept right on going. Going where, I didn't know, other than just go a little ways until she was out of sight. Then I turned around and walked back up the flight of steps to my third-floor room. I know that doesn't make any sense to the reader, and it doesn't make any sense to me, even now. But that's the way it was—at least that's the way I remember it. I think I must have called Bish on the telephone for my first date with her. We went out a number of times but never three times in a row. Up until this time, all of my relationships with girls would sort of "fade out" without my feeling any deep sense of loss or hurt. But for some reason, Bish was different. I remember we hadn't dated in several weeks when, out of the clear, I heard she was engaged to Jimmy Lester. I think he was also from Roanoke. Evidently, they were longtime friends and maybe even childhood sweethearts. Apparently, they had been seeing a lot of each other at UNC— but not behind my back; I had been seeing other girls, too. I don't believe I ever told anyone (except Louis Sutton, a fraternity brother I palled around with) about the feeling of hurt and loss I experienced, especially for the first several days. I could find no particular reason for this sunken feeling, because we were never serious in our relationship. It was just that in the back of my mind I had thought that Bish as well as Bobbie Love were the kind of girls I would like to finally end up with—down the road, of course.

Betty Bell, a Tri Delta from Greensboro, was another nice girl I dated in my undergrad days, who was special in that it took a few days or more to get over that hurt feeling when she ended up going steady with someone else.

The bottom line about my first four years of dating at Carolina is that I was slow, still shy, still "pure as the driven snow," and not ready to settle down.

The nice, good-looking girls I was attracted to were also popular with the other boys on campus. Obviously, they were a step or two ahead of me. They were ready, and I wasn't. It wasn't my time, yet.

I don't know why I'm spending so much time talking of my dating experiences at Carolina, other than I'm trying to tell it like it was. Dating did, indeed, play a big part in my college life. It was good clean fun, and I had a great time. In looking back, I think it all contributed to the general make-up of who I am today.

At this point, the reader may be thinking that all I did was go out with the girls. When did I find time to study and participate in the other activities? Somehow, I managed to keep up. I don't remember my grade point average, but it ended up somewhere between a B and a C. I was not considered smart—just a plodder and an average student.

The Men's Honor Council

The Men's Honor Council was a real blessing to me. When it was suggested that I run for the job, I was not fully aware of the responsibilities associated with it. Our main job was to hear cases involving violations of the honor code and other related matters. Bob Holmes from Mt. Olive also served on the council. I had known Bob in a casual way during the summers at Morehead. As we served together on the Honor Council, I was impressed with his sincerity and honorable approach in dealing with the matters that came before us. He later went on to medical school and practiced medicine for many years before his retirement. He is now living in New Bern with his wife, the former Betsy Gatling, a classmate of Margaret's at Salem College. I first met Betsy on a blind date at Salem. I remember her as being "lively" with a great personality.

One of my most lasting memories of the Honor Council was during the hearing of a case when a certain student was called upon to give testimony as a character witness for the accused. We were accustomed to hearing witnesses, so it was not really a big deal until this particular witness opened his mouth to speak. I don't remember so much what he said, for it was his deep, melodious voice that captured the attention of all of us. His diction was deliberate, polished, and flawless. We could not help but be is awe, not only of the tone of his voice, but also the fact that his poised countenance led us to believe he was mature far beyond his age. From the time he started talking my thought was, "He must be somebody special. How could a student have a voice like that?" At the conclusion of his testimony, he was ushered out of the room in the usual manner. Almost immediately after the door shut behind him, all of us burst forth with such comments as, "Who in the world was that?" to "I've never heard such a voice coming from a student!" to "I can't believe what I just heard!" At the beginning of his testimony, the young man had given his name as Charles Kuralt. After his departure, we found out he was a freshman whom only one or two on the Honor Council knew. It was just a few years later that his name became a household word associated with CBS television and "On the Road with Charles Kuralt."

Chapter XV

SPECIAL FRIENDS

The Order of The Grail, more commonly known as "The Grail," based its membership on leadership and character. Along with the Order of the Golden Fleece, The Grail was considered one of the top organizations at UNC. When I was a senior, some nineteen members, all of whom were outstanding men of integrity and character, belonged to the Grail. Somewhere in the material given us, I had read of a reference to the "Holy Grail," and the implication was that membership was also based on the pursuit of spiritual growth. Being the selective type of organization it was, I felt extremely humbled to be tapped into its membership, for it afforded me the opportunity to get to know several highly esteemed classmates on a much more personal basis.

Our Grail leader, referred to as the "delagata," was Eugene Oberdorfer, II of Atlanta, Georgia. His girlfriend was Saralyn Bonowitz from Chattanooga, Tennessee. She was a Chi Omega and president of the Valkyries, the leading girls' organization. Everyone looked up to them as being the ideal couple. They were both bright and of impeccable character, and their sound leadership abilities were obvious. Gene was Phi Beta Kappa and Phi Eta Sigma (Phi Beta Kappa freshman equivalent) and was president of his social fraternity, Zeta Beta Tau. In addition to being president of the Valkyries, Saralyn was also president of the Hillel Cabinet and chairman of Women's Orientation. They married soon after graduation and have had a long, happy life together in Atlanta. Although my relationship with them was not extremely close, they represented the best at Carolina, and I always valued their friendship.

Archie Forte, from Oxford, North Carolina, was the exchequer (vice president) of the Grail and a brilliant student. He was Phi Eta Sigma and co-president of Phi Beta Kappa. Donnie Evans from Charlotte was Phi Eta Sigma and co-captain of the swimming team. Steve Perrow from Virginia was another one of those all-around good guys who was a pleasure to know. These were just some of the boys I associated with in the Grail. They were all outstanding, honorable boys who went on to make a name for themselves in their various communities.

Three other Grail members deserve special mention: Arthur Spaugh, Ham Horton, and Jim McLeod.

Arthur Spaugh—and the Trip of a Lifetime

My friendship with Arthur Spaugh of Winston Salem grew stronger during the summer prior to our senior year. (Arthur would later married Mary Jo Wooten, another of Margaret's classmates from Salem.)

At that time, my longtime friend Z.A. Collins and I decided to take a trip to the New England states and Canada. We needed a third, so we asked Arthur to join us. Z.A.'s daddy told us we could use his new 1952 (or 53?) "rocket engine" Oldsmobile 88. It was a real beauty, and we were excited when we heard the news. The only stipulation was that we had to promise not to drive over 50 m.p.h. We didn't think there would be any problem with that, even though we knew the speed limit was 55 m.p.h. Z A. and I had heard that Dr. and Mrs. Paul Munsell had recently returned from a trip to New England, so we spent some time with them at their home on North Queen Street getting advice as to where to go and what to see. Dr. Munsell kept telling us, as he described the various areas of recommended travel, "That's beautiful 'count-ry' up there, beautiful 'count-ry!'" Those words he used over and over again tickled Z.A. and me, and made us all the more excited about our own trip. Arthur drove down from Winston Salem and spent the night with Z.A. The next morning bright and early, we were off on our trip of a lifetime—headed north in our brand new, rocket engine Oldsmobile. Right before leaving, Z. A.'s daddy reminded us all of our promise not the drive more than 50 m.p.h., even though the speed limit was 55 m.p.h. We kept our promise—almost to the letter! We took turns driving, always keeping in mind our firm promise. We each felt accountable to each other. The only times we went above 50 m.p.h. during the whole trip were the two or three occasions going downhill when the speedometer slipped a little past 50 to 52, 53, and 54 m.p.h. I don't think it ever got over 55 m.p.h. We all agreed we thought Mr. Collins would forgive us for those few times. We had made a firm and binding promise which we took seriously, and we intended to keep it. We took our time, and as a result, we enjoyed every minute. I was assigned to keep a daily journal of all we did and saw. We especially wanted to see several of the Ivy League schools, so we visited Brown, Princeton, Yale, and Harvard. One of our favorite spots was Bar Harbor, Maine, with its rugged coastal mountains. Z .A. was so impressed with its beauty, he commented that this was where he wanted to go on his honeymoon. Z. A. later told me that although he did not take his bride to Bar Harbor on their honeymoon, he did take her many years later. We traveled up into Canada to visit Montreal and Quebec. We enjoyed taking a walk on the famous boardwalk at the Chateau Frontenac. We came back down to Niagara Falls and were in total awe of its size and magnificence as we felt its spray and heard the deafening roar. We heard many stories of men going over the falls in a barrel. On our way home, we enjoyed seeing the horse-drawn carriages, white fences, barns, and green farm land of the Pennsylvania Dutch Country.

One of my objectives was to go swimming in one of the Great Lakes, so we set our sights on Lake Erie. Telling our grandchildren that we went swimming in Lake Erie sounded like a challenging idea—but our plans never materialized. I had pictured finding a nice little beach area with white sands and the typical swimming scene. Actually, all we could find was wooded areas and shrubs lining the waterfront—not a good place to swim. The best we could do was squat by the shore line and test the water temperature. Wow! It was cold, cold, cold—way too cold for swimming, even if we had found the right spot! In view of the fact it was late in the day, we decided at least to camp out beside the lake to get a feel for our surroundings. Z. A. slept on the back seat while Arthur and I slept in our sleeping bags on the ground directly behind the car. We were all pretty tired, so it was easy to fall asleep soon after a supper of sandwiches. After the sun set, we were left in total darkness. All went well until we were awakened from a deep sleep by a steady rain which was beginning to soak us thoroughly. Even though we couldn't swim in Lake Erie, we could at least claim we had a wet time beside the lake.

One of the main things I remember about that trip was my movie-taking. Daddy had just gotten a new 8-millimeter movie camera, which he said I could take with me on the trip. I had stocked up with plenty of Kodak film and had taken plenty of pictures along the way. But the sound of the camera bothered me. It sounded funny, and it took me only three or four minutes to use up a whole cartridge of film. Even though I had no experience in home movie-taking, I thought each cartridge should last at least 10 or 15 minutes. Be that as it may, after the first four days, I mailed three cartridges to Mother and Daddy to let them know what a good time we were having. Several days later while talking to Daddy on the telephone, he told me they enjoyed looking at the film, but we had a major problem—they were all in slow motion! Somehow, the camera was inadvertently set on slow motion, thus causing the film speed to be accelerated some five times, thereby shorting the film duration. Much to our disappointment, none of us could figure out how to correct the malfunction. Sadly, we decided to stop our movie-taking and rely on the few snapshots we took with Arthur's Brownie camera.

All in all it was a great trip for Z. A., Arthur, and me—full of fun, good times, and plenty of laughs. It was a real privilege and blessing to take a ten-day trip with my two good friends—and we did it while sticking to our promise of not going over 50 mph (except going downhill).

Hamilton C. Horton Jr.—*a Born Leader*

Ham Horton was from Winston Salem. He was easy going, soft spoken, and quietly confident as he gave his opinion on matters ranging from politics to life in general. He was an easy choice to be our president of the student body, and he won the election handily. Although short in statue, he was looked upon as being a giant among men. When he spoke, people listened. As permanent president of our class and in charge of each of our class reunions, I could always count on Ham to play a vital part in the various activities associated with the reunions. He was a natural for whatever job he was given, and he never turned me down, no matter what he was asked to do. He was smooth with words, and what he said always seemed to make good sense. His political persuasion at Carolina was generally conservative. By comparison, I think I was much more liberal in my thinking at Carolina and in my early years as a young lawyer in Kinston. (That was before I began to see the truth about liberalism and understood more fully the conservative view of politics, religion, and general life issues.) Ham, as well as a number of others (whom I will mention later), had a significant influence on my political thinking, which became much more conservative in my later years. Ham went on to serve a number of terms in the North Carolina Senate with both distinction and admiration. Even those who disagreed with him politically would readily admit he was a man of honesty and integrity who stood up for what he believed to be truthful and fair. He had a great sense of humor, which was evident in his activities as well as his words. One of my favorite memories of Ham was during a coffee break one evening while five or six of us were sitting around a table chatting and having a good time. During this time, a campus campaign was going on. We were all members of the University Party. Ham noticed several Student Party leaders entering the room and coming in our direction. He quickly got our attention and said, "Here they come, boys, and I know they're all wondering what we're up to. Here's what we're going to do. Let's huddle our heads together as if we're working on a strategic move. Then when I count to three, let's all rare back and start laughing. That'll get their attention. They won't know what in the world is going on." And that's exactly what we did. We put our heads together as if we were in some deep conversation. Then Ham very slowly counted to three. "Onnne – Twooo – Three!" We all started laughing and cutting up and slapping each other on the back as if we had really found the answer to something big. We never paid any attention to our political opponents—and I don't know what they thought of all us University Party members sitting over there in the corner. All I know is we had a good time carrying on like a bunch of juveniles, and Ham Horton was at the center of it all.

James C. McLeod Jr. — a Man of Sterling Character

Early as a freshman, I had heard a lot about Jim McLeod of Florence, South Carolina. He had the reputation being a "great guy" and one who would go far in life. Although he was elected president of the freshman class, I only knew him casually until we served together on "The Grail." Jim was born into one of the outstanding families of South Carolina. His father, Dr. James C. McLeod, as well as his grandfather, Dr. Frank H. McLeod, were both leading surgeons in Florence and the Pee Dee region. With the influence of Jim's grandfather, the state of South Carolina granted a charter in 1906 to The Florence Infirmary for the purpose of conducting "a general hospital and training school for nurses" in Florence. Dr. McLeod's dream of creating a hospital to serve the medical requirements of eastern South Carolina was a functioning reality by 1917 when the hospital had 100 beds and was drawing patients from throughout the Pee Dee region. Because of Dr. McLeod's strong identification with the hospital, the name was later changed to the "McLeod Infirmary." After the name change, the Charter named Dr. F. H. McLeod as president and his son Dr. James C. McLeod as vice-president. The McLeod father and son were not only outstanding leaders in the medical community, but also were noticeably active in civic and church affairs. Dr. James McLeod was even prevailed upon to run for governor of South Carolina. Although his only political experience had been as a delegate to the National Democratic Convention of 1944, the love of political office beckoned. In a field of eleven candidates in the primary in 1946, he finished second behind the well-known J. Strom Thurmond. In a run off election, Dr. McLeod lost to Thurmond who carried 57 percent of the votes. His bid for the United States Senate in 1948 was cut short by his untimely death. On December 9, 1947, he suffered a heart attack at his home and died a few hours later. Dr. F. H. McLeod retired in about 1940 and died in 1944. The institution, which he founded in 1906 as the Florence Infirmary, has evolved within eighty years to become the McLeod Regional Medical Center of the Pee Dee. During those years of change and growth, the institution served residents not only in Florence and vicinity, but also throughout northeastern South Carolina and beyond.

Getting a glimpse of my friend Jim McLeod's father and grandfather, the reader can understand Jim's background and the positive influence it must have had on his life. I remember having a weekend visit in Jim's home with a couple of classmates. His dear mother was a gracious hostess. Her personal attention to each of us was an example of true southern hospitality as she served us delicious meals and attended our every need. From that memorable visit, I was able to confirm my impression of Jim as a gentleman of honor. It was obvious that, as our friendship matured, he was living up to the image exemplified by his strong family background. His sister, Florie, and younger brother George were also there that weekend, and their company was enjoyable in every way. George was also at Carolina at the time and went on to make an outstanding scholastic record as an undergrad and med school student. He showed great promise as he was preparing for a career in medicine when his life was cut short by his tragic death in a hunting accident. The loss of such an outstanding young man was hard for both family and friends to take. Only through God's grace were they able to get through it.

One of my most pleasant memories of Jim was after graduation in 1953 when we roomed together on a six-week cruise to Europe with Dr. J. C. Lyons as our tour director. (I will tell you about that unforgettable trip later so as to keep the order of events in perspective.) In looking back at our days at Carolina, Jim McLeod has left a lasting impression on me. Something about his sense of humor and wit drew me to him. His values were such that he could be dead serious one minute and then, with perfect timing, have me laughing with some witty remark. When I think of a person described as having a "sterling character," I think of Jim McLeod of Florence, South Carolina. He considered going to med school, but after a fair trial he decided that the life of a doctor was not for him. He went on to law school at the University of South Carolina and made a name for himself as a hard-working trial attorney in Florence. The best thing he ever did was to marry Octavia Phillips, a delightfully charming young lady who was the daughter of a judge. One of my biggest regrets about attending UNC at Chapel Hill is not keeping up my friendship with Jim over the years. We had class reunions every five years, and many of my classmates attended. Other than the 25th, and 50th reunions, I don't think Jim came back for any of the others. At the 50th in 2003, Jim and I agreed that time is short and we needed to see more of each other. Since then, Jim and Octavia have visited in our home once, and Margaret and I have visited them in Florence. We also met at the Billy Graham Training Center (The Cove) in Asheville for a weekend of inspiration and fun. We were planning on meeting for another three days at the Cove in October of 2006, but he had to cancel because of health reasons. Hopefully, we can get together in April 2007 in Asheville. In the meantime, we plan to keep in touch by telephone every few weeks.

J. Heywood Washburn

Another great guy whom I highly respected during my years at Carolina was Heywood Washburn from High Point. I previously mentioned his name as being my freshman roommate. We were also roommates when we both successfully ran for senior class officers; he was elected as vice-president of the class. Heywood was a smart, likable friend with a good sense of humor. He pledged Sigma Chi along with Z. A. and Cooper Taylor. He was Phi Beta Kappa and majored in personnel management. He and I got along great and had many good times together. After graduation, he got a good job with a company in Tupelo, Mississippi, where he has lived ever since. Being in his company was always a pleasure, but like so many of my other classmates, we haven't been in touch as much as we would like. I feel very privileged to have met and been associated with such men of character and integrity at Carolina as Heywood Washburn, Jim McLeod, Ham Horton, Gene Oberdorfer, Archie Forte, Donnie Evans, and some others I have mentioned. From time to time, I manage to meet up with old friends Z. A. and Cooper Taylor— but not as much as I would like.

Chapter XVI

GRADUATION FROM CAROLINA

About midway my senior year I remember suddenly realizing that time was moving on. Spring was approaching, and it was my last year at Carolina! I would soon be graduating! Did I say graduating? That meant that as president of the class, I'd be expected to make a speech. I really hadn't given it much thought until that sudden revelation. I was busy with fraternity life as well as several other activities. On top of that, I was trying to keep up my grades. Then the thought occurred to me, "What if I flunked a course that last semester, I certainly wouldn't be able to graduate! Would my buddy Heywood Washburn, as vice-president of the class, have to step in and make the graduation speech in my place? That would be terrible! I would never live it down." Of course, I knew that Heywood was Phi Beta Kappa and smooth on his feet and could do a much better job than I. I remember praying about it with positive expectations. Soon the negative thoughts were dispelled, and I actually came through with pretty good grades that final semester.

In the meantime, I had to work on my speech, which I was told should be no more that five minutes. Frankly, I was somewhat scared as to what I should say. In preparation I decided to take a public speaking class from Dr. Olsen, who was the father of two of my fraternity brothers, Bill and Dan Olsen. Maybe he could help me not only with the delivery, but also with the content of my message. Dr. Olsen reminded us that Abraham Lincoln's Gettysburg address is considered one of the great speeches of all time. It was simple, to the point, and would serve as a good model to follow. He said if I followed Lincoln's format, I couldn't go wrong. The good news was that the Gettysburg Address was included in *101 Famous Poems*, the book Mother and Daddy had given me many years before. I had memorized Lincoln's words along with many of the book's poems. Dr. Olsen reminded the class that a good way to open a speech is with a specific point in time, such as a date or time of year, etc. This would be a good "attention getter" and make it easy for the listener to identify with what was to follow. Lincoln started his famous speech, "Fourscore and seven years ago our fathers brought forth upon this continent a new nation...." Based on Dr. Olsen's advice, I started my graduation speech, "June 8^{th,} 1953, will be a memorable day in our lives...."

Somehow I put it together and was ready when the big day came. In looking back over the program of events, I was reminded of the excitement of the various activities of June 8th, 1953. We officially started the day at 10 A.M. in Gerrand Hall when I presided over the last meeting of the class of 1953. The main order of business included the election of permanent class officers and an address by Dr. I. G. Greer, executive vice-president of the Business Foundation of North Carolina. I was humbled by being elected permanent class president along with my Grail friends Archie Fort of Oxford, as vice-president, and Steve Perrow of Bedford, Virginia, as secretary-treasure. After a reception for commencement guests on the lawn at the Davie Poplar, we attended the Annual Alumni Luncheon in Lenoir Hall, at which classmate Arthur Spaugh's father (class of 1920), President of the Alumni Association, presided. At the luncheon, two memorable things happened.

Comparing the Oldest and the Youngest

First, my picture was taken with Dr. M. C. Millender, a retired Ashville physician and a member of the class of 1883. The picture was featured on the front page of the next issue of the *UNC Alumni Review* magazine. The long article talked about the 70-year span that separated Dr. Millender's class on 1883 and my class of 1953. It went on to say, if I returned to Chapel Hill for my 70th reunion, "The calendar year will be 2023!" When brother Ely read that, he commented, "Dan, that's not but 70 years away—you reckon you'll be around to celebrate?" In 1953 that seemed like an eternity away, but in 2006, as I write these words, I realize it's now only 17 years away. The way time flies, 2023 "will be here in no time." The front page of that old *Alumni Review* magazine is frayed and torn, so I have preserved it by laminating back-to-back the front page and article page. If I'm able to make it back for my 70th reunion, as did Dr. Millender, it'll be right before my 92nd birthday, and I'll be sure to take my picture with Dr. Millender. That should make for an interesting story if I can have my picture taken in similar fashion with the president of the class of 2023. The Lord willing, I'll be there! By the way, in that same 1953 issue of the *UNC Alumni Review,* Felix Harvey of the class of 1943 was pictured as being recently named by the Jaycee's as "North Carolina's Outstanding Young Business Man of 1953." I might add that it was quite a handsome picture that accompanied the article. Dressed in a nice looking business suit and hat, Felix certainly looked the part of an outstanding business man.

A Conversation with Governor Umstead

The second memorable event at the Alumni Luncheon on the afternoon of June 8th occurred during a conversation I had with Governor William B. Umstead. He was there to receive an honorary degree at graduation. "Bill" Umstead was a close personal friend and classmate of my father. In fact, he had been a groomsman in my parents wedding in 1922. It was only natural that our two families gathered after the luncheon for a time of conversation and fellowship. Although Mother and Daddy and a bunch of other people were standing around talking, at one point Governor Umstead sidled up to me privately and made a statement I've never forgotten. His voice was low, out of the hearing range of everyone else. He said, "Dan, I like your smile. You'll go a long way with a smile like that." But then he added a statement which caught me totally off guard. He said, "but don't go into politics. It's a dirty business." I could tell he was very sincere; but the thought occurred to me, here was the governor of North Carolina advising a graduating senior at the University of North Carolina not to get involved in the political arena.

I sensed his friendly advice was based on his own experience of having gone through some tough political battles. In addition, it was well known that he was suffering from a malignancy and his term as governor would probably end prematurely. I knew that politics was not for everyone. At this stage of my life, I had no interest in running for political office, even though I had already had a little encouragement from several friends. It was my impression that most political figures generally encouraged promising young people at least to consider a political future, for the need for bright, young, and honest politicians was and still is so great. (Not that I was all that bright, but at least I was young and honest.) In retrospect, I think the governor was merely sharing his honest feelings with the son of a close friend, just as he would his own son. Even though I never ran for public office, I'm confident his advice had little if anything to do with my decision. Politics just wasn't for me. Some years later, my own dear mother told me in a moment of concern, "Dan, I'm so glad you're not in politics." Through the years, I've supported many politicians and political causes, but I never ran for office myself after leaving Carolina, except for running for vice-president and president of the Kinston Jaycees.

My Graduation Speech

Graduation is traditionally held in Kenan Stadium; however, on June 8, 1953, the weather was threatening, and the last minute decision was made to have it in Woolen Gym. We were disappointed, but nevertheless, we did get our diplomas. One thing I especially requested was that we march in to *Pomp and Circumstance* rather than the unfamiliar tune they had played the previous year. My request was granted, and I think the whole class was thrilled.

When it came time to give my speech, I was understandably nervous and anxious—but I made every effort to give the impression I was in perfect control and "as calm as a cucumber." I even thought if I could memorize it well enough and not look down at my notes, the audience would think I was really a big shot. I didn't even consider that the audience was so far away that most would not know if I was reading it or not. Besides that, who would care one way or the other? I was still a little over three weeks away from my

22nd birthday. In looking back to that time over 50 years ago, I am now much aware that as a 21-year-old, I was immature and "wet behind the ears" in so many ways. Be that as it may, I still remember sitting on the stage with Governor Umstead and all the other dignitaries and looking out over a packed Woolen Gym with a sea of people in the audience looking on. As I was being introduced as president of the class and taking my place at the rostrum, I saw Warren walking down the aisle to the front with camera in hand. I remember a couple of flashes, but don't recall ever seeing any pictures.

Sometime later in a conversation with Dr. Paul Whitaker, he commented that he would like to get a copy of my speech. The only copy I had was my hand-written copy on 5x7 cards, which apparently was misplaced in the process of packing to come home. As a matter of fact, the cards were not to be found for some 53 years, until I recently discovered them in a box of Carolina photographs and memorabilia as I was preparing to write this book.

It was certainly not a great speech by any stretch of the imagination—but for what it's worth, here it is in its entirety.

Commencement Address —June 8, 1953

Governor Umstead, President Gray, Chancellor House, distinguished visitors, members of the faculty, ladies and gentlemen:

June 8, 1953, will be a memorable day in our lives, for it represents the conclusion of four years of study towards an academic degree. We students are fortunate to have had the privilege of studying under some of the most renowned scholars of our day. They have helped us attain greater knowledge and insight into the problems of the future.

Not only does this day represent four years of study, but also four years of college life and making wonderful friendships—friendships which will last throughout the years. The fellowship we have had during our college days will be treasured the rest of our lives.

Let us turn our thoughts back to some of the experiences we have been through together.

A few short years ago we entered Carolina as freshmen, eager to find out what this big college life was all about. Was Carolina really what it was built up to be? Did the "Carolina Spirit" actually exist? In a short while we answered these questions for ourselves. With the passage of time an indescribable feeling was finding its way into our hearts and souls. This was the feeling we call the "Carolina Spirit," and it came from living the Carolina way of life. It came from associating our lives with the age long traditions which have made Carolina the great University which it is today.

During our four years here we have lived with a number of Carolina institutions on the campus, among them being two of our most cherished the Honor Code and the Campus Code. Under these codes of ethics we have made advancements in the fundamentals of life — the fundamentals of learning to live with other people, learning to treat our fellow man with fairness, respect, and consideration, and learning to win with grace and if we lose, to lose with equal grace.

In years to come we will look back over our Carolina days and recall such familiar land marks as the Old Well, the Bell Tower, the South Building, the Carolina Inn, and all the others that we have learned to love.

We will remember those wonderful football weekends, the German Club dances, and the incessant battle between the coed and the import; and those sunny Y Court periods in which we all gathered on the South Building steps for an hour of social studies. And we will relive those fabulous weekends at the beach in the spring. Next year, as you know, these weekends will be shorter and less fashionable due to obvious reasons beyond the students' control. Our successors will probably have to be content with sun bathing at Hogan's Lake.

All these will stand out in our memories of the past; but for the present, the foremost thought in our minds is concerned with the future and what it holds for us. Our post graduate plans will be essentially different. Some of us will begin our life's work in the business world. Others will be called to serve our country and still others will continue their education.

But when we leave this great University tonight, no matter what our particular plans may be, we will all be confronted with certain basic obligations to ourselves, to our fellowman, and to our God. Fair play and honesty will be expected of us. We will be obligated to render service to our fellowman, and above all to show proper reverence for our Maker.

The fulfillment of these fundamental obligations is the key to our search for the true meaning of happiness, and can be realized through conscientious effort and an unfaltering faith.

During our years at Carolina we have been exposed to the importance of these obligations. We have had the opportunity to develop ourselves physically, mentally, socially and spiritually.

With this preparation, we should be ready to face the uncertainties of the future.

Here's a special note about my graduation from Carolina: My friend, Paula Whitaker, was graduating from Saint Mary's Junior College on the same day. She was thoughtful enough to send a congratulatory telegram: "to the President of the Class of '53 at UNC from the President of the class of '53 at Saint Mary's."

Chapter XVII

AFTER GRADUATION

Post Graduation Trip

After graduation from Carolina, the next big event in my life was truly unforgettable. It was a six-week tour of Europe that literally fell in my lap. Dr. J. C. Lyons said he would give me the trip free of charge if I would help him encourage a group of college students to join him and his wife who would be our tour directors. He had already made a number of contacts and signed up several girls from Randolph Macon College as well as others. Actually, I did very little to help. All I did was display an exciting attitude—which came naturally when I learned that my good friend Jim McLeod would be joining us. As it turned out, we had twenty girls and eight boys. What a ratio! In addition to Jim and me, the other six boys were Bill Clark from Tarboro; Frank Davenport from Timmonsville, South Carolina; Eddie Powe from Hartsville, South Carolina; Bill Proctor from Raleigh; Jim Seely from Winston Salem; and Rollie Tillman from Lake Wales, Florida. I have so many fond memories of that trip—most of which I preserved in two large scrapbooks of photos, post cards, and other memorabilia. "Preserved" may not be the right word, because when I reviewed the trip with Jim in a visit to Florence some 53 years later in August of 2006, I discovered many of the pictures had become unglued and somewhat disorganized. But, nevertheless, we had fun laughing and reliving those glorious days.

We sailed over on the Veendam and returned on the New Amsterdam of the Holland-American Lines. Dr. Lyons had told us that half the fun would be on the ships themselves. As expected, the food was outstanding, to say the least. I think we all ate too much—but it sure was fun! Romantic music with violins was everywhere. There was always something to do. Jim and I entered the ping-pong tournament and reached the finals playing against each other for the ship's championship in the best of three out of five games. We were tied at two games each, and I had him 19 to 13 in the final game. Just two more points, and I would be the champion. Evidently, I must have been thinking too much about the gold medal or trophy or certificate, or whatever they would give me as the winner, because something happened. Jim managed to get the next eight straight points to beat me 21–19. I still don't understand how he did it. Even 53 years later, we continue to laugh about it.

It was fun being one of eight boys in a crowd of twenty girls as we ate together, rode buses and toured together, and had an all around good time just being in each other's company. We visited eight countries: England, Scotland, Holland, Belgium, Germany, Switzerland, Italy, and France. All the girls were nice, but I seemed to spend a lot of time with Ruth Farmer, a Randolph Macon girl from Macon, Georgia. As a matter of fact, that fall I entered my first year of law school and dated her a fair amount, as she was a student at UNC. I even flew to Macon to visit her for a weekend. Ruth was a very nice girl, but nothing serious developed in our relationship. Jim had an attraction for Peggy Mitchner of Raleigh. She had been the leader of the Debutant Ball a year or so prior. I recall with fondness dating her from time to time and had her over for a football game at least once. Peggy ended up marrying Jack Marcus who returned to Kinston to practice law. Jim and I also palled around with and enjoyed Jim's cousin Gina Gaston, who was also on the trip. But there was one girl who stood out above all the rest in looks (at least to me). She was Carol Waterman from Montgomery, Alabama, who spent a lot of time with Bill Clark. I was so bashful I could not make a play for her, but with her medium-length auburn hair and fair complexion, I frankly had a hard time keeping my eyes off of her. On several occasions I caught myself staring at her while she was sitting at another table in the dining room on board ship. About all I was ever able to do was enter into a one-on-one conversation on a couple of occasions. Her twin sister, Ann, who was also attractive, paired off with Eddie Powe. Four years later while living in an army tent in Korea, I got up enough nerve to write her at the same home address she had while on our trip. My thought was maybe we could correspond to help me pass the time while on the other side of the world. A month or so later, I got a letter from her saying she appreciated my writing, but she was married. At least she wished me well while serving in the army. That was that!

The lake country in England was especially scenic and memorable. In Scotland the sheep and network of stone walls that captured my attention. Several of us played golf at Glen Eagles, Scotland. I remember a lot of scenes from Glen Eagles. It was still light enough to be playing golf at 11 p.m. and there was never a time during our round of 18 holes of golf that we didn't see at least three or four big jack rabbits running around in the fairways and roughs. Most of the time we could see a dozen or so at one time. There was the enormous 18th green. I stepped off a putt of 150 feet. I don't remember how many putts it took me to get in. All I know is it was the biggest green I had ever seen. I remember the windmills, cheese, and cleanliness of Holland. In Belgium, everyone marveled at the beauty of the lace. I remember walking inside the Rhone Glacier in Switzerland and buying a Rolex watch for Warren in Lucerne. Daddy had given me enough money to buy him (and me) a nice watch. Warren still wore his Rolex from time to time up until his death in 2003. I bought a Gublin, which is still in good running condition. In Germany our trip down the Rhine River and the castles and spectacular landscape were impressive. In Italy, we enjoyed Venice and the romantic music while slowly drifting along in a gondola—also the countless pigeons in Saint Marks Square. We visited the glass factory as well as a furniture factory in Venice. I bought and had shipped home a small table with a music box inside that plays *Return to Sorrento*. I still have that table today. We enjoyed the artwork and paintings in Florence and the Leaning Tower of Pizza. We saw all the sights in Rome and attended a night performance of the opera *Tosca* in the ruins of the Roman Coliseum. The Isle of Capri was especially meaningful to me—probably because of the song and the words, "It was on the Isle of

Capri that I met her...." Although I didn't meet anybody special there, the romance of the song made our visit very interesting. We went swimming just off the island where a big rock rises out of the water some 50 or 75 feet from shore. Several of the girls swam to the rock and were sun-bathing when one of them called to me to bring her a cigarette from her purse. I assumed that was no big deal until I began to realize the problem of how to get it to her without getting the cigarette and matches wet. She said to just light it, take a puff or two, and hold it in my mouth while swimming to the rock. I then remembered that I had never smoked or taken a puff off a cigarette before. I never let on that I was that inexperienced (although I'm sure they all knew from my naïve behavior). Anyway, I lit the cigarette and tried to act like I knew what I was doing. I took a puff to be sure it was burning. Then, with the cigarette dangling from my mouth, I carefully dog- paddled my way out to the rock to complete my mission. I don't remember taking but the one puff, so I'm not sure if it was lit or not when I gave it to her. Although I later smoked a cigar or two in law school, the only time, before or since, I've had a cigarette in my mouth was on the Isle of Capri.

Although we traveled mostly by bus, we did take a night train from the French Riviera to Paris. Someone told us that comedian Jerry Lewis was in a train car or two ahead of us, so we decided to investigate. Lo and behold, there he was talking to several other people, joking and carrying on, as you would expect. It was a fun time, and I was crazy enough to enter in the conversation by making some wise crack of a joke. Jerry responded by saying, "Oh, we've got a comedian in the crowd!" That was my claim to fame with Jerry Lewis. My only other encounter with a celebrity was in our hotel in Paris when several of us rode up the elevator with Clifton Webb of *Cheaper by the Dozen* fame. Time limited us from having much of a conversation. My recollection is it was merely a "Hello, how are you'" type of brief exchange. We almost saw Rex Harrison, star of *My Fair Lady*. We were told he had been staying at our London hotel two days prior to our arrival. While in Paris, we attended the Follies. Now that was an experience! I had seen show girls dancing with perfect precision, such as the Rockets at Radio City Music Hall in New York.

But never had I seen them so scantily clad. Even at the age of 22, I still had some growing up to do in learning the realities of the world.

Ely Jr. and His Med School Diploma

As I ended my first year of law school in June of 1954, Ely Jr. was graduating with the first medical school class at Carolina. He was now Dr. Ely Jackson Perry Jr. Earning his M.D. degree is an interesting story. Let me tell you how it happened.

Brother Ely had a brilliant mind, which was manifested in his early school days. He developed into a voracious reader. Schoolwork and learning were always easy for him. He made good grades all through his school career and at UNC made Phi Beta Kappa. Of the three Perry boys, Ely was the best student. As a general rule, Warren and I had "to work" for whatever good grades we got. Ely's good grades came easier for him. In essence, he was a naturally good student. It was, therefore, only natural that Daddy encouraged him to make the most of his abilities. Warren had always had a yearning to go to law school and return to Kinston to practice law with Daddy, which he did upon graduating from law school in 1950. Ely was not sure what he wanted to do, but he knew he was not inclined to go to law school. He had done well in his premed courses, and Daddy and Ely's undergraduate advisor encouraged him to be a part of the first year class of the new medical school at Carolina.

From the very beginning, Ely was not all that smitten with the idea of being a doctor, but had a heart for farming since working on a farm one summer during high school. I remember him telling me he just didn't have the patience to be a lawyer. With law school not an option, he decided to give med school a try. If he didn't like it, he could always drop out and try something else.

The good news is that during his first year Ely worked hard and did extremely well with his grades. I don't know what his ranking was in the class, but it is my understanding he was near the top. The bad news is he still was not all that captivated with the idea of preparing himself to live the life of a doctor. In fact, he had about decided to drop out after his first year. Why should he continue on in med school if he didn't want to be a doctor?

Dr. Berryhill, who was dean of the medical school, as well as several of his teachers, saw the potential in Ely from the beginning and encouraged him to keep going. Their advice was to give it another year and maybe he'd become more interested. Of course, Daddy was his biggest supporter and encourager. Daddy's general thinking, and the thinking of the med school staff, was it would be a shame to waste all that talent and potential by dropping out after only one year. Good doctors were in high demand, and it was obvious Carolina's new medical school wanted to make a good showing by having as many top students as possible.

With all that encouragement, Ely reluctantly decided to give it another year. He apparently applied himself very well, for his excellent grades continued on through his second year. In the minds of many, the question was, "How can he be doing so well with his class work when he really doesn't like what he was doing?" This was baffling to all who knew what Ely was going through. His classmates were quite puzzled, yet very supportive. I think it boiled down to the fact that he simply loved to study and learn.

I am still amused by a particular story about Ely. One day I went to see him in his dormitory room. I knocked on his door, and upon entering, I saw Ely and his roommate, Frank Stallings from Smithfield, sitting at their desks. After a brief welcome, I asked the inevitable question. "How are you boys doing?" Without hesitation Frank, with a smile on his face, responded, "We're worrying!" Naturally, I was caught by surprise. "Worrying? What are you worrying about?" Frank broadened his smile into a beaming laugh: "We've set aside fifteen minutes to concentrate on all the things that we're worried about in school. After that we're not going to worry about it any more." We all had a big laugh. That sounded like a pretty good idea to me. By the way, I got to know Frank not only as Ely's roommate, but also when we were counselors at Camp Morehead together in the summer of 1952. He was a great guy, humorous, and always with a smile on his face. He was also a trusted friend and encouraged Ely all through med school.

But back to Ely and his medical school career. After his second year the never-ending question remained: Should he continue on doing something he really didn't like? The answer would be easy if his grades were not near the top of his class. Ely told me that the first two med school years of study concentrated on classroom academics. The last two years would be mostly focused on practical experience and actually dealing with and treating patients. Dean Berryhill and the others were encouraging him to keep going to see how he liked the practical aspect of doctoring. Maybe that would change his attitude about becoming a doctor. I remember how Ely agonized over the decision. He had already spent two years of hard work without having a sense of satisfaction with his accomplishment. Was it worth going through another year or even part of a year just to find out what he already knew? After much encouragement from all interested sources, he decided to go forward. Maybe the practical experience would, indeed, prove beneficial. It was only an outside chance, but maybe it would work.

Ely's third year was a repeat performance. He continued to do well with his grades, and I was told he had a good bedside manner with his patients. Apparently, he was making the most of a difficult situation. He kept up with his classmates in working the long hours with little sleep. I really didn't hear him complain all that much. He just plodded along with the others and gave it his best. Apparently, Dean Berryhill and the staff continued to be impressed with Ely's demeanor as well as his excellent work. When the third year ended, he was still in the same boat. Although he was making as excellent record, he still had not been won over to make medicine his life's work.

He had about made up his mind not to return for his fourth and final year, when he was convinced otherwise. Dean Berryhill and Daddy, as well as his closest teachers, made a good argument. In essence they said, "You've come this far with only one more year left. You are doing well. There is no doubt you can pass the work. Go ahead and finish up. Even if you never practice medicine, you will at least have a good education and a medical degree to prove it. You will always have the opportunity to fall back on it." Even though he did not have his whole heart in it, he finally consented to finish his degree. By this time, his story was the talk of friends and acquaintances throughout the state. As it turned out, he did get his M.D. degree, graduating in 1954 with the first class of the UNC Medical School. Ely was not the bragging type, so I never heard him talk much about his accomplishment, but I think I recall his owning up to the fact that he ended up "about 6th" in his class. I'd say that was pretty good for a young man who was never sold on the idea of wanting to be a doctor.

After receiving his M.D. degree, he then went through the rigors of passing his state and national medical board exams. He was now qualified to practice medicine. Even though it had been a frustrating four years, he could now say, in the words of Apostle Paul, "I have fought the good fight. I have finished the race, I have kept the faith."

But would he ever officially practice medicine? The answer came like a bolt of lightening—straight from the Lord. It seems that when Ely got word that he had been accepted for internship at Pennsylvania State Hospital, it all came to a head. It didn't take him long to make up his mind. He told me that when he began thinking about working with patients on a daily basis and living the life of a doctor, first as an intern and then a general practitioner, he just couldn't go on any further. Even though Pennsylvania State Hospital was considered one of the top intern opportunities, he knew his medical career had to come to an abrupt end. That was it! It was all over! The message was clear, decisive, and final! His heart then turned to the outdoors and farming which he loved. At that point, he began to read and study to learn all he could about farming.

Somehow a rumor got started that Ely took his diploma home, plopped it on Daddy's desk in a huff, and said in essence, "Well, here's my diploma and I hope that satisfies you." The rumor insinuated that Daddy had talked him into going to med school in the first place—and then insisted, against Ely's wishes that he finish. The truth is that Daddy was only one of many who encouraged him. Dean Berryhill and his teachers all saw Ely's potential and likewise gave their encouragement. A further truth is that, in reality, Ely certainly did not want to disappoint his daddy because of his love and respect for him. Warren, Ely, and I all three were taught from early childhood always to be loving and respectful toward our parents. That was a lesson we never forgot and, to my knowledge, have always adhered to. We were all three well aware of the Fifth Commandment: "Honor your Father and your Mother." It was certainly not in keeping with Ely's training and character to be anything other than respectful to his daddy.

My First Year of Law School

It was in the natural course of events that I would go to law school after my undergraduate days at Carolina. I never had any other vocation in mind. Warren got his law degree in 1950 and returned to Kinston to open his practice in Daddy's office. The following year, he married his classmate and lifelong mate-to-be, Bobbie Stockton from Franklin, North Carolina. No consideration was given to any other law school. It was Carolina from the beginning to end. I was a Tar Heel through and through.

Whereas undergraduate school presented no problem as far as scholarship was concerned, I found law school to be quite a grind. It didn't take me long to realize that I was going to have to buckle down and spend some long hours with the books. No more just sailing through and having a good time, being involved with fraternity life and other extra curricular activities, going to meetings, seeing a lot of people, socializing, and dating. My new lifestyle was going to be quite different. Well, it was time I got serious about my future. I was accustomed to hard work at Woodberry, so I was ready, but that didn't make it an easy road.

We were told from the beginning we would be studying the case method: read cases; study cases. What was the law of each case? How did it relate to the statute involved? I found the basic courses of contracts, torts, and criminal law to be of special interest with Mr. Dalzell, Mr. Wettach, and Mr. Coats as my respective teachers. They were all good teachers and presented the material in an interesting manner, but Albert Coat's class on criminal law was probably my favorite. He seemed to bring the course to life better than any of them. He captured and held our attention by telling us stories relating to the statutes and cases we studied. He often referred to his wife in a loving and respectful way, which told me that he really loved her and genuinely appreciated her support and encouragement. He told us about his vision for the

Institute of Government in Chapel Hill as a training ground for the Highway Patrol. Each patrolman needed to be well trained and versed in the law. They needed to be respected and appreciated by the public as they carry out their duties in protecting us on the highways of North Carolina. I understand that in the early days he even mortgaged his own home to raise funds to get the Institute started. It was through the extraordinary efforts of Albert Coats in the beginning of its existence that the Institute of Government developed into the renowned statewide influence it is today.

I would describe my first year of law school as interesting, but quite a struggle. I was not a good reader with any speed, comprehension-wise. I was more of a plodder. I had to spend long hours in the library in preparation for each class. Although there were others in the same boat as I, some seemed to catch on quite well. They seemed to be sailing right through. John Motsinger of Winston Salem was one of these. He was both Phi Beta Kappa and Phi Eta Sigma. When we were sitting around talking about class work, he always seemed to know the right answer. I also palled around with Bob Neill. He was my freshman year roommate along with Heywood Washburn. When it came time for the election of class officers, Bob nominated me for class president. There was no campaigning to speak of. The class just got together for the purpose of electing class officers. When it appeared that I was not included in the top two vote-getters, Bob whispered to me, "Why don't you throw your support to Jules Rousseau?" I didn't know Jules very well at the time but did know he was highly respected. He was from North Wilkesboro, and I think his father was a judge. I don't recall who the other top finalist was, but I supported Jules who ended up winning. Jules went on to be a Superior Court judge and established an outstanding record as a jurist.

Even though I necessarily had to spend a lot of time laboring over the books both on weekends as well as during the week, I did manage to have at least some semblance of a social life. Fraternity life was fairly infrequent. On football weekends, I might go by the Kappa Sig house, especially if I had a date. Other than that, it was only occasionally that I found time to visit the boys. I was still interested in girls but only on a limited basis due to my schoolwork. The one I dated most often was Margaret Underwood. She was an undergrad junior, a Tri Delt from Greensboro, and a beautiful girl. In fact, she had her picture in the 1954 *Yackety Yack* as a member of the beauty court. She was an excellent tennis player, and I enjoyed calling her for a late afternoon date for a game of tennis. The only problem was she usually beat me, although she was kind enough not to make it a big deal. From time to time, I also dated Sara Fair from Greenville, South Carolina. She was a junior transfer from St. Mary's and a Chi Omega at Carolina. She was also a member of the Yack Beauty Court. Another member of the beauty court was Sandy Donaldson. She was one of those "smiling girls." She always had a cute smile on her face, which was an attraction for all the boys. She happened to be a special girlfriend of Z. A. When he left for the Air Force during my first year of law school, he charged me with the responsibility of "looking after her" while he was away. I took her out a couple of times and would have probably asked her out more if she hadn't been a special friend of Z. A.'s. Nelson Blount was another special girl I dated while in law school. She was from a very prominent Greenville family, and her parents and mine had been friends for many years. Although she was several years younger than I, I didn't feel too old to journey to Raleigh and St. Mary's for a date with her. It is interesting to note that on one of my visits we heard a speaker (I believe he was a representative of G. E.) predict that we would have a man on the moon within ten years. I remember how unbelievable that sounded. How could we fly a man to the moon? It was just too high and too far away! Such a feat was too supernatural for my simple mind to grasp! It sounded like a Buck Rogers story out of the comic books. It was a fascinating talk as he told us about what lay ahead—a future filled with rockets, astronauts, and space travel. Although his ten-year timetable may have been a little off, my memory returned to that speech at St. Mary's when seven years later Yuri Gagarin of Russia became the first human being to travel in space by orbiting the earth on April 12, 1961. I was in downtown Chapel Hill at the bookstore on Franklin Street when I first heard the announcement on television. I was living there as a young lawyer. That memorable speech and incredible prediction in 1954 at St. Mary's again came to mind when Edwin Aldrin and Neil Armstrong made the first ever landing on the moon on July 20, 1969. The once-unheard-of space travel was now a reality.

Finishing My First Year of Law School

Although I spent enough hours studying, at times I felt like my mind was saturated with reading cases and law textbooks. I really felt like I needed a break from school. As the school year was ending, I talked to Dean Brandis and made the decision to volunteer for the draft. Mother and Daddy agreed. Although the Korean truce had been signed in July of 1953, there was still a lot of unrest throughout the world, and the draft was still in full swing. My grades were only average at best, I was tired of school, and this would give me a good break.

Chapter XVIII

MY ARMY YEARS

In August of 1954 at the age of 23, I joined the army. My induction took place in Raleigh, which included a physical exam and swearing-in ceremony. Even though I inherited my father's flat feet, I sailed through the physical without any problem. The reason Daddy joined the Navy in 1918 was because his right foot was a little too flat for the Army. I remember boarding the bus in Raleigh along with a bunch of other recruits to Camp Gordon, Georgia. I was off to my first eight weeks of basic training. The Gideons were on hand at the bus station to give us all a small Bible, which proved very helpful during my Army career.

Our greeting at Camp Gordon was what I expected. Corporal Brock sternly said he was going to take a bunch of awkward, raw recruits and mold them into a well-trained Army outfit. Even though we all "hated" Corporal Brock because he was mean and tough, down deep we knew it was for our own good. It didn't take me long to learn to go with the flow and fall in line with the training tactics.

Another Physical

A couple of early experiences stand out regarding our Army physical exams at Camp Gordon. I was sitting in the dentist chair, when the dentist seemed alarmed at what he saw. He anxiously called for his assistants to "come here, I want to show you something!" I thought he had discovered something seriously wrong. As three or four gathered around my wide-open mouth, he exclaimed, "Have you ever seen anything like that before?" As they both took turns looking in my mouth, they all seemed to gasp and sigh with amazement. My moment of relief came when I realized they were not accustomed to seeing a patient without any cavities. Evidently, most every recruit they saw generally had a mouth full of cavities. A second more traumatic event occurred when the next day Corporal Brock called me out of formation and ordered me to report to the infirmary immediately. It sounded rather urgent, so I wasted no time in reporting. I was greeted with the words, "Private Perry, your blood test shows positive for gonorrhea." My immediate reaction was one of calm confidence as I softly said, "There must be a mistake. That's impossible." I knew that I had not been exposed to any venereal diseases, for it was my understanding that such diseases are only transmitted through sexual contact. They gave me another blood test, which proved negative. Evidently, they had gotten my blood work mixed up with someone else.

Marching Was Fun

Each recruit was issued an M-1 rifle. It was made clear that we were expected to keep it clean and oil it well each night before bedtime. We also had training in bayonet, machine guns, bazookas, and some of the heavier weapons. I went along with all the shooting (we had no other choice), but the part I actually enjoyed was the marching. We had a masterful drill sergeant. I loved the way he counted cadences with perfect rhythm. I was in company C, better known as "Charlie Company." It lifted my morale and made Army life both interesting and bearable to march while the drill sergeant loudly counted, "Ya' left, ya' left, ya' left-right-left", then singing out in cadence, "Hold your head, and hold it high; here comes Charlie passing by! Sound off! One-two…Sound off! Three-four…Break it on down—one, two, three, four, one-two…three-four!" I was blessed to be able to actually enjoy marching. It was the fun part of Army life.

Whereas I considered daily marching as being fun in some respects, it was also hot, wearisome work in other respects. On one particular day while standing in formation, several men fell out because of the heat. They gave us salt pills and water, which helped—but it was still hot, being over 100 degrees on several days. One of the ways I passed the time while marching, especially on long hikes, was to quote poetry. I had brought my *101 Famous Poems* book with me, and each night I would review all my favorites such as "If" and "L'Envoi" by Rudyard Kipling; "The Builders," "Day Is Done," and "Psalm of Life" by Henry Wadsworth Longfellow; "Abou Ben Adhem" by James Leigh Hunt; "The Daffodils" by William Wadsworth; and "Keep a-Going" by Frank L. Stanton. Another one of my favorites was "Be Strong" by Maltbie Davenport Babcock. Its three short verses served as quite an encouragement to me as we marched along keeping time to the sergeant's cadenced count. Here are the words:

> Be Strong!
> We are not here to play, to dream, to drift;
> We have hard work to do, and loads to lift;
> Shun not the struggle—face it; 'tis God's gift.
> Be strong!
> Say not, "The days are evil. Who's to blame?"
> And fold the hands and acquiesce—oh shame!
> Stand up, speak out, and bravely, in God's name.
> Be strong!
> It matters not how deep entrenched the wrong,
> How hard the battle goes, the day how long;
> Faint not—fight on! To-morrow comes the song.

Entertainment?

One day during a long march, we took a break to rest and drink water. As Charlie Company was sitting and relaxing in a shaded area, Corporal Brock said, "While we're sitting here, has anybody got anything they want to say, or sing a song?" There was deadly silence for what seemed like more than a minute. I thought to myself, "Only a short while ago I was quoting to myself "Casey at the Bat." Do you reckon they would think I was crazy to recite it for them? Would a poem be appropriate?" In the silence of the moment, I gathered my courage, stood up, and said, "Well, I can tell you about 'Casey at the Bat'." My next thought was, "Lord, what have I done now? I've got to go through with it. Please help me remember it from beginning to end. Don't let me make a fool of myself." Although I was understandably nervous, I managed to remember the first line to at least get started. The Lord must have been with me, because I went through the whole poem flawlessly from beginning to end. When I got to the last sentence—"Mighty Casey had struck out!"—there was complete silence. For a minute I was a little worried, but as I sat down they all broke out with cheering and resounding applause. I must have done all right because even Corporal Brock managed to compliment me in his own stern way.

The Missing Bible

All in all, my first eight-weeks of basic training at Camp Gordon went by rather quickly. I tried to use my time wisely by reading my Bible every night along with continuing to read and memorize poetry from my *101 Famous Poems*. The Bible I read was given to me by the church when I joined Gordon Street Christian Church in 1943 as a twelve-year-old. My objective in the Army was to read it from cover to cover, starting with Genesis and ending with Revelation.

One evening I realized my Bible was missing. I knew where it was supposed to be, but it was gone. As it turned out, one of the other men told me he saw Bill Carter take it. Bill's bunk was several rows down from mine, and I knew him only casually. He was a rather friendly, black guy who was somewhat religious in his demeanor. I could tell he was not a "bad guy," for he seemed to get along fine with the rest of us. My first thought was that I'd just ask him about it to see if he would voluntarily return it. Then the thought occurred to me, he seems to "love the Lord," and he obviously doesn't have a Bible of his own. That particular Bible had special meaning to me, but if he really wants a Bible to read (and if he would read it), maybe it will mean more to him than to me. After all, I still had the Gideon Bible I was given at the bus station in Raleigh. I never said anything to Bill. Hopefully my Bible was a blessing to him—even though it was acquired by devious means.

Before the beginning of my second eight-weeks of basic training, we had a restful fourteen-day leave. Mother and Daddy and all my friends thought the

Army was agreeing with me because I was in great shape, my stomach was flat as a pancake, and I even had a few muscles on my skinny frame. While home on leave in October 1954, the big news was Hurricane Hazel. I remember standing on my front porch at 908 West Road when the wind was apparently at its peak. I was looking in a northerly direction toward the big oak trees lining the road in front of Henry Walker's house. Then, in what seemed slow motion, I saw one of those oaks, at least five or six feet in diameter, topple over to the ground. It left a gapping hole in the area around the exposed root system. It was a sight I have never forgotten.

Fort Jackson, South Carolina

My second eight-weeks of basic training was at Fort Jackson where I was assigned to Supply School. Whereas Camp Gordon (now Fort Gordon) was mostly physical activities and in-the-field training, now I was concentrating on classroom work. As a supply sergeant, I would be expected to know and be able to requisition all the weapons, materials, and supplies necessary to run a heavy weapons company. One of my instructors was Buck Ransdale who had been in my first- year law class. He knew his material well and was an excellent teacher. I sat on the front row, and, of course, recognized him immediately. He, on the other hand, was so absorbed in his teaching that on the first day I was just another face in the crowd. It was only after class when I introduced myself did he, with some embarrassment, acknowledged I was there.

I found Supply School to be both interesting and rewarding, and was pleasantly surprised to learn I ended up being fourth in the class of about 40 or so. I didn't realize it was such a big deal until my parents showed me a letter they received from my company commander saying all sorts of nice things about my outstanding performance, as well as about me as a person and soldier. I'm sure it was a standard letter, for I hardly knew who he was. They even had my picture in the *Free Press* with a long article and various quotes from that flattering letter. Even though my family and friends back home were impressed, I knew I was still wet behind the ears and had so much to learn. Horner Butner and Otha Herring, both from Kinston, were also in basic training with me at Camp Gordon. Horner went into signal corps training at Fort Jackson, but I don't remember what Otha did.

After my second fourteen-day leave, I reported to Fort Jackson for my new assignment and further orders. I learned that each in my group would be sent either to the Philippines or Korea. Naturally, we were all hoping for the Philippines, for the very name "Philippines" sounded rather intriguing, almost romantic. Upon being told it would be Korea for me, my first thought was, "How unlucky can I get?" It was only later in my search for truth and spiritual growth did I come to realize that nothing happens to me, as a believer in Jesus Christ, is attributable to luck. It's all in God's providential plan. Even though I was disappointed with my assignment to Korea, God was gracious enough to give me a good attitude. I just knew in my heart I was going to be all right; that I was going to grow and mature from the experience; and that I would return safely and be a better man for having gone. It helped to recall the experiences of the Old Testament patriarchs I had learned about in Sunday school at Gordon Street Christian Church. The Lord was giving me the assurance that I was in His care and He would look after me, no matter what the challenge, no matter how difficult the situation.

After calling Mother and Daddy to inform them I would shortly be shipping out to Korea by way of Fort Lewis, Washington, they decided to drive to Columbia to say goodbye. They took me to a fancy nightclub where we had a delightful meal and enjoyed an entertaining floorshow. The main attraction was Joni James. We heard her sing her famous song, "Little Things Mean a Lot." I can still hear her as she softly sang, "Blow me a kiss from across the room; say I look nice when I'm not. A line a day when you're far away—little things mean a lot." It was not a teary time, but rather a sentimental and somber time as we relished the moment. This would be the last time we would see each other for quite a while. It was to be a sixteen-month tour of duty. They comforted me with the assurance I would be fine and they would stay in touch by writing often. When we parted, I remember there being a bit of sadness, but nothing like that "all alone" feeling experienced when they left me at Woodberry for the first time—and I saw their car slowly drive away down the long entrance road and disappear around the distant curve.

Fort Lewis and Shipping Out to Korea

Upon arriving at Fort Lewis, Washington, we were all excited, but also anxious about what we were soon to experience. Our barracks was located right outside of Seattle, giving us a full view of nearby Mt. Rainier with its majestic snow-covered cap. It was a beautiful sight that I've never forgotten. We had a couple days of orientation in preparation for our long journey across the Pacific. One of the men said he heard we were to be on a small transport ship, and the trip over would be like "a slow boat to China."

We left Fort Lewis on a dark and dreary December 24, 1954. Being Christmas Eve made it a little more difficult than normal. As I was boarding the ship, I remember wondering what was happening back home. I wasn't particularly to the point of being homesick, but I was definitely thinking about home. On the ship we slept in hammocks three deep, and I had the top bunk. It was extremely close quarters. Many of us got seasick as we were tossed around in the rough ocean. The thing I remember about the food was the green-powered eggs we had for breakfast. Due to the stormy weather, we only went topside one time during the eighteen-day trip. It was difficult to write, but I do remember writing home that I was reminded of Longfellow's poem, "A Psalm of Life," in which he said, "Be not like dumb, driven cattle! Be a hero in the strife!" I told them I felt like "dumb, driven cattle" cooped up in the bottom of the ship, even though I was trying to be "a hero in the strife." Another memorable aspect of the voyage was that our shower water gave out after only five days from port. The other thirteen days, we got along the best we could under stuffy, smelly conditions.

Arriving in Korea

After the long trip over, we were finally glad to be on dry land as we disembarked at Inchon Harbor. Inchon is about 20 miles west southwest of Seoul and some 35 miles south of the 38th parallel, which was the Demilitarized Zone (DMZ) between North and South Korea. Inchon Harbor has an extremely high tide differential of about 30 feet, so we had to land when the tide was high. We arrived in the late afternoon in cold, snowy weather. By the time we boarded the train, it was pitch dark. That was quite a train ride as we headed north to the Replacement Center near our final destination of Camp Casey, which is about six miles south of the DMZ. I remember there being no lights inside the train itself. It was pitch dark as we slowly made our way north. When I say "slowly," that's exactly the way it was. We couldn't have been going much over 10 m.p.h., for it took about three hours to go the 30 or so miles to the Replacement Center. Peering out the train window, we could see through the snow and mist what seemed to be small, single light bulbs on posts, faintly revealing long stretches of barbed-wire fencing. It reminded me of a war movie with the troopers slipping behind the enemy lines. It really gave me an eerie feeling. An occasional flashlight was about all we had to see well enough to open our C-Rations for our supper treat. I had heard complaints about C-Rations but on this occasion it tasted mighty good to me. I remember there being very little conversation among the troops. It was a long, cold, lonely ride as we sat silently hearing the click-clack click-clack of the train inching along. What conversation we did have was softly spoken, almost a whisper. Although I knew several of the men, I recall sitting next to John Potempsky. He was from Detroit, and we struck up a good friendship that lasted our entire tour of duty in Korea.

An Unexpected Friend

When we finally arrived at the Replacement Center, it was late at night or early morning. We had been hauled from the train stop by "deuce and a half" (2 ½ ton) trucks. We were tired, weary, and ready for some much needed sleep. I remember being quartered in something like a 12-man tent with cots that surrounded a "potbelly" stove in the middle. Most of the men went straight to bed. Although I was more than ready to zip up my sleeping bag for the night, I noticed a black man sitting in a chair warming himself next to the potbelly stove. There was an empty chair available, so I decided to join him. After a brief greeting, he asked me where I was from. "North Carolina," I proudly said. "Where 'bouts in North Carolina?" he replied. "It's a little town in eastern North Carolina," I responded. I couldn't figure why he would want to inquire about such an insignificant little town half way around the world. When I told him Kinston, he asked if I had ever played golf at the Kinston Country Club? "Why, yeah, that's my home course. I played it all the time growing up." By this time I was beginning to sense he was more than just a stranger. He asked me if I knew British Long. "Yeah," I replied excitedly. "What about Slim Montgomery?" "Yeah." "What about Julian McCullen?" I was really getting excited, because I knew them all. They used to play with my daddy. "How do you know all those men?" I asked. It was then he told me he used to caddie for them when he was growing up. I told him my name and asked him if he knew Ely Perry. "I sure do," was his reply. For the next ten or fifteen minutes, we had the best time talking about the Kinston Country Club and various other things we both knew. It was so much fun, and I well remember how my spirits were boosted by merely being in his presence and engaging in such an uplifting conversation. He made me feel right at home. He named several of the caddies whom I knew, including "Big Jeep" and "Little Jeep." When I went to bed that night, I couldn't wait to get up in the morning and renew our conversation. I could hardly see what he looked like, and I don't even remember getting his name. I'm sure I must have asked him, but I just didn't remember.

The next morning, I got up and looked for my new friend, but he was nowhere to be found. Not knowing what he looked like, I couldn't identify him; and not remembering his name, I couldn't inquire as to his whereabouts. I went to breakfast hoping maybe I would run into him someway, somehow, but he was not to be found. I never saw him again. I wonder if an angel of the Lord had visited me. In my later readings about the subject, I found that God sometimes sends his angels to comfort and encourage his children. This was a time when I definitely needed encouragement, and I'm convinced the Lord met my need just at the right time and in just the right way. My low and lonely spirits had been lifted up in a most amazing way. I had been visited by an angel!

Camp Casey

After a night at the Replacement Center, we finally arrived at Camp Casey, which would be my home for the next fifteen months. The first thing I remember was going through the breakfast line and seeing the freshly cooked bacon and eggs. Boy, did it smell good! That was my first real meal since I don't know when. I can still see and hear the crackling of the bacon and the cook serving those over-light fried eggs. He greeted me with, "How many do you want?" I thought to myself, "You mean I can have as many and as much as I want?" I guess it was because I was so hungry—even the memory of those powered green scrambled eggs while crossing the Pacific was dispelled. We also had corn beef hash on toast. I don't remember what else we had. All I remember is I was full as a tick when I left that makeshift mess hall.

Our Living Quarters

I can't remember if it was an eight- or twelve-man tent, but it had the usual potbelly stove in the middle. It generally kept us pretty warm if we kept it going full blast and was close enough to it. I really don't know how cold it got in the deepest part of that first winter. We settled down at Camp Casey in mid-January 1955. Someone said he heard it got down to -40°F at one point. That's hard to believe. I think it may be an exaggeration, but, nevertheless, that's what the rumor was. Our latrine was probably 50 or so feet from the tent, which made it a rather cold trip, especially if we had to get up in the middle of the night. I really don't remember any of us complaining a lot. We didn't have any choice. After we got used to it, it became second nature to us. My first shower came 28 days after the water gave out on the ship. A couple of the "engineers" rigged up a pipe such that it would catch the water from the nearby mountain stream. I don't know exactly how they did it; all I know is we were excited when we were told we had a shower out back. It was cold mountain water, but we got used to it and got along fine. At least we soaped ourselves down and were half-way clean for a change. As you can imagine, our showers were short, sweet, and shivering cold.

"Guard" Duty

One night I had the 2-A.M.-shift for guard duty. There was very little light, but with M-1 rifle in hand, I managed to find my post. In retrospect, I wondered what I was doing out there. What was I guarding against? Was I looking for an enemy to sneak up on us? I'm sure I must have been given some instructions, but I frankly don't remember what they were. What if I did spot something suspicious—what was I supposed to do? Those memories are vague to say the least, but one thing I do remember. When my replacement came an hour later and I started back to the tent, I realized I didn't have my glasses. I couldn't believe it! Here I was, a "blind" man out there on guard duty without my glasses. I wore them all the time and would have been severely handicapped, if not helpless, in an emergency. Because it was dark, I apparently didn't miss them. It wasn't until I found my way back to the tent and removed my boots that I realized what had happened. They were in the bottom of my right boot, crushed to smithereens. I had been in the habit of putting my glasses in my boots so they could easily be found upon rising each morning. Apparently in my grogginess upon getting up at 2 A.M., it slipped my mind, and I got dressed without giving it a second thought. I remember my boot feeling a little tight, but I had no idea I had been crushing my glasses with every step I took. Heavy socks and early mourning drowsiness made me oblivious. The next day the Company Commander sent me by deuce and a half truck to a nearby field hospital where I was fitted with another pair of combat glasses. They were small and wiry with little round lenses. The ride to the hospital was bumpy. I was sitting in the back of the truck with several other men, one of whom was obviously disturbed and unsettled. He kept complaining and talking to himself in a loud voice and could not be comforted. Later I was told he was suffering from some form of "anxiety." I guess he was having a hard time adjusting to his new living conditions. He was from another unit, so I never saw him again.

Middle of the Night Nose Drops

A second experience was quite memorable. Most of the time I had stayed well and free from any sickness, but on one occasion I had been given some nose drops for the sniffles. One morning when I reached out from my sleeping bag for the nose dropper, the stopper wouldn't work. I couldn't figure out what was wrong until I realized the liquid was frozen solid. We all had a big laugh about it. After warming the bottle by the stove, it thawed out and everything was all right. But I made a big mistake. In my next letter home, I told Mother and Daddy about my unusual experience. Mother didn't think it was all that funny; in her next letter, I could tell she was quite concerned. She probably imagined me huddled up in the snow, freezing to death, and suffering from all kinds of things. She wrote, "Please tell me you're all right. Is there something you're not telling me?" I assured her I was doing fine and there was no need to worry. I thought it was rather amusing, and I was only telling of a funny incident. It was no big deal. But I learned my lesson. From then on, I only reported the "good things" and left any negatives unmentioned. Actually, in all truthfulness, I was blessed with having a pretty good attitude about my whole Army experience. That's not to say I didn't feel like complaining in certain situations, e.g., being in the bottom of a storm-tossed ship with most of us seasick and throwing up. In looking back, I know it was the Lord who gave me the ability to look at it all as a necessary experience. The good news is He helped me be aware of it at the time I was going through it. Actually, I was never in any danger, maybe a little uneasy or even scared at times, but never in any real danger of being hurt.

A Trip to the Front Line

One day when the weather was warm, Sergeant Majesky said, "Come on boys; let's go for a ride up to the DMZ." I figured that would be exciting, for the DMZ and the 38th Parallel had been in the news ever since the end of the Korean War, so four of us went for a Jeep ride. Sgt. Majesky was sitting on the passenger side next to the driver. I was in the backseat with a fellow passenger.

North Korea Communist troops, you may remember, invaded South Korea on June 25, 1950. (At the time, I was lazing around the swimming pool in Louisville, Kentucky, while visiting former Woodberry classmate, Jimmy Thompson.) Two days later, President Truman ordered U.S. air and naval forces to help defend South Korea. Three days after that, he ordered U. S. ground troops to South Korea. According to the World Book the following two years of fighting yielded U. S. casualties at 54,246 dead; 103,284 wounded; and 5,178 prisoners or missing. The fighting officially ended with the signing of the truce agreement on July 27, 1953. I arrived in Korea about six months later, in January 1954. The truce line set at the 38th Parallel was a buffer zone 1 ¼ miles wide. I understood that the entire buffer area was heavily mined to discourage troop entry.

Sergeant Majesky was a seasoned infantryman and a veteran of the war, so I felt we were in good hands. It was about a six-mile trip to the DMZ, with rugged terrain, and narrow and winding, rocky roadbeds. At one point as we were approaching a narrow passageway between two hills, we were suddenly confronted by a Korean, a young teenage boy. He ran out in front of us frantically waving his arms as if pleading for us to stop. His face was bloody, with blood on his clothing and arms. He looked like he had been hurt and needed help. I remember my first reaction was to stop and be a "good Samaritan." After all here was a human being in obvious distress. That's why I was both surprised and disappointed when Sergeant Majesky yelled to the driver, "Don't stop! Keep going! Speed up! Let's get 'outta here!" As we speedily disappeared around the next turn, he explained, "It may have been a trick! You can't ever tell what they'll do." That just shows you how inexperienced and wet behind the ears I was. It never even occurred to me that we might have been in danger. I still had a lot to learn about soldiering. Had it been wartime, I might have been more cautious. Sergeant Majesky went on to explain that even though the fighting was officially over, we still had to be on guard and not take any chances on a straggling enemy who might be trying to get even. When we got to the southern border of the DMZ, the sergeant pointed out that the North Koreans "are right over the hill." I actually couldn't see any soldiers, but he knew they were there. That was as close as I got to any North Koreans.

Accordion, Guitar, and Yodeling

Although all of us men were housed in tents, the supply room was a Quonset hut large enough to house the company weapons and supplies to be made available when needed. One day while perusing the supply manual, I noticed the listing for an accordion. I was a little surprised to see a musical instrument among our Army supplies that I could requisition. I had never played an accordion, but saw no reason why I shouldn't give it a try. After only a few days from the date of requisition, the accordion arrived and I couldn't wait to open the box. I felt like a child on Christmas Day! The right-hand keyboard being just like a piano, I was able almost immediately to pick out familiar tunes. Even though I had seen an accordion played before, the base keys appeared quite strange at first. Surprising enough, it didn't take long to figure how it worked, and by the end of the day, I was able to make enough sense of it to play a few songs. Needless to say, it provided me with many hours of pleasure. Even the other men seemed to appreciate my new found toy.

I don't know where he got it, but one of the men had a guitar. He could play pretty well and was kind enough to teach me some of the basic chords. The fact that I had played a ukulele before made the guitar a little easier. I never was too good at it, but at least I messed around with it enough to have a good time. After my Army days and soon after graduation from law school, I purchased a guitar in Raleigh in 1958. It's the same one I have today.

In addition to familiarizing myself with the accordion and guitar, I also learned a little about yodeling. On my trip to Europe, I remember hearing some of the famous Swiss yodelers display their talents. It sounded like an interesting thing to do, so one day when I was pretty much alone looking out over the nearby hills, I began to yell and switch from my regular to a falsetto voice. Nobody was around to give me a hard time, so I kept on practicing until I was able to give some semblance of a yodeling sound. My memory also went back to the Kappa Sig House and hearing one of the brothers (Herbert Dowd) yodeling and singing while accompanying himself on his guitar. He was pretty good as he sang, "I went across to Switzerland where all the yodelers be, to try to learn to yodel and go yo-da-le-e-de." I even tried to sing like he did, but somehow I fell short. At least I was having a good time trying. Even today, over 50 years later, some of my friends, and especially golf buddies, might occasionally hear me suddenly come out with a yodel or two.

A lot of times I can't resist the temptation of giving a brief yodel as we drive our golf cart through a short tunnel under an overpass, should one appear between holes. I hope it's not too annoying. I'm just having a little fun and trying not to let my so-called talent get rusty.

Other Free Times

We stayed reasonably busy training and "playing Army," but we also had some leisure time. I made a conscious effort not to waste too much of it. I kept up with my *101 Famous Poems* and even purchased a book on how to have an effective memory. A lot of it dealt with association with names, places, and objects, which I already knew about. I had also recalled a technique Daddy taught me from a *Readers Digest* article several years prior. The object was simple. Before going to sleep each night, review in your mind each and every event of the day from the time you woke up to the time you got to bed. Then do the exact opposite. Reverse the process and start with the time you turn off the light. Go backwards through each event until you come to your wake-up time. It's a good mental exercise that is not as easy as one might think. It requires a lot of concentration, which is generally hard to do, especially when you're tired and ready for sleep. Most of the time I would fall asleep before finishing the first part of the exercise.

Thoughts Here and There

I don't remember any of the men ever getting desperately "homesick," even though as time went on and we got closer to the end of our tour we all had "short calendars." Most everyone knew exactly how many months, weeks, and days we had left. I remember writing home that some of my most pleasant times were lying in bed at night and thinking about home and family and friends—and what I was going to do when I got back. I thought about returning to law school, practicing law, and eventually getting married and hopefully raising a family. We all had portable radios. Every once in a while we could hear "stateside" music, but most of the time it was Oriental—Chinese, Japanese, or Korean. We had a pretty good PX, and I bought a small Petry camera and took lots of pictures, which made it easy for Mother and Daddy to understand all about my Korean experience. My first impression of the landscape of Korea was the countless hills everywhere I looked, in all directions. Some were higher than others, but none I would classify as mountains. What little greenery there was, were wild bushes and scrubs. I don't recall ever seeing any trees—just bushes and scrubs. Most of the hills were rocks and crevices as far as I could see in every direction. The only birds I saw were a few English sparrows from time to time. I remember how excited I was as I wrote home for Mother to be sure to tell Duff Simmons (our yard man) because he and I used to talk about the different birds around home.

My Special Korean Friend

Soon after my arrival at Camp Casey, I got to know Nam He Su, one of the ROK (Republic of Korea) soldiers assigned to our company. He seemed to take to me, and I enjoyed being with him. He even taught me a few Korean words and phrases, which I still remember. Even now sometimes on the golf course, or elsewhere, I will come out with some Korean, as if I knew what I was saying. I think one phrase means "good morning" (although it may mean something else). He also taught me the first few lines of the then popular song "China Night." (I don't remember if it was in Chinese or Korean, for I wouldn't know the difference. It was all "Greek" to me.) Anyway, I still enjoy showing off my Korean from time to time.

One day soon after befriending Nam He Su, we sat next to each other for supper. As had been my custom, I bowed my head and closed my eyes in silence to ask the blessing. Suddenly I was startled when Nam He Su exclaimed rather loudly, "Look—Corporal Perry—he's asleep! Look! He's asleep!" I was quick to realize he was not a Christian and apparently had never seen anyone pray over food. When I explained that I was not asleep, but merely thanking God for the food I was about to eat as well as for all the blessings of life, he seemed to understand; or I should say he at least calmed down and never said anything about my unusual habit. Since early childhood, I had been raised to "say the blessing" before each family meal. Most of the time the whole family would say in unison, "God is great, God is good, Let us thank Him for this food, Amen." I had not been accustomed to asking the blessing in public, but my Army experience brought back those pleasant memories of yesteryear. From time to time, I just felt the special need to give thanks to the Lord and ask His blessing for the food I was about to eat. It was sometime during my Army days that I "branched out" and began to ask the blessing in my own words, not by just rote memory. It became more meaningful to express my own personal thoughts, rather than have a set blessing.

I don't remember really being afraid that I was in any danger of being in harm's way during my service in Korea, except for two times. The first I have already mentioned—the time I had a few anxious moments when we were headed to the DMZ and a bloody Korean suddenly jumped in front of us. It was all over in a matter of a few seconds as we sped out of his sight around the hilly curve. A second incident was a little more involved. One night about bedtime, we were alerted to the fact that some gunfire had been reported about a mile up the road. Sergeant Arelio Agneli was on duty and instructed us to have our M-1 rifles ready in case of an emergency. That was one thing, but when he called for two machine guns to standby, I definitely developed a lump in my throat. I had visions of exchanging gunfire in the dark with an unidentified enemy. Several of us consoled ourselves by rationalizing that, "Hey, we're here to keep the peace. The war's over! We don't have anything to worry about. They'd be crazy to try to cross that minefield guarding the DMZ." None of us had so much as fired a single shot since basic training. Even though I was the supply sergeant and not among the frontline troops, I still was expected to fill in and be ready for any eventuality. We got through the night without incident and without finding out what all the commotion was about. Other than those two situations, everything was fairly routine during my entire tour of duty.

Every Sunday our chaplain conducted a church service. Although attendance was not required, we were encouraged to go, and I don't believe I missed any of the services. Having been brought up in the church, it was natural that I attend regularly. We had a black chaplain, and he did an excellent job of conducting the service and delivering timely sermons. One of the highlights was when Billy Graham came for a one-night crusade in what was called the Bayonet Bowl at battalion headquarters. As fiery as ever, he delivered his stirring gospel message of the need to accept Christ as Lord and Savior.

Correspondence, a Phone Call, and a Record

Throughout my tour of duty in Korea, Mother wrote at least once a week—sometimes two and three times a week, depending on what was happing on the home front. Occasionally, she would enclose newspaper clippings and other items of interest. I also heard from Warren and Ely from time to time. Warren was enjoying married life and raising children with Barbara, as well as getting his feet wet as a new lawyer in town. He joined the Jaycees and also became involved with other community actives including being cub master for Pack 41, a position he held for over 20 years. Ely was living at home with Mother and Daddy enjoying helping Daddy look after his real estate and farming interests. As a young doctor, he wrote a few prescriptions for family members, but other than that he had no interest in medicine as a profession. In his letters, he would tell me how much he enjoyed the freedom of riding in the county and checking on the farms. He would always sign his letters, "Your loving brother, Ely." Daddy was not much of a letter writer, but I did hear from him from time to time. I also got a nice letter from Poo Rochelle's mother regarding church actives. I knew her only as another lady in the church, but I was thankfully impressed that she took time to write to me as a service man.

I carried on a fairly frequent correspondence with two of my "girlfriends," Nelson Blount and Margaret Underwood. They even sent me their pictures, which I prominently displayed for my army buddies to see. It was a morale builder for us to have two good-looking girls to admire. I mentioned earlier trying to correspond with Carol Waterman only to hear back that she was married.

My only telephone call home came as a result of my being a lottery winner. I forgot the details of how it came about, but my prize was a one-day trip to Seoul for the main purpose of making a phone call home. Apparently, Seoul had the closest telephone available. On the appointed day, I was given a Jeep ride for the 30 or so mile trip. I don't remember traveling on any paved roads until we got close to the city. My recollection is that it was a narrow, rocky, dirt road all the way. The sergeant who took me evidently knew exactly where to go, for in no time I had dialed the number and was all excited about talking to Mother and Daddy. After hearing it ring the fourth and fifth time, I was wondering if anyone was at home. That would be a shame to drive all that way and not even talk to them. Finally, I heard a sleepy voice answer, "Hello." I knew it was Daddy, but I was expecting a lot more enthusiasm and excitement in his voice. When he said, "Do you know what time it is?" I knew I had wakened him from a deep sleep. I hadn't given the slightest thought as to what time it was in Kinston. I think it was something like 3:00 A.M. there. Anyway, after a brief minute of small talk, he gave the phone to Mother. She, too, sounded like she was in a stupor. Their voices were weak and lethargic. No wonder! I woke them up out of deep sleep! I didn't think they hardly knew it was I, Dan, their baby boy calling from halfway around the world. I think my call was limited to only three or four minutes, so we didn't have time to say much. I just wanted them to know I was all right and doing fine. Even though I was a little disappointed in their lack of enthusiasm, it was great just hearing their voices and knowing that all the family was doing fine.

Someone said there was an afternoon performance of the Seoul opera and if we hurried we could probably get tickets. Time would permit, so why not? After all, I had seen *Tosca* in Rome a couple years earlier and at least knew a little something about opera. Besides that, it would make for good conversation and correspondence to let people know I had been to the opera in Korea. I don't remember the name of the opera or much of anything about it, other than seeing some characters on stage singing in Korean. Two things I do recall: We sat on the back row of the balcony next to a young Korean mother with her newborn baby in arms. There was nothing unusual about that, because I heard not a word or whine from either of them. What was unusual, at least for me, was the fact that shortly after I was seated, she began nursing her baby in full view of everybody. No one else looked, but my eyes were drawn to the sight. I couldn't believe it! I had never witnessed anything like that before. It was all very natural to the mother, baby, and everyone else, so they paid no attention to it. She did not try to conceal anything. I did the best I could to be casual and nonchalant about the whole thing, and I may have even appeared that way to everyone. Be that as it may, it was certainly a learning experience for me that I have never forgotten.

In December 1955, Warren decided to make a recording of family voices during out traditional family Christmas dinner. He must have found some special equipment somewhere, for making records in a home setting was something new and unheard of back then. Anyway, when the package came, it turned out to be a small, 78-rpm record. I couldn't wait to hear it! After locating a record player owned by one of the men, I was able to listen to the voices of the entire family. The only problem was they all seemed to be talking at the same time! It was hard to distinguish one voice from another. I think he must have just put the recorder in the middle of the room so as to catch the general conversation. It sounded like a general hubbub of loud confusion. There was only one voice I was sure of. Aunt Susie could be heard above everyone else. I'm not sure if I heard any actual Christmas greeting from any individual. There must have been something else on the record other than a bunch of noise, but if so, I don't remember it. All I remember is Aunt Susie's voice overpowering everybody else's. I couldn't even tell what she was saying, but she was saying it—what ever it was. By the way, I came across that record a month or so ago, and it was totally in a state of disrepair. Most all of the black surface had pealed off and had to be thrown away. Although I heard it only that one time back in December 1955, and even though it was just a bunch of noise, it was still a blessing, being that I was far from home. It reminded me of special times and family gatherings. In my mind's eye, I could see Mother, Daddy, Warren, Barbara, Ely, Aunt Susie, Dr West, Lillian, Marion, and I'm sure several others. It gave me the hope of anticipation. Next Christmas, I would be with them.

My Two R & Rs

After each six months or so of service in Korea, you were generally allowed a seven day R & R (Rest and Recuperation) leave to Japan. When I wrote

Daddy that I would soon be having an R&R in Tokyo, he wrote back that he would like for me to meet and have dinner with a Japanese couple he and Mother had met through Rotary International. The arrangements were made, and I did, indeed, meet them. Their names were Mr. and Mrs. Kobeyashi (I can't remember their first names). They were a delightful couple who were most cordial in every way. They made me feel right from the beginning that their whole purpose was to show me a good time and help me understand some of the Japanese customs. They spoke very highly of Mother and Daddy, which made me feel real good about being with them. They showed me some of the landmarks and places of interest. They even took me shopping at an exclusive store that specialized in Mikimoto pearls. Mother and Daddy had prearranged with the Kobeyashi's that I should have a nice string of pearls as a wedding present for "Miss Right," whenever she came along. Everyone in the store was nice to me and directed me to settle on the perfect gift for my bride-to-be. It was certainly not the most expensive pearl necklace, just a modest but appropriate purchase for my needs. Elsewhere, I bought a carved set of small wooden birds, and a carved set of three monkeys representing, "See no evil, hear no evil, do no evil." I even bought a small Buddha and several other souvenirs, including a Japanese smoking jacket for Warren, which he ended up making a tradition of wearing each Christmas Day. I also bought a couple of Japanese fly rods, which cousin Tony Carey advised me to get because they were supposed to be extra special. I can't remember what I bought for Ely, but everything was shipped home. Another highlight of my first R&R was having supper with the Kobeyashis. They took me to a popular restaurant where I had sukiyaki and tempura. The sukiyaki was sort of a hash or stew dish that I didn't particularly care for. The tempura was specially prepared shrimp, which was delicious. I believe this was my first real experience with chopsticks, so I was rather clumsy as they tried to teach me how to use them. I was treated royally, and the whole day was an unforgettable experience. When they took me back to my barracks, I couldn't help but ponder the thought that only a brief ten years prior to my meeting the Kobeyashis, we were considered staunch enemies. How could I or anyone else be an enemy of that fine couple? They were polite, well-mannered, and had only my best interest in mind as they showed me around the capital city of the Japanese Empire. I was beginning to see and better understand that there are good people all around the world, in every country. My traveling in Canada with Z. A. and Arthur, as well as my touring of the eight countries in Europe, confirmed that war and conflict between countries is brought about by selfish and evil leaders who take advantage of and mislead the general population.

My second R & R came toward the end of 1955. I was able to visit Kamakura and see the giant bronze statue of the Daibutsu Buddha. It was an unforgettable sight as my army friend, Richard Johnson, and I stood gazing up at the god of another religion. We were the only Americans in the crowded area of visitors. I'd be afraid to even guess how high it was—but it was mammoth and monstrous in size. We looked like dwarfs (even smaller) as we stood in awe of its enormity. I learned that its restful expression reflects the Buddhist ideal of detachment from all desires and worldly things. I also learned that, according to the preaching of Buddha, existence was a continuing cycle of death and rebirth. Each person's position and wellbeing in life was determined by his or her behavior in previous lives. For example, good deeds may lead to rebirth as a wise and wealthy person or as a being in heaven. A person's evil deeds may lead to rebirth as a poor and sickly person or even a rebirth into hell. It was interesting to hear and read about this reincarnation theory as well as about Shintoism, Taoism, and some of the other Oriental religions—but none had any attraction for me. They left me empty and dry.

I also enjoyed seeing the sights in Kyoto, but the real highlight of the entire R & R was getting up with Z. A. in Tokyo. He was stationed there as an officer in the Air Force. We had corresponded and made arrangements to spend some time together. He was a commissioned officer, and I was merely an enlisted man, a corporal at the time. I can't remember if I gave him a big salute when we first greeted each other, but I do know he "treated me kindly." We were the same old "tombstone" buddies we had always been. We rented motor scooters and had a good time riding around and cutting up just as if we were teenagers. We even played eighteen holes of golf. I didn't think either of us played very well, not having touched a club in over a year. It was both interesting and amusing to have young Japanese girls as our caddies. They spoke only broken English. Z. A. and I laughed and giggled and they laughed and giggled at us trying to communicate with them. We also went snow skiing at the foot of Mt. Fujiyama so as to be able to "tell our grandchildren" of our accomplishment. Needless to say, being novices at the sport, we took it nice and easy—but at least we had a good time trying as we took our tumbles. It was good to escape without breaking a leg. Good ol' Z. A. was good enough to get me a date with a colonel's daughter whom he knew. She was real cute. Z. A. and I enjoyed taking her and Z. A.'s date to dinner at a nice restaurant. Z. A. was probably used to taking girls out, but it was my first time in over a year. All in all, it was a fun and relaxing time being back in civilization again. Sometime during my visit with Z. A., we happened to run into R. A. Phillips, another Kinston boy who was also stationed in Tokyo. It was good chatting with him and renewing our friendship. It brought another taste of home life back to me.

Before leaving to go back to Korea, I was lying on my barracks bunk resting one afternoon when all of sudden I felt the bed tremble. In fact, the whole building seemed to shake. I didn't think too much about it because it was not that strong and it only lasted for a few seconds. Later I learned it was an earthquake. Although it was my first experience with earthquakes, it was not unusual in Japan because they experience them quite frequently.

Other Reflections

Whereas my two R & Rs were, indeed, restful and relaxing, getting back in the grind of things at Camp Casey was a little tough. The good news was it wouldn't be long before I would be heading home. As the days got shorter on my calendar, the excitement mounted. Replacements had been coming in all along as we were being rotated out. My company commander from the beginning was Captain Julius A. Frenier. He rotated out several months before I did and was replaced by Captain Dooly. Several things I remember about Capt. Frenier. In his introductory speech to us, he had said, "I'll not listen to excuses. I'll listen to reasons, but not excuses!" As long as we did things right, we were in good standing. Just don't get out of line on anything. Generally speaking, we were a pretty good company under his command. As a green recruit just joining his company, I naturally wanted to do a good job and do it right. I had recently read a story about a young recruit who was given an assignment, which he carried out in exact detail and he was rewarded for it. The point of the story was to follow your orders! Carry them out as precisely as given, to do so makes for good soldiering. But the lesson I learned taught me that there's also room for common sense, too. You've got to use your head, and in certain situations don't take everything too literally.

Shortly after my arrival at Camp Casey, Captain Frenier gave me an assignment. He knew I was a college graduate with an additional year of law school. I could tell he respected my education, and I'm sure he must have been pleased to have a new supply sergeant who had some sense and could run a good supply room. Most of the enlisted men were not nearly as educated as I. He wanted to do well on the inspections by his own supervisors, and I should be well qualified to make him look good. My assignment was to correct and retype a monthly report that my predecessor had apparently messed up—evidently in his haste to ship out, he had done a sloppy job in putting together his final report. The captain said, "Corporal Perry, I want you to go through this report with a fine-tooth comb and correct it in every detail. I want you to point out line by line everything that needs to be done to make it right and perfect." I thought to myself, "Here's my chance to follow the orders of my superior exactly as given. I'll do it right in every detail, so as to show him I'm a good soldier." It was a two-page, typewritten report in paragraph form, riddled with spelling, grammar, and spacing errors, and erasers, etc. He didn't tell me how he wanted the corrections to be made. He just said go through it in every detail and point out what needed to be done to make it perfect. He didn't tell me to retype it to eliminate all the mistakes. He just said to point out each mistake. At least that's what I think he said. He was gone, so I couldn't ask him for further explanation. My job was to carry out my assignment "to the letter of the law." And that's what I did. On a separate sheet of paper, I went through the report line by line pointing out and commenting on each misspelled word, each misplaced comma and period, each misuse of grammar, each smudge and each eraser mark, each spacing error, etc. Boy, I was going to show my commanding officer I could be depended on to follow orders exactly as given. He would surely be impressed with my thoroughness! The bottom line is when I handed him my corrections, he was somewhat speechless. In fact, my recollection is he merely looked it over with an occasional sigh or groan under his breath and then said, "O.K., now type it the way it should be to make it perfect." As he left the room, I wondered whether I had spent all that time in vain. Did he mean for me to merely retype the report without going though all that rigmarole of showing the correction on a separate sheet of paper? Maybe that's what he meant. He never said anymore about it, but I often wondered what he was thinking of his new supply sergeant. I was trying to impress him by getting started off on the right foot. Upon further reflection, he probably thought I was a real oddball without any common sense. Just following orders, sir. Just following orders!

Our Company "adopted" a little Korean boy as our mascot. He was an orphan, about nine years old when he arrived. His name was Park Jun Dong, and was nicknamed "Pak." He was a cute little fellow with a pleasant personality, which was an attraction for all of us. One of our men, Jimmy Patrick, from somewhere in North Carolina ended up officially adopting him. He took him home with him when he shipped out about six months before I did. I wrote Mother and Daddy about it, and they made a point to go by for a visit. Daddy said they were living in a poverty stricken neighborhood under very meager conditions. I've often wondered what happened to Pak and where he is today.

Finally, the big day came in April 1956. My tour of duty in Korea was over, and I was headed home. Compared to my coming, my return voyage was on a little larger ship, taking only about seven days to cross back over the Pacific. My first glimpse of land was of two cigar-like poles gradually appearing on the distant horizon. I'll never forget that sight! We were all excited when we learned that the Golden Gate Bridge was straight ahead. It seemed like forever, but when we finally docked and went ashore, I felt like kissing the very earth I was on. I remember how thankful I was to be home and how blessed I was for having had the experience of serving my country.

Reflection on Army Life

My Korean experience was, indeed, a blessing I would not trade for anything. In fact, my whole army experience was a blessing. The discipline I learned during my sixteen weeks of basic training gave me a perspective of my life that could not be duplicated or achieved any other way. Being away from home in a foreign country with strange customs under army conditions helped me appreciate my upbringing and background more than ever. From the very beginning, I knew down deep in my heart that the Lord was going to be with me and guide me in how I should respond to the various adverse conditions I was expecting to experience. Never once did I doubt the Lord was with me and would keep me safe from harm. I knew I would return a better man for having served in the army. From time to time, I am reminded of a conversation I had with Aunt Bliss and Ely shortly before I left for Korea. Aunt Bliss had made some comment about my being careful and not getting mixed up in any immoral behavior. She was gently cautioning me about the temptations of army life in a foreign country. Brother Ely's comment was, "Oh, he'll be all right. Don't worry about Dan; with his family background and training, he'll know how to handle those type situations. He'll be just fine." Ely's words of confidence and encouragement were with me throughout my army career. They served as a source of strength and general well being for his little brother. The Lord spared me from the rigors of combat, but he allowed me a wealth of much needed experience to give me an opportunity to grow and mature into the man he was molding me to be. I can truly say that my time in the army was a true blessing from God, for which I have always been most grateful.

Chapter XIX

BACK TO CIVILIAN LIFE

Making the Adjustment

Adjusting to civilian life after almost two years in the army was a little more difficult than I imagined. I was forewarned by several friends that it might take a while to get back to "normal living." Someone said it took him almost two years before he could fully make the adjustment. Others seemed to be able to take up where they left off without any side effects at all. In my case, others might not have seen any difference in my personality, but I soon realized there were some subtle changes in the way I was able to communicate in general conversations. I remember writing Margaret Underwood in one of my last letters before coming home that I sensed "I am not the same person" I was when I left. She had invited me to a party in Greensboro the weekend after coming home. It was good to see her, but I could tell there was a change in my ability to communicate. I couldn't put my finger on it, but I knew there was a difference.

I noticed the same subtle change when I went back to summer school to take a couple of law classes at Carolina. George Bell has recently been discharged from the Coast Guard, and he wanted to take a couple of business courses. We decided to room together, and were able to sublet an apartment from Nancy Bobbitt in Glen Lennox in Chapel Hill. We had a great time cooking our own meals most every night and enjoying civilian life. I remember telling George there was something different about me. George had always been a good conversationalist and took pleasure in analyzing concepts and thoughts.

I remember telling him I was a little slow in following his line of reasoning. Maybe it was my lack of focus or concentration. In retrospect I think the reason for whatever "change" there was in my personality and thought process was a result of my being cast into a totally different environment surrounded by a totally different type of people than I had grown up with. During my army experience, I had gotten accustomed to associating with a life style that was foreign to my background and upbringing. But whatever the reason, it took me about eight to ten months or more to gradually make the transition from army life back to civilian and student life.

My Last Two Years of Law School

By the time I finished summer school in 1956, I felt like I was ready to get back in the swing of law school. It was good being back in Chapel Hill and being a student again. My two-year army diversion had served its purpose. I thought maybe law school would be a little easier, having had those two years to mature and be refreshed. I found it still required long hours of study and hard work. It was interesting and fascinating in some respects, but it was still a struggle to feel reasonably prepared for classes each day. Many times I went to class feeling inadequately prepared even though I had spent enough time to be ready. I specifically remember being in equity class one day when, after posing a question, Mr. Van Hecke in his usual guff voice said, "Perry, what do you think?" I remember temporarily being almost paralyzed with fear! I managed to give him some kind of answer, even though it probably didn't make any sense. He moved on to somebody else without giving me a hard time, so I guess I didn't goof up too badly.

As our final year of law school drew to an end in 1958, we seniors were making decisions about our next step. I knew I eventually wanted to return to Kinston and be in the general practice of law with Warren. Although a lawyer by profession, Daddy's interest was not in the courtroom. He had tried it for about six months as a new lawyer in 1921, but soon found it was not for him. He didn't have the patience to wait around for his case to be called. He wanted to move on and get things done. He found his niche in the business world and in farming. I personally felt I wanted to have some experience away from Kinston before settling down to my final destination. I had heard about some openings as a research assistant for the North Carolina Supreme Court Judges in Raleigh. That had an appeal to both Tom Bennett and me, so we applied and were accepted.

I had two interesting interviews. The first was with Judge J. D. Johnston at his office in the Justice Building. He asked me all sorts of questions about Kinston and the artesian well water for which Kinston was so widely known. We had a very pleasant conversation about everything in general, but nothing specific about the law. I was thinking he would test me on certain aspects of the law. Frankly, I was a little nervous about getting into a tough legal discussion. Much to my surprise, I was very much at ease as he drew out of me things I knew. I was really impressed when he told me he knew my family, of which he had high regard. Later Mother told me she had been on a house party with him down in Elizabethtown (I don't know if Daddy was there or not). Anyway, she spoke very highly of him as a person.

My second interview was with Justice R. Hunt Parker. We met in the lobby of the Sir Walter Raleigh Hotel where he and his wife had an apartment. He was known to be a stern and serious-minded Judge who was a stickler for detail. I had been told by Marion Parrott that all the lawyers who practiced in his court highly recommended him for the Supreme Court. With tongue-in-cheek Marion said, "Yeah, we all wanted him to move on up and away from the Superior Court system. He was mighty tough on us lawyers. Everybody was scared of him."

After our brief introductory conversation, Judge Parker wrote a paragraph on a legal pad referencing a particular point of law. He then handed it to me and asked, "Dan, can you read this?" His handwriting was neat and legible, so I had no trouble reading it without hesitation. After finishing my "test," he politely but sternly said, "Good! I just wanted to see if you could read my writing, because I write out all my opinions and you need to know what I'm saying when I ask you to do some research." That made me feel good because he seemed pleased. So far so good. He then said, "So, you're from Kinston.

Do you know Marion Parrott?" My quick response was, "I sure do. He married my first cousin, Lillian West." After that, I felt like I was home free, for he spent quite a while talking about Marion and the various conversations he had had with him over the years. He told me that Marion had a wealth of knowledge about a wide variety of subjects. He told me how much he enjoyed talking to Marion about the Civil War. I later learned that Judge Parker was an avid student of the Civil War. He knew all the generals and battles and strategies, and he was eager to discuss all aspects of and historical facts about that period in our history. Someone later told me that Judge Parker was way above most folks in intellectual pursuits and there were only a few people who could really carry on a decent conversation with him. He was not a man for small talk. He was all business. He and Marion hit it off because Marion was also widely read and had a photographic memory. He could recall facts and figures in the same way as Judge Parker. They "spoke the same language."

I frankly can't remember when Judge Parker told me that I had the job as his research assistant, but I really think the reason he gave it to me was because of both his and my relationship with Marion Parrott. In fact, I later told Marion, as well as other family members, that I owed my job with Judge Parker to Marion. Tom Bennett ended up with Judge W. B. Rodman. Being the only two Carolina boys to go with the Supreme Court, Tom and I made plans to room together in Raleigh after taking the bar exam. We both felt elated over the prospects of beginning our career together.

One Last Hurdle

After graduation in early June 1958, we all had to give our full attention to the bar exam in August. Most of our class drove from Chapel Hill to Raleigh five evenings a week to attend a refresher course offered by Judge Love, in preparation for the August exam. We studied and reviewed our notes during the day, and attended Judge Love's course at night. Day after day, night after night, we studied and listened and reviewed. We knew our future depended on passing that exam. Not being one of the brightest in the class, I knew I had to really give it my all.

Finally, the big day came. I think it was a two-day exam. I do remember the tension and anxiety all us felt—or maybe most of us. Some felt more confident then others. In an effort to find some relaxation the night before, a lot of us decided to go to a movie. It turned out to be an intense story, anything but relaxing. It was "The Fly," a science fiction story about a man being in a time and space capsule that was to transfer him to another time and location. The only problem was that a common fly was trapped in the capsule with him, and when he emerged at his destination, he was part man and part fly. It was weird, but at least it took our minds off the strain we were to experience the next day.

I remember the crowded room and the instructions given us as we sat down to begin the test of our lifetime. I sat next to Ted Brown of Raleigh whom I had never met before, or at least I didn't recall having met him previously. He was so personable and acted as if we were long-lost buddies. He eventually married Peninah Powell from Tarboro, and they became good friends of my wife-to-be (Margaret) and me. Actually, Peninah and Margaret had known each other during Margaret's freshman year at Meredith before she transferred to Salem. Ted seemed real relaxed and even made me feel a little more at ease in the tension-packed atmosphere as we all labored though our two-day ordeal.

When the papers were turned in on the final day, we all were ready for a break. Some felt the exam was not too bad. Others didn't know what to think, and still others didn't feel too good about it. We were all somewhat consoled when one of the administrators told us, "You'll be all right. You probably did better than you think." I went on back to Kinston to play golf and spend some time at the beach to await the results. We were told it would probably take at least two weeks, maybe more, to get the results, which would be published in the *News & Observer*.

An Unwelcome Letter

A couple of weeks later, Mother and Daddy and I were at our beach cottage for the weekend. On Sunday morning, I noticed Daddy seemed somewhat somber as he invited me to go to Sunday school with him. For some time he had been going to Jackie Eure's class at the Methodist Church in Morehead. The unusual part about it was that Jackie was a lady teaching a class of all ladies— except for Daddy. She was known to be an excellent teacher with a wide following. Daddy saw a good thing and more or less invited himself (with Jackie's permission) to join her class when he was in town. Jackie, as well as all the ladies, seemed to enjoy having him there. When the class was over, I remember Daddy making some comment to Jackie that he appreciated the class because it related to a prayer need he had. I didn't think much about it until we got home. We were out on the porch. He put his arm around me with a letter in his hand. He softly said, "Dan you heard from the bar exam and you didn't pass." Then there was a moment of silence. I was stunned. He showed me the letter, which he said he had opened and brought to the beach to show me at the right time. I remember the empty feeling in the pit of my stomach. What did this mean? I had struggled though three, long years of law school and was looking forward to being in Raleigh in a couple of weeks as a research assistant for Judge Parker. Did this mean I was all washed up? I would have to call Judge Parker and let him know. He'd probably have to get somebody else to take my place. Mother and Daddy comforted me by telling me—it's not the end of the world—I'd be all right; a lot of people didn't make it the first time. My recollection is I called Judge Parker that same Sunday afternoon in August to let him know the bad news. Much to my surprise, my despair turned to hope. He assured me he still wanted me to come, and he would be expecting me to be there at the opening of the court session. I can't tell you how much that meant to me. It was music to my ears. I felt like I was given new life!

My Biggest Failure

Not passing the bar exam was my first big failure and disappointment. Up until that time, everything had gone smoothly throughout my whole life. Family life, school, athletics, college life, army life—they all had worked out beautifully. What little tough times and disappointments I may have had during my first 27 years of life were nothing compared to the devastation I felt by failing the bar. However, after the initial shock wore off, I was able to put it behind me gradually and move on with my life. Mother and Daddy as well as Warren and Ely gave me encouragement. It was comforting to know that I still had my job with the Supreme Court to look forward to for the next year. After that I would spend the summer studying for a retake of the bar exam. One of my letters of recommendation when applying to take the exam was written by Marion Parrott. I went by to see Marion the following week not only to let him know the test results, but also to thank him for his nice letter of recommendation. He made a statement that I've never forgotten. In fact, I've used it numerous of times down though the years to encourage others during a dark time in their lives. He said, "Adversity strengthens character." He gave me many examples of well-known historical figures who rose above their adversity to move on to greatness and honorable service to their fellow man. The encouragement I received along with my faith in a loving and gracious God helped me to keep going and look optimistically toward the future.

It is interesting to note that through the years I had never talked about failing the bar exam with anyone, except Margaret. If I mentioned it to my three children, it was only a passing comment. I had thought it was a stigma I had to live with. Frankly, I didn't have the courage to mention it to anyone until some fifty years later in 2006 when in our Bible Study of "Facing the Giants in Your Life," we were studying about the *Giants of Failure*. It was then I announced to the class my "public confession." It was good to share it openly without feeling a sense of shame. One of the main points of the lesson was we all fail at certain things from time to time. Just because you fail at something doesn't make you a failure. It's no sin to be knocked down. The sin comes in staying down and not getting up.

Judge Parker and the Supreme Court

My year in Raleigh from the fall of 1958 through the spring of 1959 as research assistant for Judge R. Hunt Parker of the North Carolina Supreme Court was truly a rewarding and enjoyable experience. I have always been grateful to him for having given me the chance to further my career without undue delay.

Seven of us served as research assistants. Tom Bennett and I along with George Saintsing of Thomasville roomed together in a small house on Jackson Street just off of Hillsborough Street, a few blocks west of the Capitol. It didn't take us long to adjust to the 8 A.M. to 5 P.M. routine of our new jobs. In the morning we were in the courtroom to hear oral arguments of the cases. Each judge would usually be assigned two or three cases, sometimes more, on which to write his opinion. Each judge would assign his assistant certain points of law to research, so as to give him a basis for his reasoning. It was actually a lot fun and a most worthwhile experience for each of us. Judge Parker was a stickler for detail. He had a photographic memory and was precise and exact as he wrote out his opinion in longhand. He wanted every comma, punctuation, grammar, and spelling typed exactly as he wrote it. Thank goodness I did his research and not his typing! He was patient but firm. His typist was Kate Humphries whom I later learned was an aunt of Carol Miller (Paul Miller's wife) from Snow Hill. Miss Humphries and I became good friends. It was a pleasure working with her, for with patience and understanding she encouraged me.

My First Blunder

From time to time, we would see lawyers whom we knew arguing their case before the court. On one occasion, while in the hallway after a session, I was asked how I liked being a research assistant. In the general course of our conversation, I was telling the lawyer how enjoyable and interesting it was. As an example, I mentioned that I was working on a case evolving a fogging machine in the Pantego area. I merely mentioned the fact that I was researching the law to find cases on point as a basis for writing a legal opinion. It was just a casual remark, and then we moved onto something else. I didn't think any more about it until later in the afternoon when Judge Parker called me into his office. His voice was calm but firm. "Dan," he said. "I heard that you were in the hall talking to someone about a case we are working on." "Yes, Sir," as I quickly recalled the incident. He was gentle, but made himself very clear as he cautioned me that it was inappropriate for us to talk about pending cases. It could open the door to give the possible impression that we could be unduly influenced to rule a certain way. No one is supposed to know which judge has a particular case until the final opinion is published and released to the public. I immediately knew what he was talking about and was totally embarrassed. I apologized accordingly. "Thank you, Judge, for telling me. I know what you are saying, and I should have known better. I assure you it won't happen again." That was the only time he ever criticized or scolded me in anyway. He was always a gentleman.

It Wasn't All Work

Each morning before leaving for work, Tom, George, and I made sandwiches for a luncheon snack. Lunch time was something we all looked forward to. Every day all seven of us would gather in the break room for a card game of hearts, officially known as "Spank Tail Hearts." I had never heard of it before, but one of the boys explained the rules and we had our game of choice every day, five days a week. It was the same game every day. For some reason, we never got tired of it. We ate our sandwiches and chips and played hearts. What an enjoyable time we had relaxing and kidding around like we didn't have a care in the world!

Another good thing about that job was we never took any of our work home. At 5 P.M., we left the building and didn't think about it until the next day. What a job! The nights were free to do as we wished. For supper Tom, George, and I enjoyed some good old home cooking at Mrs. Bizzell's Boarding House on East Park Drive. The price was reasonable for our budgets, so we ate there most every night, with an occasional diversion to the S & W Cafeteria.

At Mrs. Bizzell's I met May Robertson. She was an attractive girl whom I ended up dating a fair amount during my year in Raleigh. It was good to be back having a social life once again. Another girl I dated in Raleigh was Addie Early. She was Walter "Squirrely" Early's sister. I got to know Squirrely as another young lawyer in Raleigh. He and Addie grew up in Williamston, and Addie worked for one of the Social Security hearing officers in Raleigh. She and I dated quite a bit during that year, and we enjoyed each other's company. I even invited her home and to the beach on a couple of weekends. From time to time, I would also see her after I left Raleigh. She was a smart girl and ended up starting her own business as a Social Security consultant representing clients on appeal before the hearing officers. She later married Bill Tomlinson and still maintains an office in Raleigh with a very successful business.

Back Home to Study for The Bar

When the Supreme Court recessed in late May, I went back to Kinston to study for my second attempt to pass the bar exam. I first took a few days off to spend some time at the beach and play a little golf. Most of June and July 1959 was spent reading cases and reviewing notes. It helped to know the type of questions to expect. The previous year, they all basically had to do with solving cases. My year as a research assistant was helpful, for I was exposed to most every type of case— criminal, civil, business transactions, contracts, torts, personal property, real property, etc. I got up every day at 5 A.M. and studied for two or three hours before breakfast; then I was back at it again for several more hours in the morning, then several more in the afternoon. I did take off most afternoons for an hour or so to get out of the house to hit balls or play a little golf. By nine o'clock, I was generally in bed with the light out ready for some much needed sleep. One of the pleasures of my summer study experience was going to sleep listening to the Norman Luboff Choir singing songs of the old south, such as "Way Down upon The Suwannee River" and "My Old Kentucky Home." I had a couple of 78 r.p.m. records that sounded mighty restful as I peacefully lay there drifting first in and then out of sleep before finally fading off into dreamland for a good night's sleep—only to be awakened at 5 A.M. by my alarm clock. Day after day.

Week after week. I wanted to be ready as best I could. Several days before the exam in early August, I took off by going to the beach for diversion and change of atmosphere, so as to clean out the cob webs, and try to get ready for the big day.

The day before the exam, I journeyed to Raleigh to spend the night at the Sir Walter Hotel where the exam would be held. I decided against going to a movie, as I remembered last year and the stirred up feeling I had after watching "The Fly." This time I had an early supper and went right to bed. It was another two days of the same as the previous year. When it was all over, I remember the feeling of relief. At least it was over! I'd just have to hope and pray for the best. I certainly didn't feel overly confident I had passed, but I did think maybe I had done better than last year. Only time would tell.

As might be expected, we all were a little anxious as we awaited the results. After a couple of weeks, we began checking the *News & Observer* each morning. At least I hadn't yet received an "I'm sorry to inform you" letter. So far so good. Finally, the phone rang one morning before breakfast and before we had time to check the paper—it was Aunt Bliss. She was all excited! "Dan, have you seen the paper?" She exclaimed! Before I could say anything, she gave me the good news! "You passed the bar! You passed it." "I did? Well, great!" was about what I said at first. Daddy rushed out to get the paper, and there it was. Listed among those who passed the North Carolina Bar Exam was "Dan E. Perry, Kinston." What a feeling of relief as everybody congratulated me on my achievement. It was now time to get on with my life. My next move was to find a job. I knew I wanted to be somewhere where there was a little "action" going on, maybe Raleigh or Chapel Hill.

Chapter XX

TWENTY-SEVEN MONTHS IN BLUE HEAVEN

Finding a Job

I had three interviews, two in Raleigh and one in Chapel Hill. The first was with the Jimmy Poyner firm in Raleigh. Mr. Poyner knew Daddy, which opened the door. It was a pleasant interview as he told me about his firm and the type of practice he had. It was a big firm compared to what I really had in mind. I was thinking more of a one- or two-man firm. I had a second interview with a smaller firm in Raleigh, but I can't remember its name. In Chapel Hill I had heard the name "John Manning," and while in school, I had seen his office shingle on Franklin Street. I decided to pop in unannounced just to make contact and see if he needed any help. He had a solo practice, just he and a secretary. I didn't have any idea he would offer me a job, but anyway it was worth a try.

I was elated when Mr. Manning said he had been thinking about hiring someone to help him with an appeal of a case he was taking to Federal District Court in Richmond. My experience in researching the law would be a perfect fit for him. He said I came just at the right time, so he hired me on the spot. I couldn't believe it! I just happened to walk in his office, and the job was there waiting for me (Later I came to realize it was all in God's providential plan for my life). My first thought was, "Boy! I've got it made—living in Chapel Hill, beginning my practice of law—and with all these young girls running around. There's so much to do here. I can't wait to get started!" I told Mr. Manning I could start Monday morning. But I didn't have a place to stay. Where would I live? Well, the Lord was at work again. I went by the Kappa Sig house to check on the boys and let it be known I would be living in Chapel Hill. It so happened that Bill Olsen was there, and we got into a conversation. Bill was from Chapel Hill and graduated two or three years ahead of me. He was working with his mother in Olsen Realty Company. Being fraternity brothers, we knew each other quite well. He said, "I have a house and I am looking for someone to rent a room. You'd be the perfect one. How about it?" Well, you can believe it didn't take me long to accept his offer. All in one day I had gotten a job and a place to stay. Things were really falling into place. I was ready to go!

Living in Chapel Hill was great from the very beginning. Mr. Manning paid me $325.00 a month, which was big money to me. It was certainly enough to take care of all my needs as long as I stayed within my budget. I was on my own, and it was fun. My recollection is I was paid $300.00 a month while working in Raleigh.

Mr. Manning was a busy man. In looking back, I don't see how he was able to do what he did without help. He did it all. He loved courtroom work. He spent a lot of time in traffic court as well as general trials in District and Superior Court. On top of all that, he did title searches for the local Building and Loan Association. I don't see how he did it. He started me off doing title searches. We had never had any training in law school, so it was an entirely new field for me. He took time to show me exactly how he wanted it done. He taught me the routine of searching the chain of title and checking the grantor and judgment indexes to look for any mortgages, liens, judgments or other encumbrances. I developed a pattern for my title notes that I still use today. It was a great training ground in preparation for much of the type of work I would do when I moved back to Kinston. The county seat of Orange County is Hillsborough, which is about a half hour north of Chapel Hill. Making that trip on almost a daily basis was fun and created an enjoyable routine.

An Extraordinary Secretary

The sound of her name was catchy. It had a certain ring to it: *Twila Tullai*. She was Twila Bender who had married Fred Tullai, an assistant football coach under Jim Hickey. Mrs. Tullai was an extraordinary secretary. She was smart, neat, and organized. Mr. Manning was, indeed, fortunate to have her. I quickly learned that in order to have an efficient and well-run law office, you must have an excellent secretary, one who meets the public well and can turn out the work in a timely and nearly flawless manner. Twila was the perfect match for John Manning. What still amazes me is that she ran the whole office. She did it all. She was the receptionist as well as telephone operator. She took dictation, typed, and even drafted some of his letters, pleading, and other legal documents. Her filing system was neat and orderly. Back then we only had an IBM typewriter. Word processors, copiers, dictating machines, and computers were still a few years away. Duplications were made by carbon paper. If you had a pleading to be sent to three parties, you typed an original and four carbon copies, including an office copy. There was no easy way to make typing corrections. Today, it is only a matter of back spacing and retyping the corrections. Back then corrections were done by eraser and generally it was not unusual to have plenty of smudges and x-ed out words. Not so with Miss Tullai. It was quite the exception for any of her work to leave the office other than perfect.

My First Attempt at Dictation

Soon after my start with John Manning, I needed to dictate a fairly lengthy letter stating our client's position in a matter. I was accustomed to writing out my research assignments in longhand on a yellow pad. I had never given dictation before, so I was exploring new ground. It shouldn't be too hard, I figured, if I knew what I was going to say. That was the problem. I wasn't sure how I wanted to approach my argument. After calling Miss Tullai in, she sat down across from my desk with pad and pencil in hand. I begun and she started writing is shorthand. Giving the name, address, and salutation was the easy part. I gave her the first sentence, but after that I had to think a little. In fact, there was a long pause. The pause got longer—and longer—and longer. I was having trouble with knowing exactly what to say. I stared to the left and then to the right in deep thought. When I looked back at Miss Tullai, she was slumped over the desk. Her arms were out stretched, head down, and eyes closed. She had fallen asleep! And I mean she was out of it! My long delay, resulting in dead silence, had actually put her to sleep. "Miss Tullai," I exclaimed! "Are you all right?" These were my first words in probably two or three or four minutes. She was embarrassed, but not as much as I. I finally got on tract and was able to finish my letter, but only after an unforgettable experience of dictating my first letter as a fledgling attorney.

Mistaken Identity

One day a young man came in needing a lawyer to represent him in a criminal case. Mr. Manning was not in at the time, so Miss Tullai referred him to me. I gave him the usual greeting, "What can I do for you, Mr. Baker?" He was quite serious as he started to tell me his story. "Well, it's like this, Mr. Mason." I immediately corrected him by saying, "Oh, my name in Dan Perry." Evidently he didn't pay me much attention, for it wasn't long before he again referred to me as "Mr. Mason." I again corrected him, but I was beginning to get the picture. He thought I was the TV courtroom lawyer, Perry Mason, or at least he must have had Perry Mason on the brain. He called me "Mr. Mason" at least one more time. I didn't want to spoil his illusion. That time I just went along and enjoyed my mistaken identity. After all, Perry Mason was one of my heroes, too! Soon after moving back to Kinston, while at a party I told that story to Dempsey Hodges. He has never forgotten it, because even to this day, he still calls me "Mr. Mason." In fact, I can't remember the last time he called me "Dan." It's always, "Mr. Mason."

My First Jury Trials

I had sat at the table with Mr. Manning a time or two during a jury trial, but I had never tried one by myself until one day he said, "Dan, you've got to try this case. I've got to be some where else." He explained a little bit about the facts and the testimony of witnesses, but that was it. He said the best way to learn is just do it, and that's what I did. It was quite a learning experience, but I managed to get though it without too many blunders. At least I got my feet wet and was on my way.

In those days, the procedure in civil trials was for each attorney to read his pleadings to the jury so they would know the claims and defenses of the parties. That practice has long since changed in favor of the opening statements by the attorneys. Anyway, Mr. Manning wanted me to try a contract case in which he had prepared the plaintiff's complaint. Somehow I (we) won the case, but the thing I specifically remember is that after I read the complaint, the judge commended me in open court on what a good job I had done in preparing the complaint. He said I had covered all the bases and told the jury that Mr. Perry had made the claim clear and understandable. He probably knew Mr. Manning had prepared it, yet he appeared to be giving me all the credit. I was a little embarrassed over getting the undue recognition, so I told the judge that Mr. Manning had prepared the complaint, and I was merely reading what he had written.

The only other jury trial I vaguely remember was a criminal case in which the district attorney was a seasoned veteran from Durham County. His name was Mr. Murdock. I knew of his reputation for being a vigorous prosecutor. He, as well as I (and probably everyone else), knew I was young and inexperienced. I remember telling the jury something to the effect that, "I feel like David facing Goliath— a young boy facing a giant." The point I was trying to make was that even though my client's case may appear weak, I hoped they would look beyond the outward appearance and see the truth, that my client was actually innocent. Well, little David may have won out against the giant Goliath in the biblical account, but in this courtroom trial little Dan lost out against the giant Murdock. The jury found my client guilty as charged (and rightly so.)

The Federal Case on Appeal

My biggest project while working for Mr. Manning involved his case on appeal to the Federal District Court in Richmond. I think that was one of the main reasons he hired me, along with his need for someone to do his title work. He stayed busy in traffic court not only in Hillsborough, but also in Chapel Hill and Durham where he shared an office with another lawyer. He seemed to thrive on staying busy. He loved it and did an excellent job, but he definitely needed help with his workload. We had a deadline on the federal appeal case, and he wanted me to write the brief and prepare all the papers. He simply didn't have time. I remember spending some long hours, day and night, getting ready. We had to get it all published in booklet form at the local printer in Chapel Hill. It took some doing, but we managed to meet the deadline. Mr. Manning and I drove to Richmond for the oral arguments. He introduced me to the court for admission to practice, and we were all set. I was not thinking in terms of entering in the oral arguments, for he had not given me any indication he wanted me to say anything. Our case was called. Mr. Manning said," Dan, you go ahead and argue the first two points, then I'll finish up." After surviving the initial shock of his surprise instruction, I pulled myself together and was able to stand before the panel of judges and make a few points before "turning it over to my colleague." I guess that was the best way to do it. If Mr. Manning had given me a week's notice, I probably would have spent that time worrying about what I was going to say. Anyway, we won the case, and I got the standard certificate for having appeared before the Federal District Court in Richmond, Virginia.

Extracurricular Activities

Living in Chapel Hill was not all about practicing law. I found time to meet new friends and enjoy myself. One of the first things I did was to take the Dale Carnegie course in public speaking. I had long ago read his book *How to Win Friends and Influence People*. It had a lot of great tips and was a best seller for many years. Knowing that I had a lot to learn as a public speaker, I also felt the course would do me good as a lawyer. It met once a week for about 12 weeks and gave me an opportunity to meet and be with some other people in the community!

I also joined the Chapel Hill Jaycees. Bob Cox of Carolina football fame was a great Jaycee. He had been president of both the Chapel Hill and state Jaycees and was living in Chapel Hill as the owner of Cox's Clothing Store on Franklin Street. Bob was a real fireball as a community leader. We became good friends, and he taught me a lot about dealing with people.

One day Dick Armstrong stopped me on the street and talked to me about joining the newly formed Optimist Club, of which he was the charter president. Before I knew it, he had talked me into joining at the next day's 7 A.M. meeting at the Carolina Inn. I knew nothing about the Optimist Club, but it turned out to be a real blessing. The more I learned the more I liked it, and I ended up being elected president the following year. Dick and I became close friends as we participated in club activities and projects. The Optimist Creed was appealing because of its emphasis on helping youth. Erwin Langley was a member of the club. He was the father of Bob Scott and John Langley of Kinston. Until that time I had always called him "Mr. Langley," since he was the father of two of my older Kinston friends. In the Optimist Club, everyone called him "Erwin," so I learned to join the crowd, even though it was awkward at first.

I also became advisor for the Alpha Mu Chapter of Kappa Sigma in Chapel Hill. Although I didn't spend a lot of time at the Kappa Sig house, I did manage to go by from time to time for some of the parties. I was even invited to be the guest speaker at the next annual meeting. As part of my speech I remember quoting "The Cremation of Sam McGee" as well as "The Shooting of Dan McGrew."

But what about girls? Yes, I found time to go out with some of the coeds, even thought I was beginning to get a little age on me. By this time I was 28 or 29 years old—WOW! I couldn't believe I was that old. Soon after I started working in Chapel Hill in the fall of 1958 (I was only 27 then), I called a young Kinston girl who had just entered Carolina. I'm not sure if she was a freshman or a junior transfer. I frankly can't remember her name at this point, but I knew she was real cute. Even though she was a lot younger than I, I thought I'd call her for a date to take her to the Kappa Sig house, or movie, or something. When she answered the phone, I said, "This is Dan Perry from Kinston," She responded politely as well as respectfully by saying, "Oh, yes, Mr. Perry. How are you today?" I thought to myself, "Mr." Perry? That did it! That cut off all prospects for getting a date with her. For the rest of our brief conversation, I merely inquired about her family and how she liked Carolina, etc.—just some small talk to pass the time. I surely wasn't going to ask her for a date after that kind of greeting. I ended our conversation with something like, "Well, it was nice talking to you. Let me know if I can ever do anything for you."

Some of the older lawyers tried to fix me up with some of their secretaries and other acquaintances, but nothing ever materialized. Then one evening I was in Fayetteville at a party and Mary LeGrande Parks happened to be there. She was from Fayetteville and a student at Carolina. In the course of our conversation, I found that she needed a ride back to school. Since I was by myself and was leaving soon, I offered to give her a ride. She was nice, very attractive, and a good conversationalist. It turned out we had a delightful trip back to Chapel Hill as we talked and got to know each other. She was easy to talk to and most pleasant to be around. It was a perfect opportunity to get a girlfriend in Chapel Hill. I could call and look forward to going out with her. I didn't restrict myself by dating only her, for I still had my rule of not going out with the same girl over three times in a row. I dated other girls, too, but Mary LeGrande seemed to be someone special. She was an excellent dancer. She was smooth on her feet and "followed like a breeze." One night I took her to a supper dance in Greensboro, which was sponsored by the Regional Optimist Clubs. We had a good time shagging and twisting around the dance floor. One of the older club members from Greensboro was so captivated by her he just had to break in for a dance with my cute date. He was one of the "big wigs" and a fine gentleman. They were the center of attraction as all of us (including his wife) watched them put on a show of smooth elegance in action. It was all in fun and was like watching Fred Astaire and Ginger Rogers (almost). When their dance was over, he jokingly complimented her by saying, "Boy, if I was younger and not married, I would go after you." I think I must have thrown my "not-more-than- three-dates-in-a-row" rule out the window, for I didn't remember keeping up with it any more. I took her to Kinston a time or two and also to the beach, as well as visiting her in Fayetteville. A lot of people probably thought we were getting serious, but somehow it never worked out. The Lord had something else in mind for both of us.

Ready to Move On

Some time in late 1961, I began to have a strong feeling that my time was up in Chapel Hill. I was 30 years old, and it was time to move back to Kinston to settle down. That was where I had always known I wanted to end up. Chapel Hill had served its purpose. I got the experience I was looking for in the general practice of law. I had a good time as a single man living in Chapel Hill where there was plenty to do socially. I was able to meet a lot of wonderful people and date a lot of nice girls. I enjoyed my work and my social life. It was a wonderful and rewarding experience in every way, but it was now time to move on, and I knew it. I felt good about my 27 months in Chapel Hill, and I felt good about the prospects of my moving back home. The time was right and I was ready to go. My heavenly Father had, indeed, been good to me. He had blessed me beyond measure.

A Last Minute Trip

My official target date to begin practicing law in Kinston was January 1, 1962. I said goodbye to John Manning, Twila Tullai, and Chapel Hill somewhere around the first week in December 1961. I had left just enough time to visit my friend Bob Hook who was doing a residency in ophthalmology in New York at one of the hospitals there. We were fraternity brothers, had been on several trips together (including Florida and the Bahamas), and had been good friends since early Carolina days. I saw Bob Kirk at a party in Chapel Hill several days before I was scheduled to leave, and he was flying to New York in his Piper Cub the same day as I. He invited me to go with him, so I cancelled my commercial flight and flew with Bob. Although it was a little bumpier ride than my commercial flight would have been, it was very pleasant and it was good being with Bob. Bob Hook met me at the airport and took me to his room at the hospital where I stayed for a long weekend. He showed me some of the things he was doing at the hospital, as well as showing me a few of the sights of the big city. It was fun being with Bob before settling down in Kinston.

Ely Jr. (Bud) 7, Warren 9, Dan 2, Daddy 37, pony "Dick"—1933

The author, about 5—1936

Neighborhood buddies: John Burton, Jr., Dan, Z.A. Collins

Dan and his Spanish Catch, Morehead—1938

Devoted brothers Warren 20, Ely Jr. 17, Dan 12—1944

Ely Jr. and Warren on leave before the end of WWII—1945

Cap'm Dan and his boys, Camp Morehead—1952

Cap'm Pat, Dan, boys, and Sarah Ellen White (Archie)

*Grainger High Red Devils, Coach Bill Fay's squad
1st row, left to right: Paul Bennett, co-cpts. John Langley and Herbert Whitfield,
Jesse Aldridge, Gene Leigh; 2nd row: Vincent Jones, R.A. Phillips, Cecil Roberts
and Dan Perry; 3rd row: Bobby Neilsen, Tom Larkins, Tommy Paylor,
and Mgr. Larry Smith. Not pictured: Sterling Gates.*

Perry battles for a rebound with the Saints, Woodberry—1948

Golf Captain at Woodberry with Coach Paul Brightman—1949

Dance weekend—George Ives, Katherine Armstead, Dot Smith, Dan

Woodberry singers

Dan imitating Al Jolson—May 1949

Dan and his record 36 lb. red snapper caught off Cape Lookout—July 1949

Fraternity life at UNC
Left to right: Dan, Toddy Smith, Bobby Noble, Paula Whitaker, DeeDee Davenport

Kappa Sigma Fraternity dance

Dunes Club beach crowd—1951

Christmas Holidays at 908 West Road—1951
Left to right: Z.A. Collins, Dan, Laurence Stith, Aggie Barden, Heywood Washburn, Frank Davenport, Ely Jr.

JULY 2, 1931–DECEMBER 31, 1961   241

UNC Marshalls at graduation—1952

Gov. Umstead congratulates Dan at Graduation—1953
Left to right: Chancelor Robert House, Daddy, Mother, the Governor and UNC President Gordon Gray

At the Old Well, UNC—1953

First Shower in Korea, February—1955

Writing home from Korea

PART II

My Search for Truth and Spiritual Growth

JANUARY 1, 1962–JULY 2, 2007

Chapter XXI

LIVING AT HOME WITH MOTHER AND DADDY

The Beginning of "My Search"

It is impossible to pinpoint an exact time when my search for truth and spiritual growth began. If I had to pick a time, it would be when I moved back home to Kinston to live with Mother and Daddy. It was then I was able to observe first hand Daddy's own search. Technically, he and I both had been seeking answers to life's questions all our lives. There was a certain restlessness about both of us that is hard to explain. We knew there was more to life than just the same old routine of working, eating, and sleeping. We were basically searching for the answer to the age-old questions of *Who am I? What is life about? What is my purpose for living? Where am I going? What am I going to do when I get there?* Saint Augustine stated it perfectly when he said, "We are restless until we find our rest in God." As I write Part II of my journey through this life, hopefully I can do justice in explaining what I mean by "My Search for Truth and Spiritual Growth." It has really taken a lifetime. The interesting part is, I'm still searching and I'm sure I'll never find all the answers until that glorious day when I meet my Lord and Savior and my sovereign God, face to face.

Learning on the Golf Course

Golf continued to be my favorite past time. Our family foursome of Daddy, Warren, Ely, and me gave me the most pleasure, but from time to time I had fun playing with Daddy and some of his regular group. One Saturday morning soon after my arrival back in Kinston, he asked me to fill in for one of his friends who was unable to play. The thing I particularly remember about that game was what Daddy taught me as we were walking along side by side. We had just teed off on old hole number 5 (which is now the 8th hole) at the Kinston Country Club. As we strolled along together he said, "Dan, I want to tell you something I want you to always remember." It was a simple statement, which he quoted several times to be sure I had it firmly in mind. By the time we reached our tee shots, I had it memorized perfectly, and have never forgotten it. Here it is as he gave it to me:

> And I said to the man who stood at the gate of the year,
> "Give me a light that I might safely tread into the
> unknown." And he replied, "Go out into the
> darkness and put your hand into the hand of
> God. That shall be to you better than a
> light, and safer than any known way."

I don't remember ever seeing it in print, but that one statement has been the foundation upon which my "search" has been based. As we continued our walk together Daddy said, "That's sound advice, and if you'll put your hand into the hand of God and follow Him, He will bless you." I could see the wisdom in what he was saying, for I knew he was telling the truth. Daddy taught me many other words of wisdom both before and after that memorable day, but that particular gem has been at the forefront of my mind as a stimulus for my search for truth and spiritual growth.

Office History

Daddy's original law office was located on the northeast corner of Queen and Gordon Streets in what was known as the Perry Wooten Building. His long time secretary was Eva Wood. I believe she and Daddy grew up as classmates in school, and it is my understanding she started out with him in 1921. He had taken in several younger lawyers along the way, one of whom was Robert Stroud, a brother of Speight, Albert, Clarence, Walter, and Hugh, all of whom were outstanding citizens in the Kinston community for many years. Robert died an untimely death in the early 1930s of blood poisoning. He had nicked his face while shaving, resulting in an infection. I understand it took only a few days for the blood poisoning to develop and run rampant through his body. Today the problem could have been easily cured with an antibiotic. Back then nothing could be done. Another young lawyer Daddy took in was Phil Crawford Jr., who later had his own practice, and then became chief prosecutor in Lenoir County Records Court, later known as the District Court.

Before I came, Daddy took in John Burton, from Maryland. He moved to Kinston when he married my cousin Lillian Carey in 1936. They formed Perry Burton Realty Company, Inc. in 1952 and developed quite a successful business partnership until Daddy's death in 1968. John and Daddy complemented each other in both personality and business style. Daddy was the aggressive, go-getter who knew what he wanted and could make decisions in a hurry. John was more laid back and deliberate, with a quiet personality. Daddy could be impatient at times. Both had excellent judgment regarding real-estate and business matters. Both Daddy and John told me they liked to "argue things out" when problems arose and decisions had to be made. At first I didn't understand what they meant by the word "argue." I thought they meant they would have loud arguments resulting in heated disputes and quarreling. Although Daddy could be loud at times in making a point, I don't think I ever heard John raise his voice when "arguing" with Daddy. What they were really saying was that they liked to look at a problem from all angles and discuss the ins and outs, the pros and cons, and finally come up with a solution that was agreeable to both. I never heard or knew of them having a real argument resulting in total disagreement. They seemed to always come out with an agreeable answer, resulting in a most satisfactory and rewarding partnership as well as lasting friendship.

When Warren came back to Kinston after passing the bar in August 1950, he joined the office with Daddy, John, and Miss Eva on the second floor of the Perry Wooten Building. My recollection is the small suite was composed of Daddy's office on the corner, Miss Eva's office, and then a large reception room where John and Warren had their desks. It was crowded, to say the least.

When it became obvious that I was looking toward returning to practice in Kinston, Daddy moved the office to 106 W. Gordon Street, and that's where I started my practice. When I officially came on January 1, 1962, my office was there waiting for me. What a blessing it was to be able to step right into a family situation like that. The firm name of Perry & Perry was soon expanded to Perry, Perry & Perry. I remember Warren and I discussing whether to have a name change. He was saying, why not leave it Perry & Perry; three Perry's in a row would be redundant and a little unusual. We couldn't think of any other firms with three family names. My thought was we had three lawyers, why not use three names. Anyway, we ended up with Perry, Perry & Perry, which is what it is today.

When I moved into the office at 106 W. Gordon Street, Ely Jr. had a desk next to John Burton. He, John, and Daddy worked as Perry Burton Realty Company, and Warren and I were the two practicing attorneys. Although Daddy kept up his law license, he was never in the courtroom or involved in any court cases. His interest was in business deals and farming. Warren continued doing all the legal work for Perry Burton including title work, preparation of deeds, contracts, etc.

Settling in to My New Life

One of the first things I did was to pay a visit to all the lawyers in town. I wanted to get to know them and let them know I was a new lawyer in town. I made a checklist, and I think I ended up seeing about all of them. I saw Marion Parrott, Bill Allen, Paul LaRoque, Tom White, Brantley Aycock, Jesse Jones, Olin Reed, Tom Griffin, Jack Gerrans, John Dawson, Lamar Jones, Allie Whitaker, Fitzhugh Wallace (both Jr. and Sr.) and Bob Scott Langley, to name a few. They were all very nice, and warmly welcomed me back to Kinston as the newest lawyer in town.

A Visit with Doug Bell

Knowing that I wanted to continue to be involved in the church, I visited Doug Bell, the minister of Gordon Street Christian Church. I remember telling him that I had always been involved in the church throughout my whole life, and I certainly wanted to continue to make the church a vital part of my life. I told him I wanted to teach a class of young teens. I had never taught Sunday school before, and I wanted young people old enough to be impressionable, but not old enough to cause a disciplinary problem. Doug Bell had come into the ministry after several years in the business world. He had been a bomber pilot during World War II and had a real calling to turn his life over to Jesus Christ and go into the ministry. One of his trademarks as a preacher was to organize his sermons to last only seventeen minutes. Most of the time, they were pretty much on target. His theory was that if a sermon goes much longer he would begin to lose his audience. Most people's attention span is limited, and he wanted everybody to take in every word he was saying. Within a couple of weeks I was teaching a class, which turned out to be a rewarding experience for me. One of my strategies was to divide the class period into two time frames. The first ten minutes we would talk about anything they wanted to—school, sports, movies, whatever was on their minds. But the rest of the period would be given over to the lesson. That time would be used to learn something about the Bible or whatever the lesson emphasized. I also got involved with the CYF and similar youth work. Hopefully, I could make a contribution to their growth and development, and at the same time it would be a blessing to me.

Warren and Ely—A Real Blessing

Developing a cliental was a little slow at first. One of my first fees came from a traffic case that was really Warren's case. I can't remember how I got involved, but I felt I ought to split the $60 fee with him. As we were walking back from the courthouse, I remember him saying, "Naw, you go ahead and take it. It's yours. You earned it." A $60 fee is not much by today's standard, but back in 1962 it was nothing to sneeze at. In fact, I was thinking I had done a good day's work (with Warren's help). I use that example, because it was typical of Warren's attitude in wanting to help me get started. Ely was the same way. Each and every member of my family, Mother, Daddy, Warren, and Ely all welcomed me back with love and encouragement and were thankful for my return. I'm not saying we didn't have minor disagreements from time to time, for that is only natural. The point is both my brothers were always fair and honest with their little brother in every way. In all our years together—from my first memory, through early childhood and teenage years, as young adults and middle age, and on into our senior years until their deaths—I don't remember a single time or incident that gave me any reason to think either Warren or Ely was taking advantage of me in any way. Each one of us were (and I still am) blessed in so many ways, not only in our family and business life, but also in our relationships with each other. It obviously is the result of God's grace and mercy, and His sovereign, providential hand at work in our lives. It goes back to our loving Mother and Father setting a godly example, and instilling in each of us a sense of values for truth, fairness, and honesty.

Soon after my return to Kinston, brother Ely took me for a ride in the county to show me the various farms Daddy had accumulated. He wanted me to be aware of some of our family holdings. Ely loved land and riding around the farms. He could see the potential for land, and he followed in Daddy's footsteps by developing a feel for knowing the value of land and property. It didn't take me long to realize that the Lord worked it all out for Ely to end up being a farmer and business man, rather than a doctor. By being home with Daddy and observing his love for land and business, Ely became a great blessing to our whole family. When Daddy died in 1968, Ely and Warren were right there to take over and continue working and developing the family assets and investments. They both always had the total family in mind as they worked along with Daddy, and so continued long after his death.

One thing that really stands out in my mind about Ely is that whatever the farm and garden produced, he wanted to share equally with each of our families. In corn season he was sure each family was given an equal supply, not only for present, but for future consumption. We froze corn both on the cob and off the cob. Every spring he would bring each of us a nice supply of vegetables and fruits. During the time we raised cattle for a number of years, Ely would be sure we all shared the beef equally.

Involvement in the Community

One of the first things I did was to join the Salvation Army Advisory Board. J.T. Sutton's Insurance office was next to our law office on Gordon Street. He and his wife, Naomi, had been friends of the Perry family for many years, and he took an interest in seeing that I, as a young lawyer, became involved in community affairs. He was kind enough to invite me to join the Salvation Army Advisory Board, which met at the Hotel Kinston. J.T. was treasurer and I believe Frank Mock was president. It has been a real blessing for me to maintain my membership for over 45 years, as of the date of this writing.

I also joined the Jaycees, which was quite an active organization at the time. I saw the potential for leadership development that the Jaycees offered young people from ages 21 to 35, and I saw it as an opportunity to help me be a better citizen in the Kinston community. In the summer of 1962, I attended the Jaycee National Convention in Las Vegas with Dave Benny, a Du Ponter, and incoming president of the Kinston club. That was quite an experience! The entertainment was unforgettable. They put on a special star-packed floorshow at one of the night clubs just for us Jaycees. I've never seen so many stars together on one program: Ella Fitzgerald, Perry Como, Frank Sinatra, Jack Benny, Red Skelton, Jerry Lewis, Dean Martin, and Milton Berle, just to name a few. The list went on and on. One afternoon I saw the *Follies* and that night I saw the *Lido* show, both from Paris—both in one day. It was good to see Toy Gregory, a friend I had known from Carolina law school. He was from Los Vegas and also a Jaycee. He had known I was coming and met our bus upon arrival. I especially remember hearing about one of the national directors from Wyoming. I was told that he was not considered a gambling man, but like many of the Jaycees decided to try his luck just for the experience and to pass the time. He started out with a $5.00 bet, which he won several times straight. Each time he would leave his winnings on the table and continue to win. I was told he didn't lose a single time. Everybody was advising him to "quit while you're ahead." He thought about it briefly, but said, "No, I'll try it just *one more time*." Well, would you believe he did try one last time?—and won $40,000!! His wife was standing next to him, grabbed him by the arm and exclaimed, "No more! That's it! We're going home!" And that's exactly what they did. After collecting his money, they packed up and took the next flight home. They left the convention before it got started. We were told they were going to use the money as a down payment on a house— $40,000 was big, big money in those days, and they weren't about to take another chance on losing it!

During that first year of 1962, I was also recruited by the Boy Scout Executive to serve as Commissioner for the Caswell District. On top of that, Mayor Simon Sitterson appointed me to the Mayor's Bi-Racial Committee to serve as cochairman along with E. K. Best. Racial problems were beginning to peak throughout America, and Kinston was no exception. It was quite a learning experience for me as we met on a weekly basis for the purpose of hearing complaints and devising strategies to bring the races together on matters of concern. Some of the others serving on the committee of some 16 members included Marilyn Cogdell, George Marx, and Lowell Dupree. It was also that same year that I was appointed, along with Alex Howard, to serve as cochairman of the United Fund, now known as the United Way. In retrospect, it would appear I was too busy doing community work to do much practicing law.

Ely and Barbara Ruth

Ely married Barbara Ruth Johnson on Valentines Day, February 14, 1959. She was a perfect match for brother Ely. She had had three years of pharmacy school, so she knew something about medicine and prescriptions. Her father was the farm manager at Kennedy Home, so she knew something about farm life, which was right up Ely's alley. In one way she was a simple, unsophisticated farm girl. At the same time, she was a beautiful, intelligent young lady with a beaming smile and pleasant personality. Prior to Ely's involvement, I recall Aunt Bliss telling me about her and suggested I ask her out for a date. I had the pleasure of taking her out one time, but since I had just moved to Chapel Hill, I was not available to pursue her on a regular basis. Evidently, Aunt Bliss also told Ely about her, because the next thing I knew he was going out with her almost every night. Ely was approaching 33 at the time, and he was more than ready to settle down. Mother and Daddy, as well as all the Perrys, were thrilled to welcome her to the family. In view of the fact she was the second Barbara in the family, everybody was wondering about me. Would I end up with a Barbara, too? Soon after that, I brought Barbara "Bobbie" Love home for a weekend. (I mentioned her earlier as being one of my special girlfriends at Carolina.) People wondered if she would be the third Barbara, but nothing developed. It was just not my time. I remember "battling with the Lord" a little by asking, "When, Lord, are you going to send the right girl my way? Will I ever find her?" I had been blessed all my life in so many ways. It was hard for me to believe the Lord, my God, was not going to bless me with a wonderful wife. The answer seemed to come in a clear, convincing way: "Don't worry. I'll give you the right girl at the right time. In the meantime, be patient." Several friends, as well as Mother and Daddy, told me that she'll appear, "When you least expect it, and when she does, you'll know it." In my spirit I kept asking, "Yeah, I know all that, but when? When will she come into the picture? I'm getting a little tired of waiting."

A Special Book at a Special Time

One day Mother handed me a small book and simply said, "Here, I want you to read this." I don't recall her giving me an explanation or making any further comment. She just said with calmness, yet with certain firmness in her voice, "Here, I want you to read this." At the time I didn't know the significance of this particular book or the timing for which she gave it. It was a small, reasonably short book titled *Acres of Diamonds* by Russell Conwell. Why would she give me this particular book at this particular time in my life? Only time would tell. I don't remember rushing to read it, and I don't remember going back and reading it a second time. All I know is I read it with interest, but without attaching any significance to it until sometime later. It was the story of a man from Africa who had such a passion for diamonds that he sold his farm and went off on a futile search for them. He went from country to country, in every location where diamonds would likely be found. He was digging and searching, all to no avail. Finally, in desperation, he gave up and returned to his former home for a visit. While sitting in the living room of the new owner, he noticed a sizeable rock on the mantle. The new owner said he found it in the backyard and thought it was interesting, so he had it on display on the mantle just as a conversation piece. Upon further scrutiny, it was determined that the rock was a huge diamond in the rough. Much to his amazement, the property turned out to be the largest diamond mine in the world, right in his own backyard. Conwell used that story as a perfect illustration of the book's central idea that one need not look elsewhere for opportunity, achievement, or fortune—the resources to achieve all good things are present in your own community. He elaborated on the theme through examples of success, genius, service, and other virtues with the admonition to "dig in your own backyard." Good story with a good message. But what did that have to do with me? Did *Acres of Diamonds* have special meaning for me? Without my realizing it at the time, Mother was trying to teach me a great lesson.

Chapter XXII

THE LORD FINALLY PROVIDED

Enter Margaret Marston Taylor

Mother and Daddy, as well as most all my acquaintances, knew I had dated a lot of girls from here, there, and yonder. They also knew I had passed my 30th birthday and the time was ripe for me to be finding "Miss Right." A lot of fine, attractive girls had come into my life, many of whom were potentially the right one for me. In retrospect, I could see God's providential hand holding me off, gently yet convincingly. He was telling me in essence, "Wait, Dan. Be patient, I have picked out the right girl for you, and in my time I will reveal her to you."

My story now goes back a few months earlier to September 1961, at the wedding reception at the Kinston Country Club for Grace Walker of Kinston and Gordon Sanders of Elizabeth City. Grace was the daughter of Henry and Grace Walker, longtime friends of Mother and Daddy. The Walkers lived next door to Aunt Susie and Doctor West, just up the hill from the Perry family. It was only natural that the Perrys attend the wedding and reception of the daughter of our longtime family friends. Back then it was traditional to have guests stand in long receiving lines so the newlyweds could greet them one by one. On this warm September night, we were waiting in line on the lawn when a young girl rushed by on her way inside the club house. I was not paying much attention, but I remember Mother greeting her with something like, "Hey, how are you? You know my son, Dan, don't you?" That was the first time

I had seen Margaret Taylor in quite a while. She was the daughter of Fred M. Taylor (who died of cancer when she was ten years old) and Margaret Marston Taylor. Although her parents and my parents had been close friends for years, "Little Margaret," as she was known by many, was 5½ years younger than I, and, therefore, I never thought of her as being anyone other than a nice little girl from a nice Kinston family. But it was on that warm September evening in 1961 that I realized she had suddenly grown up and was no longer a little girl. She paused only a brief moment to speak, and then she was on her way into the club house to help serve at the reception. She and Grace were cousins as well as close friends. It wasn't until later on in the evening that my attention was drawn to her with increasing interest. She was sitting at a table with a group of friends when I saw her from a distance. I felt the urge to go over and speak. I reintroduced myself and had a brief, but most pleasant conversation. After she made it known that she was living in Raleigh and teaching second grade at Frances Lacy School, I responded by telling her I was practicing law in Chapel Hill. I remember thinking, "Here's a cute girl that's nearby. This may have some possibilities." It was only a brief conversation and my parting remark was, "I'll call you sometime and maybe we can get together." I had had similar conversations with many girls in the past, so at this point Margaret Taylor was no different from any of the rest. She was just another cute girl and another opportunity to add to my candidate list for "Miss Right." Later, as I pondered the assessment of my new "friend girl," I was reminded that she was a hometown girl from a nice family who were close friends of my family. The bottom line is I did call Margaret, and we did get together. Somewhere along the line, my thoughts returned to that special book Mother had given me. Did she have someone in mind when she gave me *Acres of Diamonds?* Was she telling me to "dig in my own backyard?" Maybe, just maybe, her message was getting through to me. At least it was worth exploring the possibility.

One Last Fling—Before Settling on Margaret

Although I did see Margaret from time to time in her Raleigh apartment as well as in Kinston, I was still seeing other girls, too. In January 1962, George Bell and I decided to go skiing at the Greenbrier in West Virginia. He was interested in a Sweetbriar girl named Lois Seward, and he was sure she could get me a date with one of her classmates. What's hard to believe is George said he could fly us up there. "Fly us up there? What do you mean, fly us up there?" was my response. "You can't fly an airplane, can you?" was my further question. I had no idea he could fly a plane, but if he said he could fly, who was I to question Ol' George "Ding Dong" Bell? I knew he didn't own a plane, so where was he going to get one to fly? He assured me that would be no problem. The next thing I knew, arrangements were made and we were on our way. I don't remember too much about the details other than George did a right good job in piloting the small plane he borrowed from his brother, Carl. Upon arriving at the nearby airport, we rented a car, picked up the girls, and off we went to The Greenbrier for a weekend of skiing. I was real impressed with my date—Betty Bonner Britt from Elizabeth City (I think). She was cute and had lots of personality. It didn't take us long to make our way to the beginners slope for a brief lesson before trying out our skills. None of us knew much about skiing, but we figured it would be no problem. It looked like so much fun. We could just see ourselves gliding effortlessly down the slopes with no strain at all. The instructors seemed to think we could all do it, and they even made us feel like we could. We were young and in good shape. Why not? The ski lift was not a ski lift as we know it today. It was merely a motorized revolving rope. The object was to grab hold the rope with your hands so as to be pulled up the hill 40 or 50 feet. Then gently ski down the hill the short distance until you got used to it. The next time you could go higher. It was a matter of learning by doing. It looked simple enough. Lois and George went first and then Betty Bonner and I were to follow next in line. Even though the rope was moving slowly, Betty Bonner's skies got tangled under her and down she went before traveling only a few feet. She was in obvious pain as we rushed to comfort her. Within minutes, a doctor was there. After a brief examination, he determined she should be taken to the infirmary for further tests. The bottom line was she had broken her leg! She was a great sport about the whole affair and after the cast was applied, she insisted that we continue with our activities. That night we had a delightful supper even though Betty Bonner was hobbling on crutches. It was one of those unfortunate things that couldn't be helped. For all practical purposes, the weekend was over before it got started. In retrospect I realized the Lord was working things out for my good. He kept me from branching out in pursuit of another girlfriend. After flying back to Raleigh Sunday afternoon, George and I dropped by to see Margaret at her apartment. I wanted him to meet her. After all, she was somebody special. In fact, after that one last fling (half-fling) at the Greenbrier with Betty Bonner, it was Margaret Taylor from then on. I had no desire to go out with anyone other than Margaret.

Who Me—a Minister?

In September of 1962 I learned a great lesson which has remained with me all these years. Dr. Elton Trueblood was invited to Gordon Street Christian Church for a week of preaching. He was a noted author and speaker. Back then if anything was going on in the church, all the Perrys were there. Mother and Daddy had set the example for us from early childhood. One of Dr. Trueblood's messages stood out above all the rest as far as I was concerned, because he told me something about myself of which I was unaware. His question to the whole congregation was, "Did you know that you are a minister?" As he was stating his case, he was pointing his finger from left to right though out the congregation. All of us Perrys were sitting to his right, and when he got to our side of the congregation, he seemed to be pointing directly at me. He went on to say, "That's right. If you are a Christian, if you believe in Jesus, you are a minister for the sake of the gospel." He further explained that the only difference between us and Doug Bell was that he was officially ordained and had been called to serve Gordon Street Christian Church. Dr. Trueblood was saying that we, as laymen, also had a ministry to serve others as God directs. I remember thinking to myself, "You mean I'm a minister? That's the first I've ever heard it put that way." Anyway, ever since then I've remembered his statement and have considered myself a minister for Christ.

Had My Time Come?

By the fall of 1962, Margaret and I were seeing each other as much as we could. She was teaching and living in Raleigh with Ellen Whitaker in the Boylan Apartments. I was in Kinston heavily involved with community and church affairs as well as trying to get my law practice off the ground. She would come home most weekends, and I would drive to Raleigh at other times. The previous summer, she and three other Salem girls took a trip out west for six weeks to see the rest of the country. They even got up into Canada briefly. It was truly a trip of a lifetime for each of them. Amazingly enough, they traveled in a compact Pontiac Firebird owned by one of the girls, who drove the entire trip. Martha Parrott of Kinston was also on the trip. Actually, I had dated Martha a number of times and had even driven to Salem to be with her before realizing Margaret was beginning to steal my heart. That six-weeks trip served a good purpose for both Margaret and me. Both of us realized we really missed each other. She called every two or three nights as the opportunity presented itself, and I was finding myself looking forward to her calls. After her return, it was all Margaret. She was the only one I was interested in dating. Had my time come? Was she the one for me? I found myself asking the Lord that very question, "Lord, is she the one you've picked out for me? Is she the one I've been waiting for?"

Popping the Question

I'm not sure when it became clear to me that, without any doubt, Margaret Marston Taylor was the girl I wanted to marry and spend the rest of my life with. This was a monumental decision, for I had never been in love before. I had dated some fine young ladies all over North Carolina and even some from out of state. I had always said I would never tell a girl I loved her until I was sure I was ready to ask her to marry me. Even though I was sure that I was in love with Margaret and pretty confident she felt the same about me, I had not told her I loved her. I was going to save those "three little words" for that special time when I asked her to marry me. I had to find a special time and a special place to "pop the question." After only a brief moment of prayer and thought, the time and place became obvious. What could be more appropriate than in church on Christmas Eve? The church was my second home since early childhood. In fact, Miss Natalie Nunn had put me on the cradle roll right after I was born. I had followed in Warren and Ely's footsteps. Christmas Eve would be perfect, too, because I was being drawn to a closer relationship with Jesus as the years went by. Margaret also grew up at Gordon Street Christian Church, and we had similar backgrounds in our search for a deeper walk with the Lord. Daddy had grown up with Margaret's mother and father, and when Daddy married Mother in 1922, all were members of Gordon Street and good friends.

It is interesting to note that Mrs. Taylor was a longtime member of the choir and had a beautiful solo voice. She also sang at weddings, civic clubs, and various social events with "Miss Jessie" Moseley as her accompanist. "Little Margaret" also sang in the choir when she was home on weekends. One of the many things that attracted me to her was the pretty little dimple in her left cheek. I remember observing her in the choir loft and thinking, "She is really cute, and I sure do like her dimple." It was a wonderful feeling to know that the Lord had led me to Margaret and that our families were so close. My folks had known her family when Margaret was born, and they knew she was of solid background, character, and reputation. Yes, things were right and I knew it —and I was confident Mother and Daddy would be pleased. I was ready and I was trusting Margaret would be ready to give me a positive answer.

It was Christmas Eve 1962. Margaret and I had made plans to attend the midnight service at the first Presbyterian Church, which began at 11 P.M. As far as I knew, there were no other such services in town. I had it all planned. I had borrowed a key to the church from Tommy Norvill, our youth minister. I'm not sure if I told him the real reason for my borrowing the key, but he gave it to me without hesitation.

After the service at the Presbyterian Church I told Margaret, "Let's ride down Queen Street and see the lights." That was nothing out of the ordinary, but when I took a left on Gordon Street and said, "Let's go by the church for a few minutes," it may have seemed a little strange. I parked the car in front of the church. Back then, in those days, it was the custom for gentlemen to walk around and the open the car door for the lady—and that's what I did. (That's something seldom done in today's world.) We walked to the side door of the church. I then told her I had a key to the church and said, "Let's walk in and sit for a while." I knew exactly where the light panel for the sanctuary was, and so without too much trouble, we managed to turn the dimmer on enough to see the beauty of the stained-glass windows as well as the entire sanctuary. I remember saying, "Let's just sit here quietly for a while." I purposely led her to the second-row pew where the Perrys had always sat. Grandmother Perry had been hard-of-hearing, so a long established tradition for the Perrys was to sit in the second row, close to the front. As we took our seats, I made a comment that, "This particular pew has special meaning for me, and I just want you to sit here with me." We quietly looked around the sanctuary with particular emphasis on the stained-glass windows. The light was dim, but we could still make out the figures and portrayal of each window. I recall making a comment about the significance of the one with Jesus standing at the door and knocking to come in. There being no knob or handle on the outside, it meant that the only way He could come into a person's heart was to be let in from the inside. Jesus was not going to force His way into a person's heart. It was a matter of response to His knocking. He wants to come in if we will but let Him. I had already accepted Jesus and so had Margaret. As we continued to sit there next to each other, sometimes in silence and other times in softly spoken conversation, I remember thinking, "Dan, this in the perfect setting. Now's the time. Go ahead and ask her. This is why you brought her here." It was then I got up enough courage to turn to her (she was sitting on my right) and say, "Margaret, I've never told a girl I loved her because I've always said I would wait until I found the right one to say it to—until I was ready for marriage. I love you, and I want to marry you. Will you be my wife?" I frankly don't remember whether she said, "Yes" or "sure will" or whatever. All I remember after that is she gave me a definitely positive response. I don't remember any pause or hesitation in her voice. Margaret Taylor had said *yes* to my proposal, and we both were elated. We knew we were in love, and we were ready to get married! What a grand and glorious feeling! My prayers had been answered. The Lord was faithful. I had waited and the Lord provided.

Much Prayer and Guarded Patience

It was not until later that we realized a lot of people had been praying for us, especially our parents. Margaret's mother told us that one morning after it became obvious we were serious about each other, her doorbell rang. It was about 8 A.M. before she was up and around for the new day. She hurriedly put on her bathrobe and opened the front door, and there stood Daddy. She said, "Ely, what are you doing here?" As he made his way inside, he said, "Margaret, I've got to talk to you!" I don't know if he took time to sit down or not, but the conversation went something like this: "We've got to do something! What's wrong with those two! What are they waiting for? Why are they taking so long to get married?" Daddy's impatience and frustration was answered with firmness and confident assurance. She said, "Ely, you keep quiet and keep your mouth shut!" She apparently had more insight than he into such courtship matters. She assured Daddy that the best policy was to, "Stay out of their business. If the Lord wants them to get together, He will bring it about." Being widowed for over fifteen years, she had learned to trust the Lord. She offered Daddy sound advice. The Lord was in charge, and she knew it. Daddy obviously felt the Lord needed some help to accomplish His will. Thanks to Mrs. Taylor, no one ever "pushed" us to make our decision to marry. We were spared knowing anything about Daddy's impatience, but became aware of the many prayers offered in our behalf.

Shout It to the World!

I well remember how excited and elated Margaret and I were as we left the church in that early hour of Christmas Day 1962. I remember it being about 12:20 A.M. when she accepted my proposal, and we left about ten minutes later. The whole proposal process didn't take long from the time we left the midnight service at the Presbyterian Church to the time we left Gordon Street Christian Church about 12:30 A.M. We were so exhilarated and energized, we wanted to tell the whole world we were in love and wanted to be married. We wanted to shout it to the mountain tops! But we knew that was not the way it was supposed to be done. There was an orderly process we had to follow. We couldn't just go out and honk the car horn and tell everybody we saw about our good news. We had to do it the right and dignified way. First, I had to ask her mother for permission to marry her daughter. Then we had to tell my parents and brothers; then Margaret's sister, Carolyn, and her husband, Graham; then close relatives and friends. That was the proper way, and that's the way we wanted to do it.

We went through most of Christmas day with our regular routine, giving the impression to our families that nothing was going on out of the ordinary. Inwardly, we were bursting with excitement but outwardly it was "business as usual." After our traditional Christmas family meal, I'm sure my folks were in the dark, suspecting nothing, when I let them know late that afternoon I was going by Margaret's house to wish her a Merry Christmas. We went for a brief ride so we could further discuss our strategy and "plan of attack." I remember being nervous as to what I should say, but when we got back Mrs. Taylor greeted us at the door. The three of us sat in her living room a few minutes before Margaret excused herself to go to the kitchen. I remember thinking, "This is it, Dan, go ahead and do it. You've got to tell her—and ask her!" I don't remember my exact words, but somehow I got the message across that I loved Margaret. We wanted to get married, and I had come to ask her permission to marry her daughter. I remember her broad smile and beaming face as she stood up and gave me a big hug. "Yes," was her obvious answer! She was so excited when Margaret came back in the room. The three of us had a great time relishing the happy moment!

The next step was to tell my folks, so off we went to 908 West Road to tell them the good news. Mother and Daddy were sitting at the card table playing their usual game of gin rummy. When Daddy heard the news, he jumped up, pranced across the room, and exclaimed, "Well, I'm a red-headed Dutchman!" (That was his favorite expression when he got excited about surprisingly good news.) The bottom line was they were both thrilled and excited that their baby boy (now 31 years old) was going to get married to a wonderful girl whom they respected and knew would make him a wonderful wife.

Setting the Date

As the word got around, the next thing was to set a date for the big day. Margaret felt the need to finish her school year, so we were thinking maybe sometime in the summer or even early fall would be appropriate. We soon found there was a big problem with waiting that long. It seemed Mrs. Taylor and her son, Fred, had planned a trip to Europe in the summer. Fred was single and had worked in India and Italy as an architect. He also had traveled extensively in Europe and wanted to show his mother the sights. Daddy especially reasoned, and even insisted, it would not be fair for the mother of the bride to go on such a wonderful trip knowing she had to face giving a wedding for her daughter upon her return. That would really mess things up. The bottom line is we settled on Saturday, March 16. That gave us only two and a half months to plan the big wedding we wanted. I should say "I" wanted, because Margaret would have been just as satisfied with a small wedding. I had just always thought in terms of a big wedding, because I had waited this long and wanted everybody to come see me take the big step. In looking back, I can see that I was quite selfish in wanting it my way. Margaret's mother had been a widow for some fifteen years, and her funds were quite limited. Of course, Daddy was willing to help out, so the plans went forward. It was a busy time for our parents as well as Barbara, Barbara Ruth, Carolyn and close friends such as Grace Walker (Sr.) as they all pitched in to help with the invitation list and other arrangements. Margaret and I were busy, too, with her engagement picture, picking groomsmen and bridesmaids, etc.

Telling the School Officials

Margaret was on Christmas vacation from her teaching job in Raleigh. She was quite nervous about having to tell her school superintendent she was quitting her job in the middle of the year to get married. She insisted I go with her. She just couldn't do it by herself. She needed some moral support from her fiancé. She called Dr. Jesse Sanderson for an appointment and off we went. I remember Margaret being real nervous about leaving her class before the end of the year. How could he get another teacher on such short notice? Dr. Sanderson was gracious enough to take the "bad news" in stride and was even able to give us his genuine congratulations and best wishes upon hearing our "good news." Mrs. Anna B. Peal, the principal, knew Margaret was going to Kinston every weekend and was serious about her boyfriend, so the news was no surprise to her. Now that that ordeal was over, everything was on go. We could proceed with our plans!

Telling Special Friends

Telling the good news to special friends in town and out of town was fun and exciting. One of several letters I wrote was to my law school and Raleigh roommate, Tom Bennett and his dear wife of a year-and-a-half, "Blossom." Even to this day, Blossom still kids me about my announcement of "Good News Inside" which I wrote in big bold letters on the outside of the envelope. The best thing Tom Bennett ever did was to marry Blossom Thompson from Morehead City, who is over ten years his junior, and the mother of their three fine children. She has a likable personality and her Christian witness and many gifts and talents include being a pianist, soloist and Bible Study leader at Bogue Banks Baptist Church. Over the years Margaret and I have kept up our friendship with Tom and Blossom, and it is always a pleasure to be in their company.

Buying the Ring

Our family and friends were very kind and helpful as plans moved forward. Daddy knew W. A. Whitfield of Whitfield Jewelers on North Queen Street, so he was the logical one to sell us a ring. Daddy made arrangements for Mr. Whitfield to come to our house with several diamonds as well as catalogues showing engagement and wedding rings for Margaret and me to look at. Daddy knew I was personally unable to pay for what he felt would be an appropriate engagement ring for my bride. He had always come to the rescue when any of us boys needed financial help, and this was no exception. He had the philosophy that one day his estate would eventually go to his sons. Why not help them along the way, while he was still living? He wanted us to know we could always count on him to help us get started, but at the same time he was insistent that all three of us boys be hard workers and support ourselves. He had helped Warren and Ely get started, and now he was helping me. All three of us always appreciated Daddy's generosity, and I never knew of any incident where any of us knowingly took advantage of his offers of assistance. Margaret and I chose a beautiful diamond with appropriate ring setting in line with what Warren and Ely chose for Barbara and Barbara Ruth. We felt so blessed to have such a beautiful outward expression of our inward love for each other. We were honored with the usual array of parties and presents one would expect from friends and family. It was indeed a happy, happy time!

Everyone Is Invited

The big wedding we planned turned out to be really big! Even to this day, when telling others about it, Margaret kids me about "inviting everybody in town"—all the lawyers, policemen, sheriff's deputies, clients, etc. Apparently, I didn't know when or where to stop. They didn't need a formal invitation. I just said, "Come on! I'd love to have you come to my wedding." Obviously, I was insensitive to the practical aspects of putting on a wedding. I remember inviting Josh Dawson, the blind merchant who sold cigarettes, snacks, and soft drinks in a little store outside the north entrance of the courthouse. His shop couldn't have been over five or six feet square, just big enough for him, a drink box, and shelves on each wall. All the lawyers and court officials enjoyed talking to Josh during their break time. Shortly before the wedding, I was telling him about the plans for the wedding, and during the course of the conversation, I told him I'd love to have him come. It was just a casual comment at first, but when he said, "Do you really mean it?" what was I to say? Although I don't specifically remember seeing him, I was told he was among the standing- room-only upstairs crowd, all dressed up in his coat and tie.

Parties and Appendicitis

We were honored at a number of parties, including one given by Alban Barrus Jr. and his family at the Barrus Construction Company farm house; also George Bell and his mother gave us a nice formal party at her house. Warren and Ely gave me a bachelor party at the Police Pistol Range on Thursday night before the Saturday wedding. Sometime Thursday morning, I began developing a pain in my side, which grew worse as the day wore on. The only answer was to have Dr. West check me out. Although I had never had appendicitis, I could imagine he was going to tell me it was an acute case and would have to operate immediately. As Dr. West began his examination on the table, my thoughts were, "Oh, no! I can't afford to have appendicitis! I've got too much going on—my bachelor party begins in about three hours, luncheon tomorrow with rehearsal and after rehearsal dinner tomorrow night, and then the wedding Saturday night. It's too late to change all these plans. What am I go'na do?" As Dr West asked, "Does that hurt?"—when probing both my sides several times, I was holding my breath for the diagnosis. Finally, the word came, "Dan, you're all right. You're just nervous. It's just a case of nerves." What a relief! In fact, it seemed like only a few minutes later that the pain went away and I was "a new man." The bachelor party went well and the remaining activities proceeded smoothly.

The Wedding—March 16, 1963

The 8 P.M. wedding was thrilling in every respect! Miss Jessie played nuptial music. Nora Jean Hill sang "O Perfect Love" and the choir sang, "The Greatest of These Is Love," "The Lord's Prayer," and prayerfully concluded the ceremony with "The Lord Bless You and Keep You." Doug Bell did a beautiful job in officiating the service. I can well remember coming in with Daddy as my best man and standing at the altar in front of all those people as I proudly watched the twelve groomsmen, all dressed in their black tails, one by one, come down each aisle to the beat of the traditional wedding march; and then came the lovely bridesmaids in their floor-length dresses of French blue georgette. As each groomsman and bridesmaid approached and passed me, I remember my smile was as wide and beaming as it could be. What a thrill it was! But when Miss Jessie let out all the stops on the organ, and all the people stood, and I saw Margaret start coming down the aisle with her Uncle Loxley Radford, I felt like singing with all the gusto of the full organ, "Here Comes the (my) Bride!" I knew this was a "once in a lifetime thing," so I treasured the moment!

Margaret's sister, Carolyn, was the matron of honor and the maid of honor was Ellen Whitaker. The bridesmaids were Barbara and Barbara Ruth, Griff Wooten Montgomery, Sylvia Courie, Peninah Brown, and Miriam Quarles. The groomsmen were Warren, Ely, Graham Hodges, George Bell, Alban Barrus, Z. A. Collins, Charles Wickham, Jimmy Tyler, Lewis Sutton, Tom Bennett, Jim McLeod, and Bob Hook. Margaret's niece, Margaret Wood Hodges, and my niece, Betty Blaine Perry, were junior bridesmaids. Special risers were built to accommodate the groomsmen.

Gordon Street Christian Church was packed to overflowing with standing-room-only both upstairs and downstairs. The reception followed in the church fellowship hall. Even though it was crowded, it was exciting to know that we had so many supportive friends to attend. Only sometimes afterward, while in a reflective mood, did it hit me that I might have overdone it. We didn't have to have it that big. Margaret, as well as our families, went along without objection, even though I recall several comments emphasizing how big it was going to be. I was obviously insensitive to any such words of caution.

Our family and friends were so gracious in wanting everything to go smoothly and exactly like we wanted it. Lillian and Marion Parrott gave us a very nice after-rehearsal dinner the night before, and Grace Walker (Sr.) provided us an after-reception get-a-way party at her home where we changed from our formal attire into traveling clothes to begin our honeymoon.

The Honeymoon Begins

Margaret and I felt blessed to have our wedding go off without a hitch. We were thankful to have had so many friends to help us celebrate not only our wedding day but also the many events leading up to it. The excitement of celebration was all well and good, but now it was time to get away from the crowd of well wishers and finally be by ourselves. We looked forward to our ultimate destination of Jamaica. Ely and Barbara Ruth had a great experience there on their honeymoon and highly recommended it to us. Again Daddy helped us with the expenses. Harvey Carrow was in the travel agency business, and he recommended we spend our first night in Smithfield at the Howard Johnson Motel. It was an hour's drive from Kinston, so it must have been close to midnight before we arrived in our "Just Married" decorated White Chevrolet Impala. I remember that proud but strange feeling of checking in for the first time as "Mr. and Mrs. Dan E. Perry." Someone had given us a bottle of wine for celebrating our first night together. We had chosen not to serve any alcohol at either the church reception or at the get-away party at Grace's, so we looked forward to a "little glass of wine" as being a nice way to relax in the privacy of our own room. The only problem was we couldn't find a corkscrew to open the bottle. We looked in every conceivable place where we thought a corkscrew might be, but none was to be found. For some reason we were unable to make contact with the front office, resulting in "no wine being served." Neither one of us were big wine drinkers, so it was easy for us to look at our plight with humor. We just laughed if off and said it would be something we could tell our grandchildren.

A Matter of Priority

Margaret and I had prayed that our honeymoon would be the special time that God meant it to be. I remember some time after our engagement we had a serious conversation while sitting on the floor in front of an open fire in the family room at 908 West Road. Mother and Daddy had told us good night and retired for the evening. In the stillness of that special time, I remember telling Margaret that I was deeply in love with her and looked forward to my life with her as my "one and only." Even though that was true, I felt that if we had our priorities right, God should be number one and she should be number two in my life—and the same with her. The point was, if we put God first, even above our love for each other, then according to His Word,

He would bless us and provide for our every need. I was referring, of course, to MATTHEW 6:33: "But seek first the kingdom of God and His righteousness, and all these things shall be added to you." We agreed that, yes, seeking God in everything we do should be our number one priority. Even though we obviously didn't always follow through with our desire to put Him first, at least we recognized that should be our overall goal in life.

On the Way to Jamaica

Our second night was spent at the Holiday Inn in Charleston. I remember the cost of the room being only $17.00, a far cry from today's prices. Daddy had told me if I allowed $100.00 a day for room, food, gas, and entertainment, I should be well within a reasonable budget. It turned out he was pretty much on target. We weren't extravagant, but we did have a good time! From there I believe we may have spent two nights at the Cloister Hotel in Sea Island, Georgia. Daddy had taken the whole family there on the memorable trip to Florida in about 1947 or 1948 before Warren married Barbara. We had taken our golf clubs and our family foursome enjoyed playing that championship course. In looking back, I'm amazed at how all five of us traveled to Florida and back with five sets of golf clubs and baggage.

As Margaret and I continued on to Miami, we stopped off at the country club in Winterhaven, Florida, just to look at the putting greens and observe the beautiful landscape. As we got out of our car in the parking lot, I recognized someone who looked familiar. It turned out to be Margaret West, daughter of Dr. B. C. and Peggy West of Kinston. She was living in Winterhaven with her husband and was about to play a round of golf. It was good to see her and to spend a few minutes chatting about acquaintances in Kinston as well as being brought up to date about her life as a Floridian.

Before flying to Jamaica, we spent one night at a luxurious hotel in Miami. My best recollection is that the cost of the room was about $45.00 or $50.00, which was about three times our Charleston room. With the night club and meal that night, our daily budget of $100.00 was shot all in one fell swoop. One night of that kind of living was enough for us small town folks.

Perfect Timing—in Jamaica

Our accommodations in Jamaica were just right in every way. The seashore setting was everything and more than we expected. I recall it being late afternoon when we checked in. The bellhop was showing us our ground floor suite of rooms with adjoining picturesque terrace over looking the calm sea. The sun was just about to set. As we stood on the terrace taking in the balmy, restful atmosphere, we noticed a man approaching from our left walking up the beach. He seemed to be dressed neatly as a waiter with white coat, black tie, and dress shoes. There was no one else on the beach. We had the scene all to ourselves, except for that one man walking toward us with a tray resting on his uplifted hand. Our eyes were drawn to him, and Margaret and I both commented and wondered why a waiter would be walking up the beach all by himself, with no one else in sight. As he got closer, we were even more puzzled when he seemed to be walking directly toward us. What was this all about? Margaret and I just stood there dumbfounded as he stopped right in front of us. As he lowered his tray his only words were, "Compliments of Mr. George Bell." I can still hear his words in broken English: "Compliments of Mr. George Bell." Needless to say, we were stunned! George had sent us a bottle of champagne for our first night in Jamaica. The timing was perfect. The setting was perfect. It was a total surprise and a moment to remember!

We had a delightful seven days in Jamaica. The weather, food, and accommodations couldn't have been better. Native singing and music featuring steel drums as well as bongo drums made us know we were in "another world"—all by ourselves. Our favorite song at the time was "Yellow Bird," made popular by Harry Belafonte. Several weeks before we were married, we took a couple of dance lessons from Doris Whitfield who taught us how to cha-cha and rumba, as well as other rhythm dances we managed to put into practice. We rode bicycles, drove to Ocho Rios in a rental car, went swimming and sailing, and even did some snorkeling in the clear, blue, coral waters of the bay. Our time was spent enjoying each other's company. It was everything a honeymoon should be. We were aware that it was all a blessing from God. We reflected upon the love of our families and friends who gave us such a wonderful send off to begin our life together.

We were in a world of our own while we were on our three-week honeymoon. Although we called home once or twice to let our folks know we had arrived safely and were doing fine, we were negligent about staying in touch on a more regular basis. After Jamaica, we took five or six more days to get home. We didn't want to rush to get back to the real world. Shortly after arriving home, Ely gently scolded me for not being in touch more often. He informed me (out of Margaret's presence) that Daddy had been hospitalized with an acute attack of diverticulitis. He said he could have died, and no one would have known how to contact us. I say "gently scolded me" because that was the way it was. He was dead serious in making his point, which leads me to say that I don't recall any time during our adult years that Warren, Ely, or I ever really got mad at each other. Even in our early childhood days when we would occasionally "get mad" (as brothers will from time to time) because we couldn't get our way, it was always short lived. Usually in a matter of minutes it would all be over and back to normal. I am reminded quite often of how blessed I was to have had two brothers I could love and trust.

For the first six weeks following our honeymoon, we lived in Margaret's house at 1104 Pollock Street. While her mother was touring Europe with Margaret's brother, Fred, we had the whole house to ourselves. In late June 1963, Daddy helped us buy Leonard and Sue Oettinger's house at 1002 Clifton Terrace. It was there we got to know and establish a lasting friendship with Betty and Hugh Stroud who lived across the street. Our other neighbors were John and "Cricket" McLean on the corner, Martha Bovinet on the corner across from them, and William and Ann Harvey next door. Down the street a little ways was Attorney Fred Harrison and wife, Ruth. Our minister, Doug Bell and wife, Glenna, were on West Road a few doors down. It was a quiet, one-block street with a good neighborhood where we could start our married life together and raise a family.

About this time, Mrs. Taylor became known as "Ma-Ma" and Mother and Daddy became "Mom-E" and "Daddy Ely." Grandchildren have a way of assigning new names. Carolyn and Graham had Margaret Wood and Bob; and Warren and Barbara's four came in rapid 1,2,3,4 succession: Wes, Betty Blaine,

Jimbo and Ashley. It was a happy and exciting morning on June 12, 1964, when I called Mom-E with the words: "Elizabeth Ann Seipp Perry has arrived!" We didn't know in advance if it would be a boy or girl. All we knew was that we were so excited and thrilled to welcome our first born, a beautiful, healthy, little girl we named Elizabeth Ann after Mom-E. Our son Daniel (Daniel Elijah Perry Jr.) was born July 23, 1966, and Radford (Margaret Radford Perry) was born June 12, 1973. We felt blessed to have three fine, healthy children.

Chapter XXIII

MY SEARCH CONTINUES

The first ten years of our marriage from 1963 through 1973, were marked with events and activities, which enhanced my search for truth and spiritual growth. The good news was that Margaret and I both were on the same wavelength. She was just as much a seeker as I. We both wanted the same experience of knowing God and His Son better. We wanted our everyday lives to reflect a spiritual walk with the Lord. We didn't know a lot of the answers, but we sensed there was something more to life than what we had, even though we had a great life together. We knew it had something to do with our relationship with God, but we weren't quite sure what it involved. We were reminded from time to time of Saint Augustine's words, "We are restless until we find our rest in God."

The Rule of 56

Soon after settling in at 1002 Clifton Terrace, I was made aware of a most unusual problem. In fact, I had never heard of this particular marriage problem before, nor have I since. Here are the facts: When I became engaged to Margaret just after midnight on Christmas morning 1962, I told her I loved her and that I had reserved those three little words for her and her alone. Although I had gone out with many fine girls during my dating years, I had never told any of them, "I love you." I had saved those special words for the special girl I was to marry and spend the rest of my life with. I remember telling her it was just the greatest feeling to look her in her eyes and say, "I love you," and really mean it. I didn't have to hold back a thing. I just let the words flow continuously while we were together. My first words to her when we woke up in the morning were, "I love you." Before we had breakfast, I must have told her several more times. At the breakfast table, several more times. Before leaving for work, at least two or three more times. When I came in the door for lunch, my greeting always included, "I love you!" The same when leaving and then returning for supper. I guess a psychologist would say I was obsessed with those "three little words." From time to time, they flowed in triplets—"I love you, love you, love you." Margaret obviously appreciated my expression of love, for she usually responded with, "I love you too," or, "I love you too, honey."

To say our marriage was going well is really an understatement. It couldn't have been better, but one day Margaret got right serious with me by saying, "Dan, I want to tell you something, and I hope you will understand what I'm going to say." At that point, I wasn't sure if I should be concerned or what. Had I said something or done something that offended her? Did she have a problem that I needed to know about? She continued by saying, "Dan, I know you love me, and I love you, too. I appreciate you telling me, but you don't need to tell me *all the time.*" It was then, for the first time, that maybe, just maybe, I realized that maybe I was overdoing it. Maybe I was telling her too many times. Maybe I was overdoing my "I love yous." We had a good laugh about it, and I jokingly said, "I'm sorry, I'll try to ease up and restrain myself. I guess it can get a little old after a while." It was all in fun when I said, "I didn't realize I was saying it so much. I wonder how many times a day I say it?" It was then I decided to go though a normal day's routine and just count the times. In order to get an accurate count, I would have to try to act normal—not make up times nor hold back times I told her I loved her. And that's what I did the next day—from the time we woke up to the time we went to bed I kept an actuate count of the times I used the words, "I love you." Well, would you believe it turned out to be 56 times? When I realized it was that many, day in and day out, I could understand her concern. Margaret had every right to lovingly "call me down." The advice often given that "you can't tell'um too much" might be thrown out the window in special cases such as mine. Daddy had told all three of us boys on numerous occasions that, "you need to tell'um you love 'um, because they love to hear it." I knew it was sound advice. I just over did it! Bankers will tell you about the *Rule of 72* as a multiplying factor in determining compound interest. Brother Warren kidded me by saying maybe I ought to call my story the *Rule of 56* as a way of establishing the limit of "telling'um too often."

The Power of Letting

One morning before Margaret was awake; I had a revelation, which I believe was from the Lord. All of a sudden, I found myself sitting up in bed. I may have been half asleep, but at the same time I was alert enough to see in my mind's eye four words in capital letters. The words were **THE POWER OF LETTING.** They were in bold print, and I've never forgotten them. I remember thinking at the time, "Is the Lord trying to tell me something?" As I contemplated the meaning over the next few days, I began to understand that God was telling me that I needed to *let* Him have His way with me. In thinking about the word "let," I understood that it also meant to *allow* or *permit* the Lord to use me, implying willingness on my part to acquiesce and submit to His will for my life. If I would only let Him have His way, He would use me to glorify Him and His plan for my life. Over the years I've tried to keep "the power of letting" in the forefront of my mind, even though I am continuously falling short of my goal in so many ways. Selfishness and ego are traits of the flesh, which stand in the way of yielding my will to His will. If I could just learn that the Lord's will is always better than my will. The object is first to find out what His will is, and then follow though by *letting* His will be done. By *letting* Him have His way, His master plan and purpose not only for me but also for all believers will be fulfilled. I was learning there is power in *letting*. The more we "let Him", the more fulfilled we become.

The Divine Plan

Sometime during the first year or so of my married life, Daddy gave me a small pamphlet by Glenn Clark titled *The Divine Plan*, which was published in 1959. It was only an eight-page pamphlet, but it seemed to go along with my "The Power of Letting" revelation and has given me many thoughts to ponder over the years. On the cover, Glenn Clark says, "The germ of this Plan was planted as a seed one spring and has been growing and unfolding ever since.... Transplant it into the garden of your heart by daily reading and meditation and it will grow and bear fruit, and great will be the fruit thereof." Over a period of time, I memorized all eight pages. In the interest of space, I will give you only the first page:

> I believe that God has a Divine Plan for me. I believe that this Plan is wrapped in the folds of my Being, even as the oak is wrapped in the acorn and the rose is wrapped in the bud. I believe that this Plan is permanent, indestructible and perfect, free from all that is essentially bad. Whatever comes into my life that is negative is not a part of this God created Plan, but is a distortion caused by my failure to harmonize myself with the Plan as God has made it. I believe that this Plan is Divine, and when I relax myself completely to it, it will manifest completely and perfectly through me. I can always tell when I am completely relaxed to the Divine Plan by the inner peace that comes to me. This inner peace brings a joyous, creative urge that leads me into activities that unfold the Plan, or it bring a patience and a stillness that allow others to unfold the Plan to me.

Over the years, I began to understand that in order for me to fully realize and benefit from *The Power of Letting*, I needed to develop my relationship with my heavenly Father. The better I know Him, the more He can teach me and lead me into following *The Divine Plan* He has for my life. I also began to see that the more I followed His unique plan for my life, the more true enjoyment and fulfillment I would experience on a daily basis. This was all confirming my understanding of Saint Augustine's words about being "restless until we find our rest in God."

Glenn Clark gives his explanation of what I'm trying to say on page seven of his *The Divine Plan*:

> I believe that the chief essential of life is to keep in touch with the Father, and let the Divinity that is in me manifest through

me. I believe that the whole world about me is full of beauty, joy and power, even as it is full of God, and that I can share it and enjoy it if I attune myself to my Divine Plan and am inwardly open toward God and outwardly helpful toward men. I shall ask my heavenly Father and Friend, who dwells within me and who has given me this vision of life, to give me His help in its realization and to help me share it with others that it may bring peace and happiness to many.

It was some years later that I began to realize that as truthful as Clark's *The Divine Plan* sounded at the time, there were a number of things missing. He didn't say anything about Jesus' sacrificial, atoning death on the cross as being a part of His Divine Plan for me. He didn't say anything about my need to accept Jesus as my Lord and Savior. One of the first scriptures I learned as a child was JOHN 3:16: "For God so loved the world that He gave his only begotten Son, that whosoever believes in Him should not perish but have everlasting life." I also learned that God doesn't desire that anyone should perish; and according to ROMANS 10:13, "For whosoever shall call upon the name of the Lord, shall be saved." By our own disobedient choices, we can thwart God's desired will that we all be saved and have eternal life.

Some years later, I began to understand the truth about God's providential plan, which includes how He causes negative things, even disasters, to work together for good for those who love Him. According to Glenn Clark, "Whatever comes into my life that is negative is not a part of this God-Created Plan." I learned that God not only *allows* negative things to come into our lives, but at times He may even *cause* certain "bad" events to happen to us for the purpose of fulfilling His provincial will for our lives. No matter what happens or what we think, the truth is God is ultimately sovereign and in control of all things. My further (though limited) understanding of that truth was not realized until much later in life.

Although Glenn Clark and his *The Divine Plan* did not present the full picture of how God works in the lives of His children, it did serve a divine purpose for my life. Even though it is full of erroneous new age philosophical thinking, it did serve a purpose in showing me that God does, indeed, have a master plan for me, which includes His providential will, His desired will, His conditional will, His permissive will, and His highest and perfect will. My job was (and is) to discover what it's all about and to follow His plan and purpose for me, so I can be the person He intended me to be from the beginning of the world. It's a life-long journey of discovery. My daily prayer, even as I write these words, is to let His master plan unfold in my life. I find it to be exciting and exhilarating, as well as challenging.

My Most Humbling Experience

I have never experienced such a feeling of humility and unworthiness as I did when I was asked to become an elder at Gordon Street Christian Church. As an elder himself, Daddy had been assigned the task of informing me. One Sunday morning in the fall of 1964 as I was about to enter for the worship service, Daddy was standing at the door of the sanctuary. He led me away from the others, saying he wanted to talk to me in private. He got right to the point. He said, "Dan, the elders want you to join them to be an elder of the church." If he made further comments, I don't remember them. All I remember is I had been asked to be an elder—a spiritual leader of the church. I was stunned, almost in shock. I didn't know what to say. In fact, I don't think I said anything. I just stood there as I thought to myself, "They want me to be an elder? But I'm only 33 years old. I'm not old enough for one thing—but most of all, I'm not qualified. I'm totally unworthy to serve as an elder of the Church." I couldn't see myself standing at the communion table on Sunday morning offering prayers for the bread and wine (grape juice) representing the broken body and blood of Jesus. I was just too young. Elders were known to be the older men of the church. They were looked up to and highly respected for their wisdom and leadership in the community as well as the church. Over the years I had admired Daddy, Galt Braxton, Jesse Olgesby, Mayor Guy Elliott, Dennis and George Loftin, Kermit Humphrey, Curtis Howard, Speight and Albert Stroud, and many other distinguished gentlemen as they served at the table. I was not even in the same ballpark with them. It even occurred to me that all of them were either graying or had totally grey hair. In fact one or two were almost bald. I thought especially of Galt Braxton, editor of the *Free Press*, who, in my eyes, had always been an old man with white hair ever since I was a little boy. How could I ever stand where he stood at the communion table? I still remember that unworthy, unqualified feeling that permeated my whole body as I stood there with Daddy. I don't remember when and where I gave him my answer. I was later told I was the youngest elder anyone could remember at Gordon Street. I remember as an adolescent in a discussion about the church, I innocently asked Daddy why he was not an elder. He said he had been asked, but had turned it down, thinking that he was not qualified. (He did accept upon being asked the second time.) Be that as it may, after prayerful consideration, I decided to accept, thinking it would be an opportunity to grow spiritually as I matured with age. My best recollection is that Leslie Noble and one or two others were also ordained at the same time in a special laying on of the hands ceremony during a Sunday morning worship service. It was my most humbling experience ever, and I shall never forget it. I remember Phil Crawford and Daddy as being two of three elders who laid their hands on my head as I knelt with the other candidates. Fred McCoun was minister at the time.

The Blanche Moseley Sunday School Class

Being asked to teach the Moseley Class at Gordon Street was a blessing, which added significantly to my spiritual development. I think it was about 1965 that Ma-Ma mentioned to me that the Moseley Class needed a teacher and they wanted me to fill the spot. I had been teaching the high school class since 1962 and maybe it was time for a change. I had understood there would be no problem in finding a replacement for me, so I accepted my new assignment as a challenge and further opportunity to study and present the lessons from a different perspective. Hopefully, it would also provide a more mature approach to teaching. As it turned out, I stayed with the Moseley Class some thirty-three years. I enjoyed the weekly study and preparation as well as the actual teaching of the class. It was composed of older ladies, all of whom supported and encouraged my efforts. I'm sure some took in the essence of the lessons more than others. At the same time, I'm also sure I learned much more than any of them.

I enjoyed and looked forward to the lessons, whether they involved studying a particular book of the Bible or a specific area of study with selected scriptures. Almost from the beginning, I opted to use the *Standard International Sunday School Lesson* series, which I purchased at the local Bible and Book Store on North Queen Street. I felt that the material coming from the national office of the Christian Church Disciples of Christ presented the lesson more from a liberal social gospel approach than from the true biblical approach. I was more interested in what the Bible had to say rather than what man's opinion about it was. I didn't want to teach a diluted version of God's Word. I wanted to teach what the Bible said, not what others thought it should say.

I shall always be thankful for the privilege of teaching the Moseley Class, for it was the forerunner of my desire to delve into the Scriptures and become involved in formal Bible study as a lifelong pursuit. As of this writing, I can think of only a handful of surviving members of the class I taught from 1965 to 1998. Most of them were faithful members of the class and seemed to appreciate my teaching style. I always started each class session with the words: "Good morning! God loves you and I love you!" Then I would say, "Let's turn our eyes upon Jesus and look full in His wonderful face." We would then all look at the picture of Jesus on the wall and sing the chorus to the familiar hymn, "Turn your eyes upon Jesus. Look full in His wonderful face, and the things of earth will grow strangely dim in the light of His glory and grace."

I made an effort to stress, particularly in the later years of my teaching, that each of the ladies should know for sure that when she takes her last breath on this earth, her spirit, will be forever in heaven with the Lord. That's what the Bible says, and that's what I taught. The Bible also teaches that the only way to get to heaven is by believing and trusting that Jesus Christ shed His blood on the cross and died to save us from our sins.

For many years, Margaret and I would have the class for a Christmas party at our home. As the ladies got older and the membership dwindled, we had to make other arrangements. Back in the 1960s and 1970s, the class roll showed about 35, and on a good Sunday we would have as many as 30 or so to fill the room. The pianists included Jessie Moseley, Helen Dail, Grace Kilpatrick, and Hattie Mae Skinner. We had a good time singing the good old hymns of the church. The ladies and I used to love the way Hattie Mae added her personal frills to make the old hymns come alive. Some of our favorites were, "He Lives," "Blessed Assurance," "Every Day with Jesus," "Love Lifted Me," "Great Is Thy Faithfulness," "The Old Rugged Cross," and "In the Garden." One Sunday as we were singing one of our favorites, "Are Ye Able Said the Master?" our minister, Buddy Westbrook, came in and started singing with us. He said we were making such a joyful noise, he just had to come in and join us!

Class members included Sutton Wells (longtime president), Lillie Wilkins (longtime secretary), Margaret Taylor (Ma-Ma), Margaret Perry (my wife and the youngest member who joined the class with me), Carolyn Hodges (Margaret's sister), Hattie Mae Skinner, Mary Lockhart, Helen Pope, Velma Humphrey, Thelma Spell, Grace Kilpatrick, Geneva Hood, Velma Lee, Margaret Gower, Mollie Hart, Nellie Pollock, Helen Fordham, Helen Watson, Ann Noble, Stella Mewborne, Mildred Johnson, Anna Harper, Marjorie Kennedy, Blanche George, Louise Cox, Sarah Bendle, Alwilda Blow, Katherine Medlin, Martha Hall, Annie Laurie Edwards, Helen Fields, and Ann Lassiter.

Full Gospel Business Men's Fellowship

The Full Gospel Business Men's Fellowship played a major role in my spiritual development. I think it was the fall of 1967 that Daddy read *They Speak with Other Tongues*, a book which emphasized the up and coming charismatic movement. Pentecostal in nature, it is the story of one man's discovery of what speaking in tongues is all about. It was fascinating to Daddy, and he passed it on to me. He and Mother had been "all around the world" searching for the meaning of life. He had read most all of the writings of Joel Goldsmith. He had been to England and corresponded with Brother Mandis and Brother Conrad. These men were considered to be mystics, at least in some fashion, and were fascinating to Daddy. From what I could understand, they believed that direct knowledge of God and spiritual truth is attainable through intuition, meditation, and insight. There may have been some measure of truth in what they were teaching, but as time went on, I began to see there was something missing. I didn't see any emphasis on the shed blood of Jesus and the need to believe and trust in His sacrificial death for the remission of our sins. Daddy thought that Joel Goldsmith had the answer, and he even gave Warren, Ely, and me each a set of Goldsmith's books. He made a brief study of Buddhism and some of the other eastern religions. In their trip around the world in 1953, he had been to India and Japan and met some top businessmen to learn about their success and religious background. One particular industrialist in India by the named of Ramnoth Podar became a special friend. They corresponded frequently up until shortly before Daddy's death in 1968.

The point of all this is that Daddy was constantly searching and reading about spiritual matters and the true meaning of life. This new book *They Speak with Other Tongues* was interesting enough that he wanted to learn more about tongues and the charismatic movement. A lawyer from Richmond by the name of Charles Maurice was mentioned prominently in the book. Daddy made a point of calling him and making an appointment to drive to Richmond to take him and his wife, Helen, out to dinner. I had also read the book, and knowing of my interest, he asked me if I wanted to go with him to meet Charles and Helen, to find out more of what they believed. We had a delightful meeting with them. Charles told us his testimony of how his life had been changed and how he had been led to make a list of all the people he had offended for one reason or another. He either called or personally saw each one to ask forgiveness so as to make things right. In answering Daddy's question about the Full Gospel Business Men's Fellowship, he said, as the Bible says, "Come see." He told us about a regional meeting in Washington DC coming up in February. He advised us to go see for ourselves.

Actually, our first Full Gospel meeting was some time prior to the regional meeting. It was a local chapter meeting in Greenville. Daddy, Margaret, and

I went. I remember two things about the meeting: a song and the speaker. It was a beautiful blond lady who sang an equally beautiful song I'd never heard before, "I'd Rather Have Jesus." The meaningful song started

> I'd rather have Jesus than silver or gold;
> I'd rather be His than have riches untold.

The featured speaker was the now renowned Pat Robertson from the Virginia Beach area. He was unknown to us at the time, but his amazing testimony told how God had used him to start his *700 Club* TV program. It was in the early stages of development and was little known by most people at the time. As his story unfolded, he told us how he had yielded his life to the leading of the Holy Spirit to do God's will. I was impressed to the point of seeing the further need in my own life to *let* God have His way with me. His point was "Not mine but Thine be done."

The Regional Full Gospel meeting was to be in February 1968, so Daddy made reservations at the hotel where the meeting was to be held. Daddy, Warren, Ely, our minister David Alexander, and I all drove up together for the memorable weekend. The atmosphere of the love of God in the three-day event was entirely different from anything we had ever witnessed. The first speaker on Friday night was David DuPlesis, who was known as "Mr. Pentecost." He supposedly was a student of the Pentecostal movement and was highly respected in Full Gospel circles. His topic for the night was, "The ABC of Christian Living." He made the analogy of how a person learning to read must first learn his ABCs. Similarly, if a person wants to learn to *love* the way Christ loves us, he must first learn to *forgive* as God forgives us. Thus the ABC of Christian living is *forgiveness*. He captivated his audience with example after example of the truth of his point. We heard every word of his hour-and-half talk, which seemed like only 20 or 30 minutes.

Before the Saturday morning session got started, we were sitting at our table observing what was about to take place in the large banquet hall. We noticed the founder of the Full Gospel, Demos Shakarian, was talking to several men at the elevated head table. Then, for no apparent reason, he descended from the stage and walked slowly in our direction. I would estimate there were some 350 to 400 people in the audience. We were seated at a table about four-fifths of the way back. I don't recall him stopping to talk to anyone along the way. All I remember is he walked directly to us, shook our hands, and welcomed us to the meeting. I remember being impressed by the fact that the number-one man in Full Gospel International would take the time to pick out a bunch of strangers to introduce himself. He was Armenian by birth, very easy going, soft spoken, and gentle in spirit. After a brief cordial conversation, he made his way back to the head table to start the meeting. The session began with singing and praising the Lord in ways we were unaccustomed to hearing. There was prophesying and speaking in tongues. The main speaker was John Osteen, who, I believe, is the father of the TV evangelist, Joel Osteen. In giving his testimony, he talked about being baptized in the Holy Spirit and speaking in tongues, etc. At the end of his talk, there was a time devoted to laying on of hands and praying for those who wanted to receive the gift of tongues. Since I was open to the idea, I was prayed for and spoke in a language not my own. Don Evans, an attorney from Rocky Mount, was one of the participants praying for me. I remember having my honest doubt as to whether it was a genuine experience, but I was told to accept it and claim I had received the baptism of the Holy Spirit. The Pentecostals believe that being baptized in the Holy Spirit is an empowerment by the Holy Spirit to enable the Christian to be a better witness for Christ. They say it is a separate experience from the salvation experience of being born again. It was later in my "walk with the Lord" and study of God's Word that I came to understand and believe that when a person accepts Christ as his Lord and Savior, he receives the Holy Spirit into his life. At that moment he is born again, and has the Holy Spirit living within him. When you have Christ living within you, you've got everything you need. It's a matter of appropriating the power that is already dwelling in us. It then becomes a matter of being sanctified, which is the process of daily conforming to the image of Christ. I later learned that God's main purpose in the life of a believer is that he be conformed to the image of His Son. In other words, God's highest will for His children is that we become in practice what we already are in position. Even though *in position* I am a child of God, *in practice* I don't always act like it, because I am still in the world and influenced by worldly ways.

A number of people we knew were at the Regional meeting, one of whom was Betsy Glenn as well as some of her friends from Greenville. After the evening session, she invited us up to her room for a party. When she said "party," for some reason I was thinking of something other that what she had in mind. When we got to her room, there was, indeed, a party, but it was not the usual social event one would expect. There were eight or ten others sitting around in her room talking about the Lord and what was taking place in Full Gospel circles. That type of unusual party became a more common occurrence as I became more involved in Full Gospel matters.

Daddy's Search Was Over

I could sense that Daddy's brief involvement with Full Gospel led to the fulfillment of his search for the meaning of life. What was his conclusion? What had he been looking for all these years? The answer was wrapped up in the person of Jesus Christ. He concluded that it was through Christ Jesus, the long awaited Messiah, that he could not only have abundant life here on earth but also have everlasting life in heaven when his earthly existence was over. He discovered that his faith in Jesus' sacrificial death on the cross was the only way to eternal life—not just *a way*, but *the only way!*

After our trip to Washington in February 1968, Daddy lived less than five months. During those last few months, it was obvious he had found the answer. His lifelong search was over. All of his looking around and reading about other religions and variations of Christian beliefs finally led him to the truth. He discovered that Jesus was right when He said,

> I am the way, the truth and the life;
> no one comes to the Father,
> but through me. JOHN 14:6

Whether Daddy knew it or not, he was fulfilling the prophecy of Jeremiah some 600 years before Christ, when he proclaimed the words:

> You will seek Me and find Me,
> When you search for Me with
> all your heart. I will be found
> by you, says the Lord.... JEREMIAH 29:13,14

I Was a Different Person

I came away from that regional meeting with a passion to witness for Christ and give testimony to the power of God in my life. I believe my first public word of testimony was to a small group of Christians at someone's house in Greenville. I had been asked to give my testimony. I remember making notes on a yellow pad. Being my first time, I was quite nervous and didn't want to forget anything. I'm sure I was not very impressive, but somehow the word got around that a lawyer from Kinston had something to say that was worth hearing. It wasn't long before I began getting invitations to give my testimony to the various Full Gospel chapters in the area. It was about this time that I became active in the local chapter and in a couple of years was elected president. I spoke at Full Gospel meetings in Greenville, Goldsboro, New Bern, Morehead City, Greensboro, Charlotte, and Wilmington. I was also asked to speak to the chapter in the Shenandoah Valley as well as Richmond. Each time I was basically giving my testimony, giving witness to the fact that even though I had achieved a certain level of success and popularity, there was a certain emptiness within my being that could only be satisfied by the power of the Holy Spirit living within me. I never thought I was much of a polished speaker, but somehow the Lord used me. When invited to speak to the Greenville, South Carolina, chapter, I made a point to get an appointment with Oliver B. Greene, an evangelist whom I had heard on the radio from time to time. I wanted to find out what made him tick. He was most cordial in welcoming me. After our ten or fifteen minute conference in his spacious office, he gave me a tour of his other facilities. I was impressed with the size of his warehouse of books and materials, including a massive printing press and all that goes with it. His daily radio ministry included the offering and distribution of what seemed like countless books and pamphlets he had written. Before I came into my "deeper walk with the Lord" I remember making fun of his preaching style when hearing his radio program. I didn't know how to appreciate what he was saying and the way he said it. Later, I learned that all he was doing was preaching from the Bible. What he said was true, even though I didn't understand it all at the time. He has long since died, but his taped radio ministry continued for many years thereafter, and may still be going strong.

Sometime in the 1970s Herbert Pate, Dave Adkins, and I and several others were invited to Raleigh to tape a five-minute testimony for Demos Shakarian's nationally syndicated Full Gospel TV program. We met at the old Holiday Inn on Hillsboro Street. The high-rise circular building still stands even though the motel ownership has changed. Soon afterward, Judge Harrell from Wilson and I were invited to appear for an interview with Pat Robertson on his *700 Club* TV program. Judge Harrell had been speaker at one of our local meetings. Other speakers we had in Kinston included Don Basham, author of *Face up with A Miracle*; Merlin Corothers, author of *Prison To Praise* as well as many other praise books; Judge Kermit Bradford of Atlanta; Dan Malachuck, International Director of Full Gospel; Rev. Jim Brown, Presbyterian minister from Ohio who later moved to Goldsboro and married Ruth Edgerton; Don Evans, attorney from Rocky Mount; Tommy Tyson; Gene Tyson; and Tommy Lewis.

Business Men's Prayer Breakfast

I don't recall Herbert Pate being present at that regional meeting, but it was about that time that he became highly interested in Full Gospel. He had some spiritual needs in his life and Full Gospel was meeting them. In 1969, he and Andy Pipkin started the Business Men's Prayer Breakfast, which met every Tuesday morning from 7:00 to 8:00 at King's Restaurant. It was a time of food, fellowship, singing, testimony, and prayer. We would have anywhere from 12 to 25 men, all with an interest in spiritual matters and growing in their walk with the Lord.

Some of the members, along with Herbert and Andy, included Warren, Ely, and I, David Adkins, Earl Hughes, Tommy Lewis, Robert Eubanks, Wallace Lewis, Ben Barrow, Paul and Pete Miller, Ben Raeford, Bobby Suggs, Bobby Brinson, Ralph Lewis, Johnny Jenkins, Quenton Stroud, Lindy Jones, Dallas Foscue, and Prescott Spigner. (I had to get some help in remembering the names by calling Herbert at his home in Morehead).

Camp Farthest Out

C.F.O. was another organization in the 1970s that attracted the attention not only of Margaret and me but also many of our friends. We met once a year at the Blockade Runner in Wrightsville Beach. We heard speakers such as Jim Brown, Tommy Tyson, Al Durance, Horace Hilton, Joe Petree, Wayne McLean and Tommy Lewis. It was a time of relaxation and spiritual renewal. I served on the board for a few years. Some of the attendees included: Bill and Virginia Hill from Wilmington (Bill was a law classmate of mine at UNC), Margaret Harvey, Virginia Evans, Sally Howard, Carolyn Dunn Miller, Nannie Hodges, John and Katherine Stackhouse, Alice Faye (Jay), Neva Wallace, Ruth Whitaker (Guthrie), Mable Mock, Thornton and Lou Hood, Carolyn Hodges, Betsy Glenn, Carolyn Massey, and Myra Hodges.

Vernon Hall Mission

One of the great ministries in Kinston in the 1970s and 1980s was that of Tommy Lewis at Vernon Hall Mission in Kinston. Vernon Hall is a majestic house located on the hilltop of a seven-acre tract of land at the corner of Herritage and Capitola Streets in Kinston. Felix and Margaret Harvey had generously donated the property in 1969 for the purpose of ministry and teaching God's Word to any and everyone who would come. Tommy Lewis had been called into the teaching ministry in a rather miraculous conversion. He had been a bicycle mechanic and repairman at Spears Sporting Goods. Even though his formal education was quite limited, the Lord anointed him with a most effective ministry for teaching the principles of the Bible. He developed incredible insight for the practical aspect and application of the true, everyday meaning of the Gospel message. People came from all over the area to sit under his teaching. On cold winter Thursday mornings, a group of mostly ladies would gather around the wood-burning stove in the den at Vernon Hall to listen to Tommy's down-to-earth proclamation of the Gospel. His simple, humorous way of expressing himself was easily understandable, yet profound, and held the attention of all who heard him. Margaret, Carolyn, Ma-Ma, Neva Wallace and her mother, Eolene Whitaker, Ruth Whitaker (Guthrie), Margaret Harvey, Dean and Steve Johnsey, and Dottie Edwards (Carter) were among those who attended. Tommy would teach to a full house on certain nights. They came from Greenville, Goldsboro, New Bern and the surrounding area to listen to the simple truth of his teaching. Most of those who came were Full Gospel members, all seeking to know more about God's Word and to learn how to put it into practice in their daily living. Tommy was also a popular speaker at area and regional Full Gospel meetings as well as C.F.O. and various church gatherings. His teaching ministry was widely known and appreciated. Dottie Edwards (Carter) became a special friend and popular speaker, sharing her testimony of how the Lord was working in her life.

Daddy's Death in 1968

I believe it was sometime in April 1968 that Daddy's chronic cough become noticeably worse. Barbara had asked me whether I was aware of his more frequent cough. He had always been one to clear his throat, but now it had developed into a more pronounced cough and was becoming more obvious to everyone. Through the years, people used to say they could always tell if Daddy was at movies or in a crowd by the way he cleared his throat. Dr. West had checked him out and ran various tests before diagnosing him with lung cancer.

I never will forget one morning when he and Mother were in the driveway before driving off for treatment. He said with a confident overtone in his voice, "Boys, don't worry about me. I'm going to win either way it turns out. If the Lord decides to heal me, that means I'll have a good chance to witness to others of His healing power. If He decides to take me home to be with Him, that's where I want to end up anyway. So I can't lose either way." With his medical background, Ely Jr. knew enough about the ravages of cancer to know that Daddy's time was short. Even though we were naturally saddened at the prospects of his coming demise, we were comforted by the preparation he had given us. He was not afraid to die, for he understood it was a part of life. We are born; we live; we die. We all have the same fate. He had told us on one particular occasion in 1962 during Elton Trueblood's week of preaching at Gordon Street, "Boys don't worry about me lying up there on that cold slab; that ain't going to be me. That'll be my body, but I'll be gone! I don't want you to cry at my funeral. I want you to sing, "Glory Hallelujah!" His confidence in knowing where he was going—that he would be with God forever—helped us all get through that difficult time.

I remember the last time I saw him at home at 908 West Road. It was shortly before he was taken to Parrott Hospital for the last time. I had gone to see him on the way to work on the morning of my 37th birthday, July 2, 1968. As I entered his bedroom, he smiled and wished me a happy birthday and then sang, "Happy Birthday." His words were clear even though a little weak. He then told me, "Dan, you've been a good son and I'm proud of you." I told him he had been a good daddy, and I thanked him for all he had done for me. On another occasion several years before, during a serious conversation, he talked about his blessings and how God had given him a wonderful wife, three fine boys, and all the comforts of life. He told me he would eventually be passing along all his earthly possessions to us three boys. I was so glad I was able to tell him in return that no matter what he leaves us when he passes on, the thing I will cherish the most is the love and spiritual example he set for each of us as head of our family. I'm glad I told him that more than once, because it was true. He may have had his faults, just like all of us, but he paved the way not only for Warren, Ely Jr. and me, but also our wives and children, to see the purpose and value of what life is all about. He taught us that money and possessions are worth nothing if you don't know the Lord. By example he taught us to work hard and always show love and respect for our family and fellow man. While in the hospital, three days before he died, he dictated several letters to some special friends he had known over the years, one of which was Norman Vincent Peale. He told him and the others of the seriousness of his condition but not to worry, for he was going to be all right. Warren, John Hines, and Simon Sitterson had helped him get his will and other affairs in order. Although we had prayed for healing, the Lord was evidently ready to take him home. On July 7, 1968, he died at Parrott Hospital with all the family around him. Mother was holding his hand as he took his last breath and peacefully slipped into the presence of his heavenly Father. Our minister, Dave Alexander, held an impressive funeral at Gordon Street Church with many friends and associates in attendance. I remember the Trustees of Atlantic Christian College, of which he was a member, sitting as a group, as did members of the Kinston Rotary Club. Although it's been almost 40 years since his death, I still think about him frequently and the influence he (and Mother) had on my life. Warren, Ely, and I were always aware of how blessed we were to have had such wonderful parents, who not only loved us, but expressed their love and example in so many ways.

Chapter XXIV

TRYING TO PUT IT ALL TOGETHER

The Essence of Christianity

I think it was sometime in the early 1970s that I first heard a particular definition of Christianity that has stuck with me all these years. My interest in spiritual and religious matters was at the forefront of my mind. Anytime there was a Christ-centered speaker in the area, I was there to hear what he had to say. I had heard that the brother of Debbie Thompson (now Wallace), would be speaking to students at Parrott Academy, and I was encouraged to go. His name was Dick Day, and he was a representative of Campus Crusade for Christ. There were several teachers and other interested adults in the crowd, so I didn't feel out of place. His basic message was centered on the need for the students to know Jesus as Lord and Savior, and to follow His example throughout life. In those days, talking about Christianity in the schools was no problem. My memory is vague about the details of his talk, except for one thing. He said, "Christianity is not a religion—it's a relationship." That was the first time I had heard it explained in those terms. He went on to say, "It's not religion we need, it's a relationship." I don't know how much the students got out of his message, but it certainly rang a bell in my heart. The truth of that statement and the thought of having a personal relationship with Jesus Christ developed over the years into the main thrust of my own spiritual growth. It was much later, as I began to gravitate toward a serious study of the Bible, that I came to understand fully God's overall plan for my life. He wants us to grow more like His Son. He wants us to conform, on a daily basis, to the image of Christ Jesus. It's a lifelong process, but it all begins with *a relationship.* Dick Day was absolutely right. "It's not religion we need, it's a relationship."

Whoever Heard of Praying with Clients?

As my interest in spiritual matters grew, I was led to carry it over into my law practice. Most all young lawyers start out with "the indigent list," and I was no exception. This was a list of lawyers who were appointed to represent indigent clients charged with crimes. They were unable to pay, so the state paid the lawyer's fee to represent them. The pay was not all that great, but it provided an opportunity to get exposure and experience in the courtroom. I found it both fascinating and interesting work as I interviewed clients seeking to determine the true facts. Sometimes this was difficult, but as I tried to understand their background and develop a relationship with them, most of them would open up and tell me the truth (even though there were some exceptions). My standard initial approach was "I can help you better if I know the truth."

The more I dealt with those in trouble with the law, the more I realized they needed something more than just legal advice. They needed spiritual advice. They lacked peace and joy in their hearts. I could tell they were confused as to their sense of values. Like so many of us, they were worldly in their life style. They thought that money and possessions were the source of all pleasure and contentment. Their lives were geared toward violence, deception, sex, and drugs. They were looking in the wrong places for the wrong things. Although the background of these indigent clients may have been different in some respects, they all seemed to have the same basic need for spiritual counseling and advice. As I began to explain how Jesus had changed my life and given me peace and joy, "which passes all understanding," many responded positively and knew exactly what I was talking about. Others knew very little about Jesus and required further explanation. I don't remember any of them being turned off to the point of refusing to listen to a simple explanation of the Gospel message.

In most cases when I interviewed clients in jail, I would take them to a private room where we could discuss their case. I first tried to get to know them and establish a relationship of trust and understanding to help them open up and tell me the full story. Then I would lead into my personal testimony and their need for a personal relationship with Jesus. I was able to point out their need for forgiveness of their sins. For those who were obviously guilty, I would tell them they would have to suffer the consequences for breaking the law. I also told them that if they were in the right relationship with Jesus, God would forgive them and give them a new start with a new life that could and would be fulfilling and rewarding. I most always ended with a prayer. For those who did not know Jesus as Lord and Savior, I would first lead them in the sinner's prayer.

I also represented clients with domestic problems. Some involved separation agreements, others divorce and property settlements, and others with just plain marital squabbles that needed advice and counsel. In most of these cases, I applied my rule thumb, "They don't need legal advice as much as they need spiritual advice." Some did need legal advice, but they needed spiritual advice more. In looking back, I'm sure my legal advice may not have been as effective as it should and could have been. As lawyers, we each handle our clients differently. Some are wiser than others. Some are more successful than others. It's the same way with doctors and politicians and preachers. Some are better than others. We're all different. As an honest assessment of my success as a lawyer, I would certainly not put myself in the category as being near the top, or even close to the top—maybe average or even below average. Maybe if I had spent more time in studying the law and in preparation for trials and in the representation of clients, I could have been more "successful." The main thrust of my interest was in spiritual matters and raising a family. Even as I sought to "put first things first," I can see where I made plenty of mistakes along the journey through life—and I'm still making them.

I think my most successful day in court was the time I had three criminal jury trials in Superior Court, which took up the whole day's calendar. All three were "not guilty" verdicts. You win some and you lose some, but on that particular day everything fell into place. Whether they were truly innocent, no one knows except the client. Under our system of laws, when the jury finds you not guilty, you are deemed to be innocent as charged. I had plenty of guilty verdicts along the way. There were times when I was embarrassed by not being able to answer the judge's questions or by the way I represented my client; but the time I had three "not guilty" jury verdicts in one day was my most successful as a trial lawyer.

Moving to 1209 Sutton Drive

We lived at 1002 Clifton Terrace from June of 1963 until we moved to 1209 Sutton Drive in the spring of 1969. We had always admired Ruth Bowles' house, not only for the nature of the brick house itself, but also because of its unusual appearance. It was white, but red brick showed all over the place. To the casual observer it needed painting, but to Ruth it was a matter of design with a purpose. Ruth was known to be a lady of great taste, and apparently she liked the "unfinished look." There was a certain appeal about it that is still admired even today, long after we moved in 1975. Elizabeth was five and Daniel was three at the time. We loved our neighbors. Tom and "Buzzy" Benton were next door with their children, Greg and Amy. Across the street were Ed and Mary Lassiter and their children, Keen and Leigh. Adjoining us at our backyard were Tom and Woodard Heath on Walker Drive, with their children, Tom, Louise, and Woody. We had many fun times raising our children on Sutton Drive. The Lord was good to us, and we will always treasure those times. We may have remained longer had not Radford come along. Her first bedroom was Ruth's old sewing room. That's where we put her crib. When she grew out of her crib, we managed to find just enough room for a small youth bed. It was a perfect fit, but leaving hardly enough room to move around.

Elizabeth kids Daniel, even to this day, about the early morning of June 12, 1973, when they heard they had a new baby sister. I was with Margaret at the hospital awaiting the delivery of our third child. Mom E was staying overnight with Elizabeth and Daniel who slept in a separate room. When I called Mom E to tell her the good news, she woke Elizabeth first. She was very excited at the thought of having a baby sister born on her ninth birthday!

When they woke Daniel (age seven), all he could say was, "You woke me up to tell me that?" He pulled the cover over his head and went back to sleep in a gruff. Boys will be boys! Margaret remembers that Elizabeth weighed 7 pounds and 11 ounces at birth. Radford was born in the morning at 7:11, exactly nine years after her sister, almost to the minute.

Jaycees Kept Me Busy

Although I was heavily involved with Full Gospel and church matters, I was also busy with the Jaycees and other community affairs. I found the Jaycees provided an opportunity to develop leadership skills in dealing with people and community projects. We called ourselves "Young Men of Action," for our purpose was to pursue actively various projects that would benefit the community as well as the state and county. I wanted to be president of the Kinston club not only to promote myself, but also Kinston and Lenoir County. Although I had been a Jaycee only a year, I ran for vice president, thinking I might as well get started. The next step would be president. Boy, did my ego suffer a blow when I found I had lost the election! I was on my honeymoon when I called home to get the word. I had lost to Bob Curtis! I realized later that suffering such a defeat served a good purpose, just as did failing the bar exam. I was not accustomed to failure. The lesson learned was to use failure as a means for growth rather than a direction of defeat. The next year I ran for president and won. I am reminded that Cabell Ramsey of the Kinston club became president of the State Jaycees only after losing the previous year. We all learned a lot of valuable lessons from membership in the Jaycees, for which I am grateful.

One of the things our Kinston club was known for back then was that we had nationally known speakers for our annual Distinguished Service Award (DSA) banquets. We had such notables as Edward R. Murrow, Paul Harvey (twice), Norman Vincent Peale, and Catherine Marshall. I won the DSA when Edward R. Murrow spoke. I remember being speechless when responding. About all I could say was "thank you" as I sought to make a few acceptance remarks. Some years earlier, Warren had also won the Distinguished Service Award. We were privileged to have had both Norman Vincent Peale and Catherine Marshall stay with Mother and Daddy at 908 West Road when they spoke in Kinston. My parents had developed a close friendship with Dr. and Mrs. Peale and were even invited to accompany them on a trip to Jerusalem and the Holy Land.

Shortly after aging out of the Jaycees, I joined Rotary in May 1968, only a couple months before Daddy died. Our minister, David Alexander, joined at the same time. Warren, Ely Jr., and I enjoyed our brief membership in Rotary with Daddy, for he and some of his cronies provided a lot of spark and camaraderie for the weekly meetings. Daddy, Warren, and I each served as president of the Kinston Rotary Club. It was a little unusual to have a father and three sons in Rotary at the same time. It was probably even more unusual to have four brothers—Speight, Albert, Walter, and Hugh Stroud—as Rotarians all at one time.

I Was Too Busy!

With all the many organizations and activities, I was busy, busy, busy! If I wasn't going to Full Gospel meetings, I was going to a church committee meeting. If it wasn't the Jaycees, it was the Salvation Army. If it wasn't the Boy Scouts, it was the Flynn Home. If it wasn't this, it was that! But what about Margaret and our two, and later three, young children? Margaret was mighty patient with me, in fact maybe a little too patient. I seemed to be away from home too many nights, and even mornings, going to meetings, all in the interest of being a good citizen in the community. On Tuesday mornings I would be at the Prayer Breakfast; Tuesday night it was supper with the Jaycees; Wednesday mornings it was the Elder's Prayer Breakfast. Then it was Rotary for lunch on Thursdays. Scattered in between were all these other meetings. They were all worthwhile, but there comes a point when enough is enough. At times Margaret might make a comment indicating maybe I ought to slow down, but it was Barbara Ruth who really got my attention. Evidently, Margaret had shared her feelings with Barbara Ruth about my being away from home so much. Barbara Ruth was calm yet firm as she told me privately one day of Margaret's concern. I immediately knew what she was talking about. I don't know how much slowing down I did, but at least I became aware (and rightly so) that I needed to spend more time with my wife and children. They should come first. I had to learn that even in religious matters I can be too busy. Even if I am president of every organization in town and receive all the top awards and recognition—and even though they are all related to spiritual growth—they amount to nothing, if my love and relationship with my wife and children suffer. One of the greatest lessons I learned in life (and am still trying to learn) has to do with priorities and putting first things first. This was brought to light not only in my family background with Mother and Daddy's example, but also in reading what became known as "the little red book" and memorizing the thirteenth chapter of 1st Corinthians at an early age.

Scouting Played a Major Role

When we three boys were growing up, Daddy encouraged us to join the Boy Scouts and work toward achieving the highest rank of Eagle. He knew the value of scouting and its positive influence for building character in the lives of young boys growing toward manhood. I think it was 1939 when Warren was one of the first boys in the Kinston area to get his Eagle Badge. He was in Troop 43 with J. T. Sutton as scout master. Ely Jr. reached Life Scout but for some reason didn't get the final few merit badges required for Eagle.

When I was presented my Eagle Scout badge in a special ceremony at the Court House in 1946, Daddy gave me a $25 Savings Bond. Ever since then until he died in 1968 he made a point of giving every Eagle Scout to go through the Caswell District a similar bond. His purpose was to encourage young boys to go into scouting and benefit from the many character-building lessons it teaches. He also wanted them to be diligent and persistent in their pursuit of the highest rank of Eagle, and then to reward them for their accomplishments.

The Little Red Book

In 1956 Daddy came across a little red book entitled *The Greatest Thing in the World* by Henry Drummond. It is based on Saint Paul's great dissertation on love, the thirteenth Chapter of 1st Corinthians. In the first paragraph Drummond asks the question, "You have life before you. Once only you can live it. What is the noblest object of desire, the supreme gift to covet?" His conclusion was the same as Paul's: "And now abideth faith, hope, love, these three; but the greatest of these is love."

In essence "the little red book" says—and Daddy wanted every Eagle Scout to know—that you can win the Eagle badge, you can win all kinds of other awards and trophies, and do all kinds of good things, and be given wide publicity for your efforts and accomplishments, but if you don't have love in your heart for God and your fellow man, it all amounts to nothing. Listen to the King James Version of how Paul states this familiar chapter:

> Through I speak with the tongues of men and of angels, and have not Love, I am become as sounding brass, or a tinkling cymbal. And though I have the gift of prophesy, and understand all mysteries and have all knowledge; and though I have all faith, so that I could remove mountains, and have not Love, I am nothing. And though I bestow all my goods to feed the poor, and though I give my body to be burned, and have not Love, it profiteth me nothing.

The Bond, The Book, and The Picture

In addition to the savings bond and the little red book, Daddy also inserted a wallet size picture of Jesus in the book. On the back of the picture was the well-known inscription "One Solitary Life," which starts out: "Here is a man who was born in an obscure village, the child of a peasant woman...."

When presenting the picture he would often quote the last paragraph:

> I am far within the mark when I say that all the armies that ever marched, and all the navies that ever were built, and all the parliaments that ever sat, and all the kings that ever reigned, put together have not affected the life of man upon this earth as powerfully as has that one solitary life.

In his last will and testament, Daddy made a provision stating his desire that his family continue the tradition of presenting each Eagle Scout to go through the Caswell District a savings bond, a little red book, and a picture of Jesus. Down through the years, this has become known as the *Ely J. Perry Memorial Award* and is, to this day, a part of each Eagle Scout Court of Honor. It has been our special privilege as a family to be able to honor Daddy Ely's wishes, for we, too, recognize the value of scouting in the lives of young boys.

Distributing the Little Red Book

Before he died, Daddy told me he had passed out literally thousands of these books, together with the picture of Jesus and "One Solitary Life," throughout many parts of the world. The only place he could get the pocket edition of *The Greatest Thing in the World* was in England. He would order them by the gross. I think almost every member of Gordon Street had a copy. Each time he went to a meeting or spoke to a group, he would give a book and picture to everyone. In his travels, he would carry an ample supply. He told me that on one occasion while he and Mother were traveling in Europe, he was sitting next to a man on a train. In the course of their conversation, he gave him a little red book. To his surprise, the man responded, "Hey, I already have one, and I believe you are the same man who gave it to me two years ago in Germany!"

It was his tradition to write in each book the following:

Keep this with you and read it often. Let it become a part of your
daily living, and when you do, you will find the greatest thing
in the world.

As time permitted he would personally write in each book, but by necessity most of the time his secretary would do it, stacks at a time. After Daddy's death, we continued to order the books from England by the gross for our own personal distribution. For many years at the last Rotary meeting of the year, Warren, Ely, and I would present a book and a picture to each new Rotarian joining the club in the previous 12 months.

Several years ago they stopped printing the pocket edition as well as the traditional picture of Jesus with *One Solitary Life*. We still give the smallest copy of *The Greatest Thing in the World* we can find to the Eagle Scouts as well as the best substitute picture of Jesus and *One Solitary Life*.

The Little Red Book in Russia

Back in 1982 Warren and Barbara traveled to Russia on a tour with a group of lawyers and judges. They took fifteen little red books with them. This was seven years before the wall was torn down ending the Communist rule. When the KGB in Moscow searched their luggage, they confiscated thirteen of the books leaving two for Warren and Barbara. When asked to explain what the books were all about, Warren told them they were about the greatest thing in the world—love. The KGB was apparently trying to link Daddy's handwriting to some type of code or message about plotting against the Communist government. The KGB asked them if the books have anything to do with the writings of Tolstoy, their one-time friend and now enemy. The bottom line is that after several hours delay, not only in Moscow but also in Leningrad, they were able to get back 11 of the 13 confiscated books in Leningrad before leaving the country. The KGB kept two books, for what purpose I don't know. Hopefully they may have read them and discovered that love, not man's selfish ambition and power, is *the greatest thing in the world.*

A Thank You Letter from a Casual Friend

It is amazing how God has used the little red book and the message of I Corinthians 13 to change the lives of those who come to understand the truth of its power. Shortly before Mother died in May of 1983, she gave me a letter she received from a man to whom she had given a copy of the little red book. She and the man happened to be attending an inspirational meeting where they were to hear a particular speaker.

The handwritten letter speaks for itself. It is postmarked August 20, 1974 (with a ten cent stamp). The return address shows "Inter-Church Team Ministries, P.O. Box 34, Bridgewater, Mass. 02324." It was addressed only to, "Mrs. Elizabeth S. Perry, Kinston, NC 28501." The stationary heading reads, "From the desk of Albert R. Freeman."

The letter reads:

Dear Elizabeth:

It is over two years since I have seen you and I think it is about time I wrote to you to let you know about the little red book you gave me on July 2, 1972.

That book changed the course of my whole life and ministry. Before going to sleep on July 2, 1972 I read the book through. The Lord awakened me at 3:00 A.M. the next morning with these words ringing in my ears. "Albert, I have not called you to preach, I have called you to love."

The world is more in need of loving than preaching and the Lord has been pleased to make me a lover of mankind and all his creations.

The little red book is with me constantly and I have distributed about 200 copies around New England.

How I praise and thank God that He led you to give me that book. It is one of my most prized possessions. I long to see you again and to share with you once more the love of Christ which is shed abroad in our hearts.

God bless you and keep you in the center of His great love.

I love you and praise God for letting me know you and receive of His love through you. Albert.

I read the letter to several of my Eagle Courts of Honor to emphasize the importance of love in the lives of all of us. Some ten years or so after Mother gave me the letter, I tried to locate Mr. Freeman by telephone and correspondence but never could make contact. I suppose he'll never know (at least on this earth) what a blessing his letter was, not only to Mother, but also at a later date to me and many others. Yes, love is truly *The Greatest Thing in the World*.

Chapter XXV

FAMILY LIFE AT 1305 PERRY PARK DRIVE
1975–2002

When Radford came along as our third child, we were prompted to build our house at 1305 Perry Park Drive. One day back in the early 1950s, Daddy took Warren, Ely, and me to show us available lots in the Perry Park Subdivision. All that area was mostly undeveloped at the time. Warren picked a beautiful lot on Sweetbriar Circle backing up to Catfish Branch and the country club. Cousin Jack Carey designed his family's house, in which they were blessed to raise their four children (Wes, Betty Blaine, Jimbo, and Ashely), to adulthood. Their first house was at 1506 Perry Park Drive, which was later sold to Jesse and Jack Fields. Ely picked the lot at the corner of Perry Park Drive and Greenbriar, which was later sold to Jim and Dot Tyler and built at 1104 Walker Drive. Ely and Barbara Ruth were blessed to raise their two children, Ely III and Ruth-E, to adulthood. Their first home was at 1603 Waverly Drive and later moved to Ruffin Terrace before they built on Walker Drive. Ely had gotten William Harvey to design his house, and we did the same. Ely and I both had Calvin Jackson and son Bobby to build our houses, and it was a real pleasure working with them.

Margaret and I and our three children have many pleasant memories living at 1305 Perry Park Drive. We probably wouldn't have built until much later (and maybe never) had not we felt we needed the extra room when Radford came along. We raised rabbits both at Sutton Drive and Perry Park Drive. Our first dog was Frieda, a miniature dachshund, who had one litter of puppies. I don't remember if we sold them or gave them away, but it was fun for all of us to watch the puppies grow until they were weaned. Later Muffie, a black, sweet-tempered cock-a-poo, came into our lives. She was absolutely the best pet we could have had. We spent many hours throwing a tennis ball for her to retrieve. I enjoyed her as much as did the children, for she would greet me with a wagging tail and bark when I came home from work. She would sit beside me at my easy chair in total contentment as I read the paper and watched the news. The first of our two cats was Tootsie followed by Calico.

We Had a Lot of Good Help

To be able to raise three fine children was a special blessing for us. A second blessing was in having Calonia Davis, who worked for us for over 20 years, not only doing domestic work in our home, but also helping us with the children. She was a willing and able friend who was loyal in every way. Everybody loved "Nonie." She was always kind and gentle with the children. She stayed with us at Morehead when it was our turn to use the cottage at 1701 Shackleford Street. She loved to fish with us on the pier, for she was one of the family. When thunder and lightning caused concern and even fear for us and the children, Nonie could be found in her room sitting quietly in her chair. She'd say not a word, but just sit quietly—her way of calming the storm.

We were also blessed over the years with a lot of other good help. One early morning in 1936, Duffy Simmons showed up at our back door at 908 West Road. Our former yard man had recently died, and Duffy was asking to take his place. Daddy gave him a chance, and it turned out to be a long-lasting association. Duffy was with us for 32 years until Daddy died in 1968, and then an additional ten years or so until age caught up with him. I remember spending many good times with Duffy as he worked in the yard and taught me many things along the way. He even helped with some of my Boy Scout merit badges, teaching me how to identify various birds, cattle, and plants. Evans Miller worked for Warren for many years, but was also helpful for all of us. He was a good, solid worker who was friendly and kind to all the Perrys. Louise

Bannister worked for Mother for many years in the home. Her specialty was cooking deep-fried cornbread so thin you could see through it. I'm sure it wasn't all that good for us, but it was so delicious—almost like eating dessert with collards, corn-on-the-cob, and field peas (and don't forget the tomatoes, cucumbers, and scallions). All the family used to gather at Mom-E's at least one day a week for that good ol' country eating. After Louise had a stroke and was unable to work, Beulah Becton worked for Mom-E for a number of years. She was another good worker who became a member of the family.

Elizabeth and Tootsie

When our cat Tootsie was run over by a car, we all felt the loss, but Elizabeth had an especially hard time. In my effort to console her, I went to her room with a piece of candy. I thought maybe I could be of help in her time of grief. Sometimes our good intensions are not good enough. When I entered her room, she was on the bed teary eyed and sniffling with her face buried in her pillow trying to be a big girl, dealing with her loss. As I sat on her bed beside her, my first words were, "Elizabeth Ann, I have a piece of candy for you." As she slowly raised her head, I was glad to see her stop crying. Maybe I was on the right track—but I soon learned better. When she saw the candy, she suddenly started bawling louder than ever. I immediately realized my mistake. It just so happened that the piece of candy was a Tootsie Roll. Even though my intensions were good, that innocent reminder was just too much for her! I guess she could still see poor Tootsie lying in the street, never to be played with again.

Daniel and the Big Carrot

One of our favorite stories about Daniel was when he was about six years old. We had heard about the new Hyatt House in Winston Salem and had seen a picture of the glass elevator and its spectacular view of the spacious surroundings inside this luxurious hotel. We decided to splurge by taking the children for a weekend experience. The elevator was all it was cracked up to be as we rode up and down, time and time again. The food was equally impressive and enjoyable as we basked in the lap of luxury. The first night we went through the highly decorated buffet line with all types of food and amenities. Daniel had liked raw carrots since he was a little fellow. Maybe he got his taste for carrots from watching Bugs Bunny chomp on a big one as he uttered his famous words, "Aye, What's up Doc?" As we went through the line, we noticed one of the table decorations included a monstrous carrot with its green shoots prominently displayed. It looked like it had come right out of the garden without having been washed. As we took our seats at our table, we saw Daniel with his tray of food with that big display carrot in the middle. Apparently, we hadn't paid much attention to what Daniel took, but he sure thought that carrot was his for the taking. After we all had a big laugh at Daniel's innocent blunder, I sheepishly returned the oversized carrot to its proper place on the buffet table.

I was captivated by the man entertaining us in the dining room as he played some of my old favorites on the Hammond organ, such as "In the Good Old Summertime," "Let Me Call You Sweetheart," and "By the Light of the Silvery Moon." I loved his style, which reminded me of the dances at the old Dunes Club when I was growing up in the 1940s and 1950s at Atlantic Beach. I was both surprised and thrilled to learn that he was, indeed, the one who had played for many of those dances. When I told him I was from Kinston, he said, "Oh yes, I also used to play the organ at the old Paramount Theater there in Kinston." I then recalled those wonderful times growing up back in the late 1930s and early 1940s when he would thrill the audience both before and after each picture show. He was a real attraction. Many times I was just as excited about his organ music as I was about the picture show itself. (Note for the modern-day reader: What you call a "movie" or "cinema" today was called a "picture show" or "moving picture" back in the old days.)

Radford and Crutches

When Radford was in about the second grade, she came home from school one day complaining that her leg was hurting. I was at work so I was unaware of the incident. Margaret checked her out pretty carefully, but was unable to determine the nature or exact location of the pain. All she knew was Radford kept complaining that her leg hurt, and obviously something was wrong by the way she was limping. Margaret was at her wits' end. Radford kept complaining, "Oh my leg hurts. It hurts so bad. Call the doctor, Mamma! Call the doctor!" It was late in the afternoon, but maybe Dr. Ed Cooper would see her before he left his office for the day. Margaret had no choice but to give it a try. Ed, in his usual accommodating way said, "Don't worry about coming to the office. I'll drop by your house on the way home and take a look at her."

What a relief it was to have Ed make a house-call on such short notice. Not every doctor would take the time to show such interest. After a cordial greeting, Ed began to examine his patient with the usual questions: "How did it happen?" "Where does it hurt?" "Does it hurt when you move it this way?" "How about this way?" Margaret could tell by his puzzled look that the good doctor was somewhat baffled at Radford's responses. Ed then very casually said, "Now, let me see you walk to the other side of the room and then return here." That was a logical request, so Radford proceeded to follow the doctor's instructions by slowly limping across the room. With every step, she moaned and groaned with pain. Ed then asked her, "Which leg did you say was hurting?" "This one," she replied as she groaned still again while holding her left leg.

Margaret says that Ed tried to restrain himself so as not to embarrass Radford, but when leaving the house, he let go with a big laugh at what had happened. Radford had limped on the wrong leg. She limped on her right leg, not her left. Ed was laughing, but Margaret was mortified at the thought of having her friend make a house-call for no reason at all. Ed assured her she need not be embarrassed, for it was worth it to him to have a big laugh. He said it made his day!

The bottom line is that Radford had a friend at school who showed up on crutches that day. Apparently, all of her fellow students were sympathizing with her to the point of making her the center of attention. It made her feel good to have friends feel sorry for her. Radford could possibly have gotten away with her scheme of having crutches prescribed had she known to hold her right leg rather than her left. Ed and Margaret, and all of us, still get a big laugh when we relive the day Radford set her heart on going to school on crutches.

A Personal Miracle

I think it was sometime in the mid 1970s that I experienced a miracle. I had heard many of the Full Gospel speakers tell how God had healed them of various diseases and physical ailments, but I had never experienced a personal healing. Oral Roberts and his healing ministry were widely known. I had read Katherine Khulman's book, *I Believe in Miracles,* relating accounts of how God had used her as a channel for His healing power. Her book basically was an account of numerous documented cases of miraculous healings.

When we heard she was to hold a healing crusade in Greensboro, we decided to go see for ourselves. The service was held in the large hotel banquet room, which was packed to overflowing. Miss Khulman was standing on stage ministering about God's love and healing power. It seems like she spoke for only a few minutes when all of a sudden she stopped and said something like, "Someone is being healed of a hearing loss in his right ear. Come on up and claim your healing." Then she continued: "Someone over here is being healed of blindness in her right eye." Then pointing to the other side of the room, she said, "Someone over here has had a spinal condition. You have been healed. You don't need your back brace. Come on up and claim your healing." Time and time again she would call people to the stage to tell of their healing. Margaret and I sat in amazement. We had heard about such miracles, but now we were seeing them first hand. Then it happened! She said, "Someone has been healed of bursitis in his right shoulder." After a few seconds with no response from the audience, again she said, "Someone has been healed of bursitis in his right shoulder. Come on up and claim your healing." My thoughts were directed to a situation in my own life that had temporarily slipped my mind. For several months, I had been suffering from increasing pain from bursitis in my right shoulder. It didn't bother me unless I raised my arm up to shoulder level. The higher I raised it, the more excruciating the pain became. In fact,

I couldn't raise it more than a few degrees above the horizontal plain. As Katherine Khulman kept insisting that someone had been healed of bursitis in his right shoulder, I thought to myself, "Could she be talking about me? I didn't come here for a personal healing. I just came to see if somebody else would be healed." I looked around to see if anyone else was coming forward. Instinctively, I raised my right arm to see if it was true. What a feeling of relief and amazement I had as I began pumping my fist high above my head! My shoulder and arm felt as light as a feather. I continued to pump it up and down, sideways, backward and forward. I was totally pain free for the first time in probably six or eight months. In a matter of a few seconds, I found myself running down the aisle up to the stage, still moving my arm in every direction. After a brief testimony as to my former pain and present healing, I returned to my seat, filled with lingering amazement as well as thanksgiving. We saw many other people come forward to claim their miracles during the one-and-a-half to two-hour session—people with crutches, walkers, and braces; the lame, the deaf, and the blind. They all appeared to be genuine at the time, even though I have no way of knowing for sure. But this I do know: I was healed of my bursitis apparently in an instant, for I had felt it earlier that morning. That was over 30 years ago, and I have been pain free ever since. I have no explanation other than it was a miracle from God.

Chapter XXVI

PRECEPT BIBLE STUDY COMES TO KINSTON

It is my understanding that Precept Bible Study came to Kinston in 1984 through the influence and efforts of my nephew and nieces Jimbo, Stewart, and Betty Blaine. Jimbo had for many years been interested in spiritual growth and Christian-related activities. Somehow, he found out that Caroline Colson was teaching a Precept Bible Study in Greenville and suggested that Stewart, who was also interested, join the class.

Betty Blaine and husband, Les Worthington, had moved to Greenville because of his job in the tobacco market. Their stay of some eight years was long enough for the fulfilling of a Godly purpose. Betty Blaine was working in the alumni office at ECU when God's providential hand led her to join the class along with Stewart. It was called "Precept upon Precept," by Kay Arthur, who had been dramatically converted from a life of immorality, frustration, and depression. It was an in-depth study of God's Word, and the concept was to learn verse by verse what the Scripture says, then determine what it means, for the purpose of applying it to the student's life. The three basic questions in the study were, "What does it say?" "What does it mean?" and "What does it mean to me?" It was a matter of *observation, interpretation,* and *application.* It took a lot of serious word study to understand the true meaning of the original Hebrew and Greek words as found in the Old and New Testaments. By learning one precept at a time, and then building on it, precept upon precept, the student would gradually come to know the Creator of the universe and His love for all mankind through His only begotten Son, Jesus the Christ.

When Betty Blaine returned to Kinston, she and Stewart persuaded Caroline to drive to Kinston once a week to lead a Precept class for a small group of ladies at Vernon Hall. Caroline agreed on one semester only, after which they would have to find another leader. Betty Blaine and Stewart Perry knew that Kinston needed a teacher of its own, and after much prayer and soul searching, Stewart talked Barbara Ruth into leading a class that met weekly at Vernon Hall. In addition to Stewart and Betty Blaine, others in the class included Margaret, Juliet Barrus, and Betty Stroud along with several others. Her class later moved to Saint Mary's Episcopal Church. B-Ruth became seriously dedicated to the task, and it wasn't long before a handful of ladies soon blossomed into a room full. She later moved the class to her home on Walker Drive where she now teaches two classes each week, one on Monday afternoon and the other on Monday night.

My Personal Involvement

Soon other teachers came forward, and formal Bible Study in Kinston was well on its way. Margaret had been involved first as a student and then as a leader. I was busy with work, Full Gospel, church, and community affairs as well as trying to be a good husband and father. I could see the interest and excitement in Margaret as well as all the others as Bible Study was beginning to be "the talk of the town," at least in certain circles. Not everyone was taken by it. Some of our church friends were turned off. I think they thought it was too fanatical, and certainly too time-consuming.

My first Bible Study was with Ruth Bock in the spring of 1987. She had a class that met at her house on Tuesday nights. It was a Kay Arthur study course called "In and Out," which was not as in-depth and time-consuming as the more rigorous "Precept upon Precept" study. The idea was to "take it in and live it out." I think it was a study of II Peter. Whatever it was, Ruth did a great job in leading us through the lessons. I remember Ely, Leonard Oettinger, and Alice Tingle as well as Ruth's son, Jonathan, being in the class of about 15 or so. I knew I was where I should be. I became increasingly aware that a study of God's Word was essential for spiritual growth and development, to become the kind of man God intended me to be. It wasn't long before most all the Perry family living in Kinston was involved in formal Bible study, either as a leader or student: Barbara and Warren, Ely and Barbara Ruth, Margaret and I, Wes and Stewart, Betty Blaine, Jimbo and Joan.

Precept Training in Goldsboro

Goldsboro was catching on to Precept Bible Study about the same time as Kinston. Margaret and I decided to attend a two-day Precept training course at the Presbyterian Church in Goldsboro. Representatives from Precept headquarters in Chattanooga were on hand to lead the sessions. It was both interesting and informative. On the way back to Kinston, Jimbo and Betty Blaine rode with us. As we discussed the day's activities, I remember Jimbo telling Margaret and me that he hoped that some day we would lead a Bible Study class. My first thought was that I was a Sunday school teacher and had more then I could handle with all my other activities. I also was thinking that even if I personally got involved as a leader, it would probably be for no more than a year, just to have the experience.

As it turned out, Margaret started leading a class in our home beginning in the fall of 1987, at which time we studied two semesters of the Book of John followed by two semesters of Genesis, two semesters of Hebrews, and four semesters of Romans. She continued by leading classes in Daniel, II Thessalonians, Revelations I and II, Habakkuk, Covenant, Philippians, The Beatitudes, The Life of Joseph, Spiritual Warfare, Ephesians, Psalms, and Knowing the God You Worship. During those 12 years as leader of those "In and Out" courses on Tuesday nights, she was also taking Precept courses each Tuesday morning, first under Barbara Ruth and later under Ruth Bock. Most of her time was spent either preparing Precept lessons and attending classes, or preparing "In and Out" lessons and leading classes. That took us through the fall of 1999. It was a busy, busy time for her, and quite rewarding for both of us.

I Was Weaned Away from Full Gospel

In the midst of our personal study of the Bible, the Lord was apparently weaning me away from my activities in Full Gospel. F. G. B. M. F. I. served a needed purpose in my life, for it provided the background for my search for spiritual truth as presented in the Bible. But as time went on, I found that many of the speakers, in giving their personal testimony, tended to concentrate more on the gifts rather than Jesus as the Giver. There were plenty of exceptions, for we did hear some excellent teaching from time to time. I guess the bottom line was that we wanted to concentrate more on the study of God's Word rather than hearing personal testimonies. It was a matter of the direction of our focus and attention. We also found that some who were interested in a deeper walk with the Lord were more comfortable with the Pentecostal approach, while others tended to be more reserved. Both approaches can be beneficial and rewarding, depending on the individual and how each believer is led. Our church background was such that we just felt more comfortable going in a different direction. But whatever the reason, we were weaned away from Full Gospel circles as we sought to spend more time in Bible Study. I served as president of the local chapter for nine years, and I shall always be grateful for the many friendships we developed and enjoyed during our time in Full Gospel. Herbert Pate stands out as one who benefited greatly from Full Gospel. He went on to be a field representative and later national director. His leadership and powerful testimony have been a blessing to many throughout the years. David Adkins, a member of the Pentecostal Church, was one of the first men I met in Full Gospel. His main emphasis was on Jesus and His love. He could be as loud as anybody in proclaiming the Gospel, but he could also be gentle and loving in dealing with people in need. He was known for the "compassion chain" he kept in his truck and how he pulled a stranger's car out of a ditch. He was especially nice to Daddy and our entire family during his last illness. On several occasions he read us an appropriate meditation from *Daily Blessing* as he ministered and encouraged us all. I could mention many others, including Earl Hughes, who thoroughly enjoys the freedom of his spiritual walk with the Lord, both in worship and friendships. Yes, Margaret and I were indeed blessed through our association with Full Gospel and the many friendships we enjoyed. It served as a stepping-stone to an even deeper walk with the Lord.

Chapter XXVII

OUR SPLIT WITH GORDON STREET

As a member of the "Cradle Roll" at Gordon Street Christian Church, I was a life-long member, as were all the members of the Perry family. Sunday school and church were always a part of my life. Through my church upbringing and God's grace, I was led to accept Christ as my Lord and Savior followed by baptism in 1943 at the age of 12. I taught Sunday school most all my adult life. Gordon Street and the Christian Church (Disciples of Christ) were about all I knew until I got into a serious study of the Bible.

Through a concentrated study of the Bible and much prayer, all the members of the Perry family were led to leave Gordon Street and the people we loved. It was probably the most difficult decision I have ever made, but at the same time, it was obviously what God was leading us to. When the decision was made, it was clear in our hearts and minds we had done the right thing.

When Randy Spaugh came to Kinston as minister in 1989, we had been in Bible study a few years. In his sermons, we appreciated the fact that after reading the morning Scripture he would say, "This is the Word of God and it can be trusted." He believed, as we had learned to believe through study, that the Bible is the inspired Word of God, infallible and inerrant in its entirety. We knew that the Christian Church had its beginning in 1804 through a Holy Spirit revival, and that at its inception it was biblically based. The founding fathers believed that the Bible was inspired by God and was inerrant in its content. But as time went on, we found that through liberal philosophical thinking over the years, the present day leaders of the denomination had come to believe that it only "*contained*" the Word of God and that certain parts were flawed and in error. In essence, they were saying the Bible cannot by trusted in its entirety. Although some parts may be true, other parts were not true.

Disbelief in the Virgin Birth

Questioning biblical truth was brought to our attention rather dramatically by one of our interim ministers prior to Randy coming in August 1989. During the summer, we had only one large Sunday school class, which met in the fellowship hall. In the course of one particular lesson, we were discussing the virgin birth. The interim was a retired, highly acclaimed leader and minister in the Christian Church, who voiced his opinion that the biblical word for virgin meant "young girl" and not what we think of as a virgin today. When I questioned him about it, he argued that it is impossible for a virgin to have a child. There must be some contact between a man and a woman; and besides that, he said that the word "virgin" is only mentioned one time in the entire Bible. If Jesus had really been born of a virgin, much more would have been said about it. I could hardly believe my ears! This man was highly respected in the Christian Church and didn't believe in the virgin birth! He was not the only Disciples of Christ minister I had known to disbelieve the virgin birth of Jesus. Even though I tried to be as respectful as possible, I pointed out that if the doctrine of the virgin birth is not true, Jesus was a fraud and the whole Christian faith would fall apart. The fact that Jesus was conceived by the Holy Spirit and not by Joseph made Him God-in-the-flesh, and, therefore, He was qualified to be the perfect sacrifice. Without the virgin birth, Jesus would be just another man, and, therefore, a sinner unable to be the perfect sacrifice for our sins. The bottom line is, if Jesus was not born of a virgin, we would have no hope for eternal life. I further pointed out that although the Bible teaches He was 100 percent man, it also teaches He was 100 percent God. He was the God-Man. He was God-in-the-flesh walking the earth as a human being.

A careful examination of the Bible, taken as a whole, makes it clear that

Jesus was God's Son, not Joseph's. Numerous references support that claim, but I'll just mention two of the most familiar:

(a) For God so loved the world that He gave **His only begotten Son**.... (JOHN 3:16)

(b) But when the fullness of time had come, God sent forth **His Son**, born of a woman, under the law. (GALATIANS 4:14)

One of the strongest pieces of evidence for Jesus' virgin birth is found in Matthew's gospel when he refers to Joseph as, "the husband of Mary of whom was born Jesus who was called Christ." (MATT. 1:16) Here the Greek word for "of whom" is feminine singular, indicating clearly that Jesus was born of Mary only and not of Mary and Joseph.

Matthew continues with a detailed explanation:

This is how Jesus the Messiah was born. His mother, Mary was engaged to be married to Joseph. But before the marriage took place, while she was still a virgin, she became pregnant through the power of the Holy Spirit. Joseph, her fiancé, was a good man and did not want to disgrace her publicly, so he decided to break the engagement quietly.

As he considered this, an angel of the Lord appeared to him in a dream. "Joseph, son of David," the angel said, "do not be afraid to take Mary as your wife. For the child within her was conceived by the Holy Sprit. And she will have a son, and you are to name him Jesus, for he will save his people from their sins!" All of this occurred to fulfill the Lord's message through his prophet:

Look! The virgin will conceive a child! She will give birth to a son, and they will call him Emmanuel, which means "God with us." (Here the angel is quoting ISAIAH 7:14)

When Joseph woke up, he did as the angel of the Lord commanded and took Mary as his wife. But he did not have sexual relations with her until her son was born. And Joseph named him Jesus. (MATT 1:18-25– New Living Translation)

Not Confident About Heaven

The interim minister amazed me even more by his response to our discussion about heaven. I had made the comment that a believer in Jesus Christ could know for sure that he was going to heaven when he died. He said that he had never known anybody, except some people at Gordon Street, who could say positively and without a doubt that they knew they were going to heaven. That's something that can't be determined in advance. He went on to say he himself wouldn't know for sure until he got there. It would be assuming too much. It was his opinion that there is simply no way to know for sure where you will end up after you die. In essence, he seemed to be saying that, "God will judge me for the way I've lived my life. I'm a longtime member and minister of the church. I've served Him well and done a lot of good things during my lifetime. Not that I've been perfect, but if He finds that my good deeds outweigh my bad deeds, then He will let me in. I probably will go to heaven because of the way I've tried to serve Him on earth, but I won't know for sure until I actually get there." He seemed to be saying that the Lord would honor his modesty. Just do the best you can and hope for the best.

The Sunday school class came to an end, limiting more discussion, but I knew I needed to talk to him further. However, this was his last Sunday, and he would be leaving the next day. I didn't want him to leave town without one last talk, so I called Barbara Ruth to discuss it with her. She had been in Sunday school and was equally disturbed. She agreed to go with me for a visit. I had called to see if we could drop by to see him that afternoon. He and his wife were most gracious in receiving us, even though they were in the middle of packing. Barbara Ruth and I pointed out several references to the virgin birth we had looked up in both the Old Testament and New Testament. He listened, attentively, but still held on to his opinion that to be born of a virgin was impossible. It has never happened before or after and it couldn't have happened 2000 years ago. I reiterated my argument that Christianity and the whole Church itself is without foundation without the virgin birth. That didn't matter. He just didn't believe it!

Barbara Ruth and I tried to explain that the Bible makes it clear that Jesus was the perfect blood sacrifice who died that we might live, and by trusting that He paid our sin debt for us, we can know for sure we are going to heaven. It is not a matter of how good we are or how many more good things we've done as compared to the bad things. It is sound biblical doctrine that we don't go to heaven because of our good works. We read several scriptures in support of our claim, mainly EPHESIANS 2:8, 9, which says:

> For by grace you have been saved through faith, and that not of yourselves; it is the gift of God, not of works, lest anyone should boast.

We also tried to make it clear that the Bible plainly states that God wants His children to know for sure they are going to heaven. In fact, John wrote his first letter specifically for that purpose:

> These things I have written to you who believe in the name of the Son of God, **that you may know that you have eternal life,** (emphasis mine) and that you may continue to believe in the name of the Son of God. (1 JOHN 5:13)

Nothing we said seemed to break through or even make a dent in his belief. He was kind enough to take the time to listen, but when we parted, Barbara Ruth and I were both shocked and disillusioned by a man of such stature in the church. Something was radically wrong, and we knew it. It really boils down to whether you believe the Bible or not.

In the Wrong Church?

The above incident was only one example of our growing disenchantment with the hierarchy of the Christian Church (Disciples of Christ.) We soon discovered that many of our Gordon Street friends were in the same boat and didn't believe in the inerrancy of the Bible. They could accept some things as written in Scripture but not others. Some of the miracles were just too far-fetched to believe. For instance, the parting of the Red Sea was impossible even though there were many Biblical references to it. How could Jesus feed

5000 people with only five fish and two barley loaves, and then have more left over than when He started? They argued that some of the miracles may be true, but certainly not all of them.

As time went on, it became obvious that all those at Gordon Street who were in Kay Arthur's Precept Bible Study were on one side of the fence and most everyone else was on the other. It would serve no useful purpose at this point to rehash the various other differences. Suffice it to say, a Resolution Committee was formed to listen to members with concerns about the direction and future of Gordon Street. Members of the Committee were Charles R. Brown, Philip A. Crawford, III, Helen E. Goins, Edna M. Loftin, Dan E. Perry and G. Ray Respess. After many hours of listening to 28 members of the congregation on an individual basis and considering some 55 different letters, the Committee compiled a report to the General Board identifying 12 general areas of concern. For each concern, the Committee wrote a "Committee Response and Recommendation." Our prayer was that the document would be a "starting point" for bringing all members of the congregation back into the folds of Gordon Street Christian Church (Disciples of Christ) as one in Christ.

Although our prayer for unity may have been noble in concept, there was awareness in my mind that to unify believers and unbelievers in the inerrancy and trustworthiness of the Bible was like mixing oil with water. There were many hard feelings expressed in the open Board meetings which were regrettable, but true. It was, indeed, a time of strain and testing for everyone. Of the 12 areas of concern, I was most interested in the issue of the Bible being the inspired Word of God.

As a family, Warren, Ely, and I and our wives searched our souls to find some common ground that would override the liberal agenda of the Christian Church Disciples of Christ denomination. We found the gap far too wide to overcome our dissatisfaction. We wrote the state office and Lexington Theological Seminary seeking answers, without satisfaction.

Our concerns were brought to a head one morning at the Elders Prayer Breakfast when we saw the spring 1998 issue of the *Disciple Renewal,* a publication openly opposed to the liberal trend of the Church. It had as its front-page headline, "Disciple University Embraces Witchcraft." It showed a large photograph, from the February 1998 issue of the *Los Angles Times*, of three young women in long robes consecrating the ground for an all-faith chapel at Chapman University. Chapman is a Disciples of Christ-affiliated university, funded, in part, through Basic Mission Finance (BMF). According to the account, the caption under the photograph read: "Wicca faithful (the names of the three witches were listed) bless the ground of a planned Chapman University Chapel." The article went on to say that the president of the university, "defended the witches' participation based on the Disciples emphasis on toleration and diversity." The article in the *Disciples Renewal* rightly questioned, "Does he assume that witchcraft is a legitimate religion? That would seem to be a logical conclusion to draw based on their active participation in the ground blessing service. It would appear Disciple diversity does indeed embrace witchcraft as a legitimate spiritual practice."

The writer of the *Disciple Renewal* went on to say, "I thought I was beyond being shocked by the beliefs and practices of Disciples leaders. In the past eleven years we have seen the General Assembly of the Christian Church (Disciple of Christ) refuse to affirm Jesus Christ as the only Savior (Res. 8728, 1987), and then vote down a resolution affirming the Bible to be the highest authority of the church (Res. 8944, 1989). After the Denver Assembly (1997) it became crystal clear that the denomination openly promotes gay and lesbian lifestyle (Res. 9719). Still I must admit that the witches' story was something of a shock."

The article continued: "Thank God for the several dozen students who quietly protested. The article states the students felt that an 'all-faith chapel is contrary to the university's Christian roots.' These young Christians had the courage to stand up and protest, but apparently to no avail. The LA Times quoted one student as saying, 'We want to return the university to its Christian values and ensure the spread of the Gospel of Jesus Christ.' The leadership of the University ignored this plea."

Warren, Ely, Barbara, and I were all at that elders breakfast and sat both amazed and shocked at what we were hearing discussed. It was becoming more and more evident that the denomination of the Christian Church (Disciples of Christ), which we once knew and loved, had drifted away from the vital principles of biblical truth for which it once stood. We were faced with the decision of either staying in an atmosphere we knew in our hearts was opposed to our interpretation of the Scriptures we had studied, or leaving our many church friends we had known and worshiped with most of our lives.

A Matter of Apostasy

According to *Webster's New World Dictionary*, a short definition of the word, *Apostasy* is, "An abandoning of what one has believed in, as a faith, cause, etc." This describes exactly what has been happening over the years not only in our denomination, but in many church denominations throughout America. Even the casual observer of the history of our country can see that we were called into existence as a great nation. God gave our Founding Fathers the vision and inspiration to structure our early existence on biblical principles and a trust in our heavenly Father to lead us in our governmental affairs. The Holy Bible was the first text book in our schools and colleges. But over the years as we have prospered, we have drifted away from our rich heritage. We have followed too much the devices and desires of our own self-centered nature. This apostasy is prevalent not only in governmental and church affairs but in most all aspects of life in America today.

The Bible Shows Us What's Happening

There are a number of Scriptures that give us a picture of what has happened throughout America as I see it. Let me mention a few:

(1) II TIMOTHY 3:16–17

All scripture is given by inspiration of God and is profitable for doctrine, for reproof, for correction, for instruction in righteousness, that the man of God may be complete, thoroughly equipped for every work.

The key starting point is the Bible itself. The basic question is, "Do you believe that the Bible is the inspired, inerrant Word of God?" The word usually translated "inspiration" is more accurately "spiration," or "God–breathed." In essence, it is actually saying that all scripture is "God– produced." Many in our culture do not believe this.

(2) II PETER 1:20, 21

> Knowing this first that no prophecy of Scripture is of any private interpretation, for prophecy never came by the will of man, but holy men of God spoke as they were moved by the Holy Spirit.

Man tries to give his own private interpretation of the Bible. Due to his own personal desires and lifestyle, he wants the Scripture to conform to his way of thinking, rather than determine the truth of what it actually says and means.

(3) II PETER 2:1-3

> 1. But there were also false prophets among the people even as there will be false teachers among you, who will secretly bring in destructive heresies, even denying the Lord who bought them.
> 2. And many will follow their destructive ways, because of whom the way of truth has been blasphemed.
> 3. By covetousness they will exploit you with deceptive words....

We can see the truth of Peter's words coming to light in the teaching and preaching not only in various churches, but in the liberal media of television, radio, and newspaper.

(4) II TIMOTHY 4:2-4

> 2. Preach the word! Be ready in season and out of season. Convince, rebuke, exhort, with all long suffering and teaching.
> 3. For the time will come when they will not endure sound doctrine, but according to their own desires, because they have itching ears, they will heap up for themselves teachers;
> 4. And they will turn their ears away from the truth and be turned aside to fables.

Here Paul is clearly admonishing young Timothy to preach the truth, for the time will come when some will not want to hear it. They will fall away and become more interested in seeking out teachers who will teach what they want to hear, rather than the truth of God's Word.

(5) COLOSSIANS 2:8-10

> 8. Beware, lest anyone cheat you through philosophy and empty deceit, according to the basic principles of the world and not according to Christ.
> 9. For in Him dwells all the fullness of the Godhead bodily;
> 10. And you are complete in Him, who is the head of all principality and power.

Paul is warning the church at Colosse to beware of false teachers who will teach, "according to the basic principles of the world and not according to Christ." He's saying that if you teach the truth about Christ, you will have all you need, for *you are complete in Him.* The message of Christ is the plumb line for truth and all biblical teaching.

Without question, leaving Gordon Street ranks as one of the major decisions in the life of each member of the Perry family. We left with absolutely no hard feelings toward anyone at Gordon Street for we loved and still love them all. With us it was purely a matter of our not being able to conform to the basic beliefs of the denomination. In good conscience, we could not continue to support financially something we did not believe in. On the following page is a copy of our letter in its entirety that we sent to each member of the congregation explaining our decision.

As best we can determine, approximately 110 men, women, and children left Gordon Street at about the same time.

Some Thought We Were Too Judgmental

Back when I was growing up, if someone had asked, "What is the most quoted Bible verse in all of Scripture?" the obvious answer would have been JOHN 3:16: "For God so loved the world that He gave His only begotten Son, that whosoever believes in Him shall not perish but have everlasting life." Those words give us the Gospel in a nutshell.

But today things are different. The truth has not changed, but worldly thinking and liberal influences have changed our perception of the truth. Today we are told that the most quoted Scripture is MATTHEW 7:1: "Judge not,

LAW OFFICES
PERRY, PERRY & PERRY
POST OFFICE DRAWER 1475
KINSTON, NORTH CAROLINA 28503-1475

FILE COPY

WARREN S. PERRY
DAN E. PERRY
JAMES STOCKTON PERRY
ELIZABETH P. WORTHINGTON

December 1, 1998

ELY J. PERRY (1896-1968)

RETIRED:
BARBARA S. PERRY

OFFICES:
518 PLAZA BOULEVARD
KINSTON, N.C. 28501
PHONE (252) 523-5107
FAX (252) 523-8858

The Congregation of Gordon Street Christian Church
c/o Mr. Pete Pully, Chairman Elect of the General Board
118 East Gordon Street
Kinston, NC 28501

Dear Friends:

With sadness and after much prayer, we feel the Lord is leading us to leave the Disciples of Christ denomination, and thus to leave Gordon Street Christian Church. Although it is most difficult and heartbreaking, we can no longer be under a denomination which does not honor the authority and sovereignty of God's Word.

We know that the Disciples of Christ say their watchwords are "in essentials unity, in nonessentials liberty and in all things charity". However, after corresponding with the General Minister, and head of Lexington Theological Seminary, our Regional Minister, and others, we cannot identify what the essentials are.

The recent events that have happened at Gordon Street have been a wake-up call which we cannot ignore. This has pointed out that our basic beliefs are not in keeping with those of the denomination, so we feel it is best that we leave.

Though we will worship in a different place, we want to maintain our friendships with you because we love you and pray for God's guidance as you continue your worship at Gordon Street Christian Church.

In Christian love,

Warren S. Perry
Barbara S. Perry
Ely J. Perry Jr.
Barbara J. Perry
Dan E. Perry
Margaret T. Perry

cc: General Minister and President Richard Hamm
President Richard L. Harrison, Jr. Lexington Theological Seminary
Rev. Rex L. Horne, Regional Minister

that you will not be judged." It appears that the liberal mindset of many church leaders today takes this verse out of context in an effort to rationalize the tolerance of all beliefs, whether they are in keeping with the true intent of God's Word or not. When Jesus said, "Judge not, that you be not judged," He was merely warning the hypocrites to get their own lives straight before they start judging and condemning others. Jesus Himself would be the ultimate judge of all mankind. He was not opening the door for tolerance of false teachers or the worship of other gods. Some felt the Perrys were being too judgmental and that we should be more tolerant of the beliefs of others. Because of His great love and compassion, Jesus may have been the most tolerant person who ever lived, but, in another sense, He was the most intolerant. Most in the world today do not believe in absolutes. To them there is no right or wrong. Regarding the Bible, they say you can believe what seems right to you, thereby giving their own private interpretation of what Scripture says.

There are times when a person must stand up for what he believes to be true, and this was one of them. Our decision to leave the denomination forced us to leave our many friends at Gordon Street. I'm sure many were shocked when, at the last minute, I rejected the recommendation of the Resolution Committee, of which I was a member. Our differences were too fundamental. There was no way I could continue to support the denomination and church I grew up in. We had to make a complete break. I sense there may be many who still don't understand why we left. If there are any hard feelings among them, I pray their forgiveness. We made our decision as a family, based on what we felt was God's will for us. We believe He has honored our obedience.

Praying in Jesus' Name

I will mention another situation of less magnitude that tested my resolve in standing firm for what I believed to be right and in keeping with my faith. It involved giving the blessing in Rotary. From time to time, I have been asked to invoke God's blessing on the food. My usual habit in any prayer is to conclude by praying in Jesus' name. On one occasion several years ago, I was politely asked by one of our members to respect the beliefs of others by not mentioning the name of Jesus when I prayed. The idea was that it might be offensive to those who were not of the Christian faith. I knew that there were several in the club who were not Christians, and I certainly didn't want to be disrespectful in any way. At the same time, I didn't feel I should change my belief system for fear of offending someone else. I was reminded that this was a picture of what is happening in America today. The liberal agenda advocates that we be "all-inclusive." Let's don't offend anybody because it might make them mad. We want to get along with everybody. Not to pray in Jesus' name would be a compromise of my own faith for the sake of not offending a few. I respectfully told my Rotary friend that if I prayed it would have to be in Jesus' name, because it shows honor and respect for the very character of my Lord and Savior who has the power to answer prayer. If I was going to be restricted from using the name of Jesus, they would have to get someone else to ask the blessing. My further comment was to "Let them pray like they want to by not mentioning Jesus, but when I pray I will not be afraid to use His name."

The Bible warns us that the time will come when some people will not want to hear the name of Jesus. In today's culture, even among many Christians, the tendency is to talk about God, but not about Jesus. There's something about the name of Jesus that creates a stumbling block in the minds of many. And yet the Bible tells us that there will come a time when, "That at the name of Jesus every knee shall bow…, and that every tongue shall confess that Jesus Christ is Lord to the glory of God the Father." PHILIPPIANS 2:10, 11.

Until that time comes, I will stand with the Apostle Paul when he said in ROMANS 1:16, "For I am not ashamed of the gospel of Christ for it is the power of God to salvation for everyone who believes…."

Fond Memories of Gordon Street

In looking back over my 67 years at Gordon Street, I can see many good things. My lifelong habit of attending Sunday school and church was developed from the very beginning. Margaret and I both were nurtured at Gordon Street by family and dear friends who loved us and wanted the best for us. Mother, Daddy, Warren, Ely, and I all taught Sunday school at one time or another.

We loved Gordon Street and its people. As organist and choir director, "Miss Jessie" Moseley set a standard that was second to none. Her prize student and understudy, Joanne May Heath, followed beautifully in Miss Jessie's footsteps by maintaining her high standard of excellence. As a teenager and college student, Margaret, and her mother, sang in Miss Jessie's choir. Some years after Miss Jessie's retirement, Joanne began leading the choir. Margaret continued with Joanne as time permitted. One of my most rewarding experiences at Gordon Street was singing in the choir with Margaret, beginning sometime in the mid 1980s. Joanne was an excellent director and was able to get the most out of her choir. She was ably accompanied on the organ by Gail Cooper. Kenneth Hardy, Rex Cooper, John Hickman, and Marjorie Moore were among the standout soloist in those days.

Gordon Street was, indeed, blessed when Gail and Rex moved to Kinston sometime in the 1970s, for we not only got Gail as organist, but also Rex as a tenor soloist. In addition, both were always on board to help with the youth programs. That was quite a team to have Joanne and Allan Heath as well as Gail and Rex Cooper and Marjorie and Bob Moore giving tirelessly of their time and effort as youth sponsors. Many others were also involved, but they are the ones who stand out in my mind for quality and length of service.

Joanne also developed a bell choir that became widely known throughout many states along the eastern seaboard. We are thankful our daughter Elizabeth and her best friend Penelope Stroud had the experience of participating in the early stages of Joanne's bell choir. As the ringers became more proficient, they went on summer tours playing in New York City, at the White House, Disney World, and many churches and locations in between. Other than the precision ringing of the bells, one of the main attractions of the Sanctuary Bells was, and still is, Joanne's daughter, Beth Heath, as she performs as soloist. It is simply amazing to watch her put it all together, flitting up and down the seemingly countless array of bells lying neatly on the table before her. It's equally amazing to realize she is now an Eighth District Court Judge mixing in among the teenagers of the church.

For over 80 years, one of the outstanding programs at Gordon Street has been the Boy Scouts. Troop 41 and Pack 41 are known throughout the area as two of the best around. A lot of credit should go to Ernest Thornton as longtime institutional representative. He was the chief recruiter in charge of seeing that the various committee and leadership positions in both the Troop and Pack were always filled. Much of the time he worked behind the scenes to see that everything ran smoothly. I was cub master when Daniel was in Cub Scouts. My recollection is that Allan Heath was his original scoutmaster followed by Duane Griffin when he got his Eagle. Wes Perry also served as scoutmaster for ten years. His father (my brother) Warren was cub master for over fifteen years beginning in the 1950s, shortly after he returned to Kinston to practice law.

I, as well as the entire Perry family, have many pleasant memories of our association with Gordon Street Christian Church. It was an important part of our lives, for which we will always be grateful.

It Was My Turn to Lead Bible Study

When our daughter Radford announced her engagement to marry Chad Pharr of Asheboro, we decided to give Margaret a much needed rest as our Bible Study leader so as to prepare for the wedding on May 13, 2000. Margaret and I both had been blessed to have had a group of some 20 to 25 friends in our home each Tuesday evening. We knew we needed to continue with the class. We were learning that every aspect of the Bible was true. We knew in our hearts it was the inspired Word of God, and the more we studied it, the more we were convinced we should stay involved with Bible Study the rest of our lives. It is through a daily pursuit of reading and study of the Word of God that we can grow and mature into the man and woman He wants us to be.

Since we had taken about all of Kay Arthur's "In and Out" courses offered at the time, we decided to try other studies. Beginning in January 2000, I led my first formal Bible Study class at our home on Perry Park Drive. It was based on Bob George's book *Classic Christianity*. That was a good one to start with, for it presented all the basic principles and doctrines of the Bible along with supporting Scriptures. From there we studied a course on *Grace Discipleship*. In the fall of 2001, we had our first David Jeremiah study called,

Christians Have Stress Too. All three of these studies were based on selected Scriptures and provided us with insight into living out the Christian life. After a study on the Resurrection in the spring of 2002, we embarked upon a three-year David Jeremiah study of the Book of Romans. I had a good time leading the class, for it was full of fundamental doctrines of the church that are essential for a solid background for basic knowledge of biblical truth. This was followed by a study of I John in the fall of 2005, and a two semester study of *Facing the Giants in Your Life*, followed by Ecclesiastes in the fall of 2006. Our last study, as of this writing, was called *What You Always Wanted to Know About Heaven*. I mention our family involvement and the courses by name so that the reader can get a flavor for the Perry family's serious attention to the study of God's Word over the last 23 years. It has been a rewarding experience in every way, for we've been learning about eternal values as they relate to the meaning of life. With each passing year, as we look down the road to the end of our earthly existence, we can face the future with confidence. We know we are going to heaven, not because of any good thing we may have done during our time on earth, but because of our trust and faith in what Jesus did for us on the cross. According to the Great Commission, we as Christians are to spread the good news of Jesus Christ throughout the world.

Chapter XXVIII

LIFE TAKES ON NEW MEANING

Faith Fellowship Became Our New Church

It was not clear in the beginning that we wanted to be involved in starting a new church. My first thought was to look around at various other churches to see if we would fit into the beliefs and structure of another denomination. It didn't take us long to realize that many of the mainline churches were having similar problems as those we had just experienced. The bottom line was we decided on a new start without having to answer to a denominational hierarchy. In December 1998, Randy and a small group of followers started meeting in a building on Sussex Street owned by Gordon Vermillion. In a few months, as our attendance grew we moved across the street to Vermillion Catering Service banquet room. Members of other congregations began to show up. Randy's preaching was stressing the truth of God's Word and was beginning to attract worshipers from various backgrounds. Margaret and I joined a small group of choir members led by Pam Nichols (Respess). Other members I recall included Ozzie Shackelford, Nicole and Felix Croom, Charlotte Smith, Mary Cauley, Bonnie Cribbs, Gil Respess, and Mary Repess. Our first pianist was Zelia Sneed.

Within a year or so, we were blessed to have Dr. Alan Armstrong come as our part time choir director. Alan's fulltime job is head of the music department at Mount Olive College. He is multitalented in many areas of music and ministry. He and Anita live on the Kinston side of Goldsboro making his commute to the College and Faith Fellowship at least bearable. Not only does he lead our choir and praise team, sing and play solo on the piano, organ, cello. and bagpipes, but he also knows the intricacies of our sound system. In addition, when Randy is on vacation, he also does an excellent job filling the pulpit.

Our New Church Building

In the early weeks, our group was without an official name. After considering several possibilities, we finally settled on Faith Fellowship, because we were a group of Bible believers who were venturing out on faith. The Lord provided temporary housing through the kindness of Gordon Vermillion, but now it was time for a more permanent, spacious building. A site committee, as well as a building committee, was appointed, resulting in Felix and Nicole Croom generously giving us a beautiful ten-acre tract of land on Paul's Path Road.

After many months of hard work on the part of the building committee, headed by Tony Mallard and J.T. Pratt, we had our first service at the new building in January of 2005. Other members of the building committee were Allen Parrott, Ann Oliver, Mary McCarter, Robbie Norville, and myself. The builder was Farrior and Son out of Farmville. The aesthetics committee in charge of furnishings and decorations was, and is, Mary McRae Parrott, Margaret Perry, Marie Gerrans, and Marie Singleton. As of May 2007, our membership had grown to 330. We are not tied to any denomination.

It is interesting to note that five years before the founding of Faith Fellowship Church, another group of "Bible believers" broke away from their denominational ties and formed Grace Fellowship Church. In the fall of 1993, they began meeting in various homes, moving to Vermillion Vending in the winter of 1993. The following April, they called Dean Woodward out of Texas as their first pastor. They also met at Northwest Elementary School and later in the renovated theater at the Kinston Plaza Shopping Center. In April 2007, they moved to their newly constructed facility on Academy Heights Road under the leadership of their current pastor, Jason McKnight. The "founding families" of Grace Fellowship were Gram and Diane Spear, Jimbo and Joan Perry, David and Bonnie Grigg, Tom and Gayla Vermillion, Paul and Ginger Cleavenger, Glenn and Carla Gannett, and Ray and Cindi Shimer. Both Grace

Fellowship and Faith Fellowship share the common belief in the inerrancy of the Bible as the inspired Word of God.

Developing a Structured Routine

Two things happened on January 1, 1999, which I deem to be of major importance in my life. That was the beginning of two disciplines in which I have developed vital interest: journaling and daily Bible reading. I had known for a long time that most all the great "giants of the faith" did what is known as "journaling." I knew basically what it was, but was not familiar with the details until one weekend in October 1998 when Margaret and I heard David Jeremiah speak at the Cove in Asheville. During one of his sessions at the Billy Graham Training Center, Dr. Jeremiah told how during the past two years journaling had blessed him so richly. He told how his quiet time with the Lord starts early each morning (I recall 4 A.M. as being his rising time). His daily routine of study, prayer, and preparation for his pastoral, radio, and television ministries takes many hours of meditation and quiet time with the Lord so as to seek His direction and wisdom. He was telling us there is no right or wrong way to journal, just as long as you are, in essence, using it as a tool to worship God. Journaling can be in the form of a prayer or a psalm. It can be a diary of past activities or present aspirations. It is a way of coming before the Lord to seek his wisdom and guidance. It can be a means of private confession and seeking direction for one's life. It can be used as a time of prayer not only for personal needs but the needs of family, friends, the church, our country, and the world. The idea is first to pray, then get started. Just sit down before the Lord and write whatever comes to mind.

Dr. Jeremiah said he journals on his computer each morning for about an hour, sometimes more, sometimes less. He said it's interesting to look back and see how the Lord answers his written prayers from the previous year. The telling of his journaling experiences motivated me to give it a try. I knew it was something I had to do, to fulfill my desire for a deeper walk with the Lord. I was not into computers and would have to write rather than type. Dr. Jeremiah said the idea was to do your own thing. Let the Lord lead you in the way you should journal.

About that same time, I was beginning to see the need to get into a daily routine of Bible reading. I had been studying my Bible Study lessons and looking up related Scriptures, but I was not on a daily routine. The Lord seemed to be telling me, if I was to know Him better, I needed to be in His Word more. I had heard of the *One Year Bible*, which structured a program of daily reading of the entire Bible in one year. That would seem to be the best way to accomplish my purpose of daily reading of the Word. After much prayer and seeking God's wisdom and guidance, I decided to begin my new routine of journaling and Bible reading on January 1, 1999. But I also knew I would have to get up earlier to do it!

Ever since about 1988, Margaret and I had been in the habit of praying together on our knees. We were accustomed to reading a daily meditation along with a short prayer early in our marriage, but it was not until 1988, at her suggestion, that we began praying by our bed, side by side on our knees. I remember how awkward I felt the first few times we tried it, but soon it seemed second nature to us.

I would emphasize to any couple, young or old, that if you really want to get closer to your spouse and develop a deeper relationship as husband and wife, try praying together *on your knees.* There's something about humbling yourselves *on your knees* together before the Lord that will be honored by your heavenly Father. It will make a difference in your marriage! We both value our prayer life together as we seek to know the Lord better and His will for our lives.

Developing a Morning Routine

Soon after I added journaling and Bible reading to my daily routine, I realized I needed to get up earlier if I was to fit it all in my schedule. I was accustomed to rising about 6:30 each morning, so I moved it back to 6:00. My journal was a 200-page college-ruled composition book. Generally, it took about 15 minutes to write one page, plus 15 minutes for Bible reading. I had also developed a routine of spending at least a half hour in the bathroom immediately upon rising each morning. In addition to doing all the normal things of shaving, etc., I spent time memorizing Scripture. Over the years,

I've developed a card file with some 150 or so cards and notes filled with various Bible verses and wise sayings, which at one point I have memorized. I find that I lose them if I don't review them from time to time. The real reason I started the Scripture box was not only to learn Bible verses, but to exercise and improve my memory. As I have gotten older, Margaret has gently "accused" me of not remembering certain things, so I thought this was not only a great way to learn the Bible, but also a good way to improve my memory. As new verses and thoughts come to mind, I add them to the box. Even though I don't look at the cards every single day, the box sits by my sink as a daily reminder to stay in the Word.

One day several years ago, the Lord reminded me I needed even more quality quiet time in the morning if I was to accomplish what I wanted to do. Margaret had been part of a small group of girls who prayed weekly at Vermillion's. On this particular day, Margaret knew several would be absent, so she invited me to join them. As I recall, in additional to Margaret and me, the only other two were Jamie Crisp and Audra Hargitt. In the course of our preliminary conversation, Jamie mentioned that she got up between 5:00 and 5:30 most every morning. She needed that extra quiet time for personal meditation and prayer. Her comments served to inspire me to realize that 6:00 was not early enough for me. After that I set 5:00 A.M. as my goal to start each morning's activities. My present, approximate routine is:

5:00 A.M. rise and spend at least 30 minutes in the bathroom.

5:30–6:00 journal and read Bible.

6:00–6:40 prepare Bible Study lesson or other reading or meditation.

6:40–7:05 prayer time with Margaret.

7:05–7:28 listen to David Jeremiah on 100.3 FM radio while stretching and exercising.

7:28 listen to news and weather—we usually continue stretching for an additional five to ten minutes or so.

8:00 (or whenever we can get ready) breakfast

I generally try to have lights out at 9:30 P.M., which will give me seven-and-a-half hours sleep. That seems to suit my lifestyle just fine.

I am quick to remind the reader that this is just an approximate routine we generally shoot for. It may vary from day to day, depending on circumstances. I have found that by having a goal, we have something to go back to when circumstances cause a variance in the set routine. Since I began writing this book I find myself getting up many mornings between 4:00 and 4:15 A.M. Once I got use to it, I now look forward to accomplishing something worthwhile in those early morning hours.

Building at 1902 Holding Place

As much as we enjoyed raising our children and living at 1305 Perry Park Drive for over 25 years, the time had come when we knew we had to down-size. All the children were gone. Warren, Ely, and I each had a lot at the end of the cul-de-sac on Holding Place, thinking that possibly one day we might build smaller houses. Warren and I ended up selling our two lots to Hoyt Minges. Ely kept his lot, but was not interested in moving from Walker Drive. He was kind enough to offer it to me, so after much prayerful planning, we set about building our perfect house at 1902 Holding Place. We had asked the Lord to show us exactly what He wanted us to build in every detail so as to glorify Him. At the time Ely III and Bill Simmons were in the construction business under the name of Perry Management. They gave us a stack of design books with all kinds of floor plans. Margaret knew our needs and desires, so it wasn't long before she was able to combine several floor plans with our own ideas to come up with the perfect plan. It was centered on a spacious combination family room/dining room area, large enough to accommodate comfortably our Bible Study group of some thirty five or so people. We made room for an office-study for me with a large built-in corner desk. I had looked at Barbara Ruth's upstairs study for ideas. She was most helpful in giving me her thoughts as a starting point for my own personal design. Margaret and I felt led by the Lord in every respect as the overall plans for our house developed. She had a cut out drawing of the larger pieces of furniture at Perry Park Drive, drawn to scale to fit in each room of the Holding Place plans. Room sizes were adjusted to suit the placement of the furniture we brought with us. We decided on a large, circular drive in the front to accommodate parking for our Bible Study group. Before the house was built, we knew where I would be standing to lead the group as well as the placement of the various chairs and each piece of furniture. We prayerfully turned it over to the Lord from the very beginning, and He was faithful to lead us all the way. It was an enjoyable experience to work with Drew Dalton of Dunn and Dalton Architects, who drew the final plans based on our own particular needs. Ely III amazed us with his thoughts and suggestions as to how to put it all together. Bill Simmons was the contractor in charge of the construction work. It was such a blessing working with him and his talented crew of Jeff Turner, "Big Al" Mercer, and Aaron Powell. Everything seemed to fall into place without any major hitch. Instead of being tiresome drudgery, it was a pleasurable experience to build our perfect house. Soon after moving in, we called all the family and office staff together for a celebration to dedicate our new home to the glory of God. We give Him praise and thanksgiving for it.

With the development of my structured morning routine, I look forward each morning to getting up early and entering my secluded study for a special quiet time with the Lord. It's my own private time set aside for journaling, Bible study, meditation and other study. The Lord has given me the time and place. Now I need to give it back to Him. I have found that when the Lord gives me a worthwhile goal or ambition, He will also provide the way and means by which to accomplish the task. If I am willing to follow His will, He will lead. Therefore, my prayer is, "Lord, I am willing to be led by you!" There is, indeed, something to be said for "The Power of Letting," which I learned so long ago.

Chapter XXIX

LOOKING BACK

Looking Back at Golf

As I was growing up, many adults encouraged me to keep up my golf game, because it would be something I could enjoy the rest of my life. How true that was, for I have enjoyed playing golf all my life. From the time Warren introduced me to the game at the age of six, on through school, throughout my adult years, up until the present time, golf has been my number one hobby. The family foursome of Daddy, Warren, Ely, and me was always a privilege. Competing for the Perry Family Birthday Trophy was something we three boys, along with our family- (or friend-) guest looked forward to three times each year on our birthdays. From the very beginning of my work life in Kinston, I always scheduled Wednesday afternoon as my golf day, playing with various groups and friends.

Beginning some time in the 1970s, Carlton Oliver asked me to join a regular foursome along with Ray Rouse and Walker Sugg. Those were fun times as we gathered for our 12:30 tee time each Wednesday afternoon. "No news is good news" was our slogan, meaning unless we heard differently, we'd be there at 12:30 ready to go. Carlton and I played as partners against Ray and Walker. We played a 25-cent Nassau, plus a quarter for birdies, greenies, and sandies. You couldn't win or lose any more than a dollar. I had a little book in which I recorded our individual scores along with team winnings for each week from January 1 through December 31 of each year. It was fun writing a year-end report giving a resume of our games. Most of the time, there was only a dollar or so difference for the whole year. One year we were exactly even going into the last game of the year. We battled for 17 holes and were still tied. Finally, on the 18th hole, Carlton made a five-foot putt to win a quarter for our team for the whole year's play. I'd say that is about as close as you can get!

By the way, Carlton will always be remembered for his personalized "curse words." After missing an easy putt, he could be heard yelling out "Sock-a-ma-roo-cha!" which was most always followed by, "Side-a-vaze!" We kidded Ray about being so negative about everything. To listen to him complain, you'd think he never made a good shot. But on April 14, 1987, he proved himself and us wrong. On that day he made what seemed like every putt he took. They all seemed to go in—even the long ones—20, 30 feet. The one on the par three #15 was all the way across the green. It was amazing! Even years later, we would remind him of that memorable day in April 1987. Walker was a left-hander, and we kidded him about hitting from the wrong side. When he'd make a good shot, I'd tell him, "I'm gonna' have to get me one of those left-handed clubs." I guess I was known for spouting off several Korean or Japanese phases I had learned in the army when missing a putt. I don't know how to spell it, but it went something like, "aan-ya-haash-a-me-ka!" followed by, "nanan-taan-she-nal-sala-haam-ne-da!" And then there were some others, depending on how close I came to making the putt. A lot of times I would leave the green mumbling those and other such phases under my breath to show my disgust with myself for making such a stupid shot. I had long forgotten what it all meant, but it was fun just cutting up and making out like I knew what I was talking about.

In 1990 Walker had to drop out because of physical reasons, so we got Myron Hill to join us. He and I have continued playing together on Wednesdays and other times ever since. I always kid him about being "the best putter in the club." He has a long, smooth, sweeping stroke—and when he keeps his body still, he generally makes a bunch of 'um.

Carlton and I use to have a good time counting our blessings while riding together on the golf cart. We would talk about the beauty all about us—the picturesque setting of the holes and fairways, the smooth greens, the chirping of the birds, the flight of the hawk as he swooped down on an innocent squirrel, unaware of the pending danger. We enjoyed admiring God's beauty about us. From time to time, I would kid him by saying, "I bet you haven't even noticed how pretty it is out here!" To which he would reply, "Oh, yes, I have, Dan. Did you know that 20 years from now we might not be playing golf together?" We would always agree to "savor" the moment and appreciate the privilege we had of playing together and enjoying the beautiful scenery all about us. The Lord may have given us a few more than 20 years, but since then Walker died and Ray and Carlton have both dropped out. Today our regular Wednesday foursome includes Myron and Payne Dale against Charlie Brown and me. Ken Rouse or maybe Warren Whitehurst joins us when Payne is out from time to time. Since I've slowed down at the office, I've been able to play at other times, when time permits. On Monday mornings usually Jim Smith or Frazier Bruton joins me as a twosome at Falling Creek. We play early so I can get back to the office after an early lunch. When we play on Fridays, Myron and I are sometimes joined by either Barney Jones, Payne Dale, Ken Rouse, or Warren Whitehurst, depending on who's available.

I've had so much fun playing with the Kinston Seniors group once a month as we compete with other seniors from nearby towns. For quite a few years, Myron has been the Kinston representative to make the arrangements for our group. When I'm able, I also join with a group of the old Kinston High Red Devils as they get together once a month and play various courses in the area under the leadership of Amos Stroud. Back in the 1980s and 1990s, four of us used to go on three-day weekends with our wives and compete for the DARR Trophy named after Dan (Perry), Allen (Parrott), Rudy (Mintz), and Roy (Jones). It was fun having Margaret, Mary McRae, Connie, and Brenda along with us. They shopped while we played golf, then at night we would enjoy a nice meal together. Some of the courses we played were at Pine Needles, Raleigh, Myrtle Beach, Swansboro, and three times at Williamsburg. Oh what fun we had!

I've had three holes-in-one—one at Kinston, one at Myrtle Beach, and one at Falling Creek. I've had eight or ten eagles, the longest of which was a

220-yard. three wood shot for a two on number seven (after hitting a tree on my drive) at the Kinston Country Club. That was on October 4, 1982, playing with Carlton, Myron, and Charlie. (I've got the pinnacle ball mounted to prove it). The only time I ever shot my age was four years ago in 2003 when I shot 71. If I sound like I'm bragging, I am—because I haven't even come close since then. In fact, today I have a 20 handicap at Kinston Country Club and a 16 at Falling Creek. It's been all downhill since then, and now I have a hard time breaking 90! I never thought I would be that bad. Age has taken its toll! But just you wait—I'm not giving up! I keep telling myself I'm gonna break 80 again, "one of these days!" As Carlton used to say, I need to, "Take a BC and come back strong." Every time I see Leroy Pittman, he asks me to come back and play with him with his "shoot out" group of Frank Sabiston, Lennox Britt, John Hickman, Phil Sanders, and some of those boys, just like in the old days. I've always got an excuse not to play with them—but the bottom line is I'm too embarrassed. But just you wait, I'm gonna take that BC and come back strong. Just you wait and see! Dennis Michels, my neighbor across the street, gave me a little encouragement the other day when I saw him practicing chipping in his front yard. He said once you've been a good player, you may lose it—but you *can* get it back. Don't give up. You can get it back. I told him I'd keep trying. Maybe I can get at least a little of it back.

Looking Back at Traveling

I've always enjoyed traveling—going to other places and seeing new things. In school it was fun playing basketball and golf away from home. It was refreshing as well as challenging to play new courses. I've either visited or driven through most every county in North Carolina and most of the states in the United States.

Margaret and I took the children on the usual family trips to the mountains, Land of Oz, Carowinds, Six Flags over Georgia, Kings Dominion, Disney World, The Lost Colony, Cherokee, as well as Williamsburg, Boston, and New England to visit Uncle Buddy, and many others. The Lord has blessed us to be able to enjoy traveling and being together as a family. We took Daniel to France and joined up with Elizabeth who was in Paris ending up her experience with a family as an au pair. We toured Rome, Florence and Venice. Daniel and I went to the top of the Leaning Tower of Pisa and felt like we "almost fell off" as we climbed out on the unprotected ledge and waved to Margaret and Elizabeth. Probably our most memorable trip with the children was to the west coast in 1984. We flew to Phoenix and took a Tauk bus tour and visited all the notable attractions in the area, including Las Vegas where I showed the children how to lose $5.00 on the slot machines as they, being underage, watched from a distance. We took a scary helicopter ride around the awesome Grand Canyon. We saw tract star Carl Lewis win three of his gold metals at the Olympics in Los Angeles. In San Diego we toured the Queen Mary and Howard Hughes's Spruce Goose. For the last half of the trip, we rented a van and drove along the scenic coastline from California to Washington State. Daniel and I played golf at the famous Pebble Beach course. I told him this would be a once in a lifetime experience, because it cost us over $300.00 for the 18 holes. Today I imagine it would cost at least three times that much for two to play. We visited Yellowstone and Yosemite National Parks. It was, indeed, a blessing and privilege to be able to take such a family trip together.

Margaret and I had a great experience traveling to the Holy Land with Dave and Ann Alexander, which was their first of many trips as tour guides. Actually, Dave was considered the tour guide, and he was an exceptionally good one. We also had several nice trips with Margaret's brother and sister, "Aunt Carolyn" and "Uncle Buddy." The most memorable one was probably to England and Scotland. We particularly wanted to see the Cornwall section of England because of our interest in Ross Poldark and the BBC Poldark television series. The breathtaking scenery was something we had to see for ourselves. Margaret and I have also enjoyed meandering along the coastlines of Maine and Nova Scotia as well as taking a getaway trip to the Bahamas. Allen and Mary McRae Parrot and J.T. and Jean Pratt joined us for a delightful David Jeremiah cruise to the Caribbean. We heard some inspiring teaching and enjoyed the ship's entertainment and island tours.

We've had a couple of birthday trips with Jeff and Ellen Whitaker (she and

I were both born on July 2) to the Outer Banks and Canada. We've been to Williamsburg with Allen and Mary McRae Parrott. Tom Bennett and I took off for a week to attend a golf school in Florida and play several courses in the area. We've had several nice trips with Everette (Sonny) and Suzanne Wooten, the most memorable of which was to Washington, DC to hear Johnny Mathis perform at Kennedy Center. He sang all the old favorites, including "Misty," "Chances Are," "The Twelfth of Never," "A Certain Smile," and a bunch more. We stayed at the infamous Watergate, which was in walking-distance from Kennedy Center. Another memorable trip with Sonny and Suzanne was back to the Washington area to hear Pavarotti. We also took an overnight bus ride with them and some other Kinston folks to New York City to see several plays, the Metropolitan Opera, and our favorite, Bill Cosby and Sammy Davis Jr. on stage in *Two Friends*. We had front-row seats, and it was simply hysterical, to say the least.

I suppose we've traveled the most with Gerald and Dinah Sylivant from Snow Hill. We've had many memorable trips together, including the great times we had in Bermuda, New Orleans, and Savannah. On one of our several trips to Charleston, we had a most unusual experience. While the girls were shopping for ladies' stuff, Gerald and I decided to look around in the men's department. As our eyes drifted over the necktie display, we began to look through to see if anything caught our fancy. Finally, Gerald said, "Dan, you need to make a statement. We're going to take those girls to a high-class restaurant tonight, and you need to wear a tie that'll make a statement, something different that'll stand out." After a few minutes of silently observing the various options, Gerald finally exclaimed, almost with a shout, "Here it is! Here's what you need!" As he proudly showed me his discovery, he said, "Now, that'll make a statement. Nobody's ever seen one like this before!" He was right, because the colorful, swirling pattern was different from anything I'd ever seen. After buying the tie at Gerald's insistence, I thought to myself, "I'll have to wear it now whether it'll match my coat or not." As we left the store with the girls, Gerald kept bragging about my new purchase: "Dan's got a tie that's really gonna' make a statement tonight."

We stayed at the Elliott House, which was right next door to Eighty-Two Queen where we had our reservations for the evening. The girls were all dressed up and looking pretty. Gerald and I were wearing our blue blazers, and I was sporting my "statement" tie. As we were being shown to our table, we admired the charm of the dimly lit, outdoor garden setting. We were seated under a large gazebo with overhead vines surrounded by various flowers and decorations. At first we were so captivated by the beauty of our surroundings, we didn't notice the tablecloth. Finally with obvious excitement in his voice, Gerald exclaimed, "Dan, look at the tablecloth! Then look at your tie! They're exactly the same!" He was right! I couldn't believe what we were seeing! I put the end of my tie on the table and it seemed to disappear right before our very eyes. I'm sure we upset the mood and elegance of the evening for others, as we got louder in our comments. I'm not sure what the guests at the surrounding tables thought as we laughed and giggled and carried on. They probably thought we were drunk! We simply couldn't control ourselves. Although we enjoyed a delicious meal, the topic of conversation for the whole evening was our disbelief in my disappearing tie. Gerald was right from the very beginning. I had bought a tie that was going to make a statement. From time to time, we still get a big laugh when we relive the night my tie disappeared.

Then there was the trip with the Sylivant's to Savannah when we went to dinner at an atmospheric restaurant with a small combo band. During a break in the music, Gerald had gone to the restroom leaving the three of us at the table. For some reason the pianist remained after the others left. Then without telling us a thing, Dinah got up and went over to the pianist and appeared to be whispering in his ear. Margaret and I had no idea of what was going on. The next thing we knew, we heard Dinah singing, "You made me love you, I didn't want to do it, I didn't want to do it...." Gerald was just returning from the restroom and stood across the room flabbergasted. He was beaming from ear to ear in shock as she continued singing directly to him. It was a total surprise to all of us. Needless to say, the whole restaurant burst out in applause as Gerald and Dinah rejoined us at the table. Dinah then told us it was something she'd always wanted to do, but never found the right time and place. Our trip to Savannah was in celebration of the 20th wedding anniversary of Gerald and Dinah, as well as Margaret and me. What a perfect time! What a perfect place! What a perfect song! Everything was perfect. It was an experience the four of us relive quite frequently—even 25 years later!

Looking Back at My Many Blessings

Looking back over my life, I see obviously that the Lord has blessed me beyond measure. Many times when people greet me with the usual question, "How are you doing?" I'll reply, "Better than I deserve, that's for sure!" Some don't know exactly how to take that. They don't understand. They think we all deserve something, especially if we've stayed out of trouble and been at least fairly successful in life. Actually, we don't deserve a thing, no matter how good we've been or how many good things we've done. We're here in this life only by the grace and mercy of God.

Let me mention just a few of my countless blessings:

1. HERITAGE AND FAMILY

    The Lord blessed me with a mother, father, and two brothers who loved me unconditionally all my life. Then when the time was right, in God's perfect timing, He gave me a beautiful wife to love and cherish. Her love and faithfulness to me has been forever present. We've had many laughs with only a few tears. We've been blessed with three fine children who not only love us, but also love each other (sometimes that's a rarity these days). We have a wonderful son-in-law in Chad Pharr—and the cutest little granddaughter, Virginia Carolyn.

2. MANY FRIENDS

    It has been said that to have a friend, you must be a friend. Although I've tried to be a friend to all, I am aware that at times I've turned a few friends off—some by the way I've acted and others by what I've stood for. When Margaret and I first saw our need for a deeper walk with the Lord, we began to see friendships change. We naturally gravitated toward those who shared similar beliefs and interests with us. When the Apostle Paul said that he wanted to be "All things to all people," he was not saying he would conform to the lifestyle and beliefs of those about him. His purpose was to mix in among all people for the purpose of proclaiming the Gospel to them. In any event, the Lord has blessed us with many good friends we love and hold dear.

3. MANY MENTORS

We are thankful for the many "giants of the faith" we respect through reading, radio, television, and tape ministries as well as hearing them speak from time to time at the Cove, churches, crusades, and other gatherings. As an evangelist, Billy Graham, heads the list. As a pure in-depth Bible Study leader, Kay Authur stands out. There are many I could mention as being a blessing to us down through the years. James Kennedy is known for applying biblical principles to governmental affairs, and how we as a nation have fallen away from the original concepts of our founding fathers. But the two who have blessed me the most over the years are David Jeremiah and Charles Stanley. We listen to Dr. Jeremiah every weekday morning on the radio as we do our stretching exercises. We've been using his Study Guide and tapes to lead our home Bible Studies for a number of years. I personally find his teaching to be clear, perceptive, and right on target in helping us discern the truth of God's Word. We listen to Charles Stanley on television most Sunday mornings and also on the radio during the week, as time permits. I find that both David Jeremiah and Charles Stanley are fully prepared as they deliver their messages, which seem always to be appropriate and meaningful for life application.

4. OFFICE AND WORK

We moved to our present office at 518 Plaza Boulevard in 1986. At first Warren and I were concerned about being much further from the courthouse than our old location on Gordon Street, which had been in easy walking distance. But things worked out beautifully at our new location with easy access to all the needed conveniences of home, drug store, grocery store, bank, gym, and the Plaza Shopping Center. The four- or five-minute drive to the Register of Deeds and courthouse is no problem at all.

Our 5000-square-foot office is divided with the lawyers on one side and Perry Management on the other. It has always been a pleasure working with Warren, Jimbo, and Betty Blaine in the legal field. After Warren died in 2003, Betty Blaine moved into his office. Barbara also maintains an office even though she retired some years ago. It was fun to have brother Ely and the Perry Management staff on the other side. After Ely died in 2004, Ely III ably assumed the full leadership role for Perry Management. We have been truly blessed over the years with loyal employees. Bill Simmons, who is a jack-of-all-trades and master of many, recently retired after 47 years. He and Gram Spear, who works closely with Ely III, are like family to all the Perrys. They have two highly qualified and loyal employees in Michelle Wetherington and Amanda Barajas. Ashley Perry's husband, Burton Rudolph, formerly employed as an engineer with the East Group, worked with Perry Management for several years before moving his family to Florida. Linda Davitt, who serves as our receptionist, also does a good job with typing and special projects. Although Danelle Roberson works mostly as Jimbo's paralegal, she also does work for Betty Blaine and me. She is always willing to lend a helping hand whenever needed. The one who does most of my paralegal work is Marie Sessoms. She's been with us almost 20 years and is truly outstanding in her field. We work well together as a team. I do all the title searches, and she does all the detail work of putting the packages together and scheduling the loan closings. She sure makes life easy for me, for she's willing to do whatever it takes to get the job done efficiently, correctly, and on time. Several years ago I nominated her, and she won, the Administrative Professional of the Year Award. Both her daughters, Ann Marie Lokey and Nikki Bourré, have worked for us and have that same work ethic.

Over the years in working with Warren, Jimbo and Betty Blaine on the lawyer side, and Ely Jr., Ely III, Burt, Gram, and Bill on the Perry Management side, a personal observation emerges: They all have been people of integrity, honesty, and of the highest work ethic. In their personal and family lives, each has been exemplary in many ways. Each is respected and a true blessing throughout the community.

It has truly been a privilege to have worked for over 45 years in my hometown of Kinston. It's been an added special pleasure working with family members and a supportive staff I love and respect. Not everyone can say they enjoy going to work every morning, as I have been privileged to do.

Looking Back at Warren and Ely

Just a brief post script: The older they got, the more they recognized their need for a closer relationship with God and Jesus as their Lord and Savior. That's the way it was with Daddy and seems to be with most Christians. Warren and Ely both became faithful Bible Study members. For the last 10 to 15 years of their lives, I could see them loosening up and not being afraid to talk about spiritual matters. Each of them acquired a favorite verse. Warren's was PSALM 118:24, "This is the day the Lord has made. Let us rejoice and be glad in it." He began quoting that verse at mealtime and any other time he was asked to pray. I remember the first time I heard him quote it in public. He was asked to give the blessing before the meal at a Rotary meeting. He said, "Let's all join hands and raise them above your head, and join me in quoting PSALM 118:24." That was the introduction to his prayer. For those who were unfamiliar with it, it didn't take them long to join in, for every time he prayed at Rotary he would always quote that Psalm. It became his "trademark." In fact, I remember visiting the New Bern Rotary Club soon after Warren died and one of the members told me he will always remember being in Kinston at one of our meetings when Warren gave the blessing. The way he told the incident, it was obvious Warren's witness made a lasting impression on him.

Ely also had a favorite portion of Scripture he quoted quite frequently, "Christ in you, the hope of glory." COL 1:27. But there was a particular saying by Dr. John Hunter that became Ely's trademark. It was, **"For this, I have Jesus."** This took on special meaning for Ely as his health began to deteriorate. For several years he suffered from an injury to his ankle that caused him almost constant pain. He and Barbara Ruth traveled to see doctors both in-state and out-of-state, but there was no relief. Yet, Ely was upbeat and maintained, **"For this I have Jesus."** Barbara Ruth led the homework review of their weekly Bible Study, after which Ely taught the 30-minute lecture lesson. It was a team effort. She says he would always conclude his lesson with, **"For this I have Jesus."** Barbara Ruth mentioned to me just recently that a member of the class told her (over three years after his death) how blessed they were to hear Ely say, **"For this I have Jesus."** The Lord used his keen mind as a gift for teaching the Bible, and this was life-changing for brother Ely.

Margaret and Dan—March 16, 1963

Our three wonderful children Elizabeth, Radford, and Daniel

"MaMa" and Radford—1980

"MaMa" (Margaret's mother) and "Mom E" (Dan's mother)

Nonie liked to fish with Elizabeth and Daniel, Morehead—1972

Radford with her Uncle Graham and Aunt Carolyn—1974

Family Foursome, Kinston Country Club—1966

Original Wednesday foursome: Dan, Carlton Oliver, Walker Sugg, Ray Rouse—1970s

The golfing DARR boys and wives at Pine Needles—1988
Front left to right: Mary McRae and Allen Parrott, Brenda and Roy Jones;
Back: Connie and Rudy Mintz, Margaret and Dan

Dan shoots his age (71!) with Myron Hill, Dan, Carlton Oliver,
Charlie Brown—September 6, 2002

Perry Brothers and wives Margaret, Dan, Barbara Ruth, Ely, Barbara and Warren—2000

Radford and Chad's Wedding—May 13, 2000

C.C. and Carrie Pharr, Virginia's paternal grandparents

Little Virginia with her Gran and Grandan—2006

A happy family: Chad, Virginia, and Radford

"Aunt ZeeZee" with Virginia (Elizabeth)

Daniel Jr.

Margaret's sister Carolyn Hodges and brother Fred Taylor—2007

The Perry brothers were honored by the Boy Scouts

With Octavia and Jim McLeod—2004

Good Friends: Ford and Vickie Coley, Jeff and Ellen Whitaker, Sonny and Suzanne Wooten, Margaret, Gerald and Dinah Sylivant

The incredible disappearing tie, in Charleston with Gerald

Faith Fellowship Choir Party

Bible Study Group—Fall 2007

Bob Holmes and Dan enter Kenan Stadium at 50th reunion, UNC—May 2003

Arthur Spaugh, Cooper Taylor, Zollie (Z.A.) Collins and Dan at their 50th reunion

Perry Attorneys and Staff—2007
Left to right: Denelle Roberson (paralegal), Betty Blaine (niece), Dan, Lin Davitt (receptionist), Jimbo (nephew), and Barbara (sister-in-law)
(Not available for picture: Marie Sessoms)

Perry Management and Staff—2007
Left to right: Amanda Barajas, Bill Simmons, Michelle Wetherington, Gram Spear, Linda Davitt, Ely Perry III, Burton Rudolph, Dan Perry

In memory of
Marie Sessoms
February 16, 1950–August 8, 2007

(Paralegal for 20 years)

Dan and his sweetheart
—More than I deserve—

PART III

21 Lessons I've Learned along the Way

Chapter XXX

21 LESSONS I'VE LEARNED ALONG THE WAY

I have just celebrated my 76th birthday. In looking back over my life, there are a number of things I've learned that I feel are deserving of passing on to others who have life before them. Here is the list:

1. Take life seriously, but not too seriously.

Somewhere in this life there is a balance that can be achieved. Sometimes when we seek to experience God on a deeper level we might tend to, as some would say, "go off the deep end." We could become fanatical to the point of losing our perspective on life. There's nothing wrong with being a fanatic for Christ as long as it's kept in proper perspective. After all, sports fans yell and scream as the tailback crosses the goal line after a long run to win the game. But sometimes they can go overboard. Developing and maintaining a good sense of humor creates a healthy mix as we seek to find meaning and purpose in life. Sometimes I catch myself getting a little too serious. My advice to myself and to others is to lighten up and enjoy life.

2. Enjoy life but obey God's commandments.

King Solomon in his great wisdom shows us that we should enjoy life, but this does not exempt us from obeying God's Commandments. A footnote in my *Life Application Study Bible* goes on to explain: "We should search for purpose and meaning in life, but they can not be found by human endeavor. We should acknowledge the evil, foolishness, and injustice in life, yet maintain a positive attitude and strong faith in God." The footnote concludes, "We need to (1) recognize that human effort apart from God is futile, (2) put God first—now, (3) receive everything good as a gift from God, and (4) realize that God will judge every person's life, whether good or evil. How strange that people spend their lives striving for the joy that God gives freely." Bottom line: We will find meaning in life only in a proper relationship with God.

3. Live a life of response to God's goodness.

The starting point in developing a proper relationship with God is to live a life of response to His love, grace, and mercy. We experience His *grace* when He gives us something we don't deserve. We don't deserve salvation from our sins, but through His unconditional love He freely offers it to all those who will receive it. We experience God's *mercy* when we don't get something we do deserve. The Bible says we deserve death because of our sin nature, but because of His mercy He doesn't condemn us to death if we respond properly to His gift of salvation. If we understand and appreciate God's goodness in our everyday experiences we can find joy even in the midst of difficulty and hard times. It's a matter of attitude and how we respond.

4. The bible is the source of all truth.

In my life long search to discover the truth about life I came to this conclusion: The Bible is the starting point. It is the one thing you can count on as being without fault or error. It is God's Word and it can be trusted. It is the plumb line upon which all truth is based. The writer of Hebrews tells us, "For the Word of God is living and powerful and sharper than any two-edged sword, piercing even to the division of soul and spirit, and of joints and marrow, and is a discerner of the thoughts and intents of the heart" (HEB. 4:12). God's Word is called the Sword because of its piercing ability, operating with equal effectiveness upon sinners, saints, and Satan! It has the power to reach to the innermost parts of one's personality, and discerns and judges the innermost thoughts. ISAIAH 40:8 says, "The grass withers, the flowers fade, but the Word of God stands forever."

5. Jesus is the central theme of the bible.

In my reading and rereading of the Bible from cover to cover several times, I discovered that the Old Testament points toward Jesus. It is amazing to read how the prophets prophesied His coming hundreds of years before His birth. I also discovered that the New Testament looks back at Jesus to tell His story and the effect He can have on those who believe in Him and the reason He came. He is the beginning and the end (the Alpha and Omega). He is the centerpiece of the human race and the fundamental principle of the universe. He is the ultimate revelation of God, the living picture of God and His holiness. I once heard my friend Steve Johnsey say, in essence, "If we can understand who Jesus really is, we can understand the truth about a lot of things." The Apostle Paul tell us in his letter to the Colossians, "For in Him dwells all the fullness of the Godhead bodily; and you are complete in Him who is the head of all principality and power." (COL. 2:9-10) No wonder Jesus is the centerpiece of the human race and the central theme of the Bible.

6. Jesus is the only door to heaven.

In a little booklet by Charles Stanley, he points out that Jesus was extremely precise when He discussed the issue of the salvation of man. He made a statement that some may consider close-minded, but He made no apology for it what-so-ever: "Enter by the narrow gate; for the gate is wide, and the way is broad that leads to destruction, and many are those who enter it. For the gate is small, and the way is narrow that leads to life, and few are those who find it." (MATTHEW 7:13-14) Jesus is saying there is only one door into heaven. Some may say, "That's very narrow-minded." Stanley tells it like it is when he says, "Truth is narrow. Two-times-two equals four, in the 15th century or the 20th century, in the western hemisphere or the eastern hemisphere." God is single-minded about the way to heaven because there is only *one way*. Jesus came straight to the point when He said, "I am the Way, the Truth, and the Life; no one comes to the Father, but through Me." (JOHN 14:6).

7. We have to be holy and perfect to live with God.

God is holy and perfect in every way. He knows no sin and can not live with sin in His presence. Therefore, if we want to live with Him throughout eternity we ourselves must be holy and perfect, without sin. But there's a problem. We were born physically alive but spiritually dead with a sin nature which we inherited from Adam, and unless something is done we will die in our sins, eternally separated from God. We are hopeless unless there is a change in our sin nature. What's the answer—the solution to our problem? How can we be made holy and perfect? The Bible tells us we must be "born again," and the only way to be born again is through Christ Jesus and His sacrificial death on the cross. When Jesus (who was without sin) shed His blood and died He did it for all mankind. He paid our sin debt for us. He took upon Himself our sin nature along with all our daily sins, and in exchange He gave us His righteousness, His holiness, thereby giving us our ticket to heaven. This is called "The Great Exchange." He became Sin for our sake and we became Holy for His sake. We owed a debt we could not pay. He paid a debt He did not owe. We can expect to go to heaven and live eternally with our Holy God when we accept this free gift through faith and trust in what Jesus did for us on the cross.

8. God is sovereign over all things.

In our study of *Habakkuk* under Wayne Barber's teaching video some years ago, we learned five basic truths that will give you encouragement, and hold you in times of trial and testing: (1) God is in control, He rules over all, He's in charge of history; (2) All history centers or pivots on two groups of people, Israel and the church; (3) Whether or not we see it or understand it, there is a purpose in what God is doing; (4) Our times are in His hands. We are on His time table; (5) Fear and doubt are conquered by a faith that rejoices. Our study guide was entitled, "Lord, Where Are You When Bad Things Happen?"

Charles Stanley further developed these truths by giving us six principles to live by when you go through hard times: (1) God is with us in our dark times; (2) God has a purpose for allowing this present darkness; (3) The darkness will last as long as is necessary for God to accomplish His purpose; (4) We learn more in the dark than in the light; (5) Even in dark times we are moving toward the light; (6) What we learn in the dark we share in the light.

9. We are all moving toward eternity future.

One of the hardest things for many people to realize is that we all are destined for an eternal existence in either one of two places. The Bible teaches that we will either exist forever with God or exist forever separated from God. Eternity is composed of three categories: Eternity Past, Eternity Present, and Eternity Future. God the Father, Son, and Holy Spirit were all living in Eternity Past, even before the foundation of the world—they have no beginning and no end. All of us living now are in Eternity Present. For those of us who have accepted Christ as Savior, we were given eternal life the moment we received His gift of salvation. We will spend eternity future with the Holy God of the ages. For those who have not received this gift of eternal life, they are still spiritually dead, even though physically alive. They will remain spiritually dead unless they receive God's free gift of eternal life through Christ during their earthly existence. If they leave this earthly existence without having received Christ, it is too late to change their destiny. They will spend eternity future in hell separated from God. The Bible teaches there is no second chance after we die.

"Behold, now is the accepted time; behold, now is the day of salvation." (2 COR. 6:2).

10. We are new creations in Christ.

2 COR. 5:17 says, "Therefore if anyone is in Christ, he is a new creation; old things have passed away; behold, all things have become new." In our Grace Discipleship course there were five basic things we learned, along with supporting Scripture, regarding the newness we have in Christ:

A. *You Have a New Life—Eternal Life.* 1 JOHN 5:13—"I write these words to you who believe in the name of the Son of God so that you may know that you have eternal life."
B. *You Have a New Past—Total Forgiveness.* HEB 10:14—"Because by one sacrifice He has made perfect forever those who are being made holy."
C. *You Have a New Future—and a New Identity.* ROM 6:6—"For we know that our old self was crucified with Him so that the body of sin might be done away with, that we should no longer be slaves to sin."
D. *You Have a New Power—by the Spirit.* GAL 5:16—"So I say, live by the Spirit, and you will not gratify the desires of the flesh."
E. *You Have a New Inheritance.* COL 1:12—"giving thanks to the Father who has qualified us to be partakers of the inheritance of the saints in the light."

11. Our number one purpose is to know God.

Why is it so important to know God? Because the more we know God and His holiness, the better we are able to live our lives for Christ. In our study on "Knowing the God You Worship," we looked at the elements involved in knowing God:

A. *Make knowing God a priority.* Don't just talk about it. It takes time to really get to know God. JOHN 17:3 says, "And this is eternal life, that they may know you, the only true God and Jesus Christ whom you have sent."
B. *Convert that priority into practice.* We come to know God through prayer, His Word, and through Jesus Christ.
C. *Get into a program of study.* A study group will cause you to grow and move toward knowing God.
D. *Get someone to check-up on your progress.* Be held accountable.

The most important principle in getting to know God is this: God will take your search for Him to the exact same degree to which you seriously search for Him. God will never leave anybody short who really wants to know Him. You will not be disappointed. God will meet you at the point of your search.

12. The two basic Christian doctrines.

In our three-year study of Romans, we learned many of the doctrines of the church. They all seemed to boil down to two basic doctrines. It still amazes me that even though I went to church all my life, I never recall having heard the terms "justification" and "sanctification" being preached from the pulpit.

A. *The Doctrine of Justification.* In essence the term "justification" means "to be made right with God, or to be made righteous in the eyes of God." Someone has said it means to be made blameless, "just as if you had never sinned." The Bible teaches we are "*justified by faith*" in Christ and not by our works. It is the same as being "*born again.*" Being "*justified by faith*" qualifies us to have eternal life with God.

B. *The Doctrine of Sanctification.* After a person is *justified* by being born again, he becomes a child of God. He has been adopted into the family of God through faith. God's main purpose for His new child is that he grows into the likeness of His only begotten Son, Jesus the Christ. This is the process of "sanctification." It is the process of being daily conformed to the image of Christ. For the believer, it is becoming in practice what he already is in position. In position he is a righteous and holy child of God, but in practice he is far from acting like it. God's overall objective is for him to mature and live out who he is in Christ.

13. It takes time to grow toward maturity in Christ.

In our various Bible studies over the years, we have emphasized the fact that if we are to grow and mature in Christ, we need to spend *sufficient quality time* getting to know God and His will for our lives. He wants the best for us, and as we've already said, He wants us to get to know Him better as our heavenly Father. We get to know God by spending time with Him, prayerfully talking to Him, and listening to Him talk to us. We get to know Him by reading His Word, not just from time to time, but on a consistent basis. The more we read His Word and have sincere conversations with Him, the better we can get to know our creator and heavenly Father. 1 PETER 2:2 tells us, "As newborn babies, desire the sincere pure milk of the Word that you may grow thereby." Through prayer and the reading of the Bible, we can get to know God and His son Jesus on a personal basis so as to *grow thereby*. But it takes time; not just time, but quality time; and not just quality time, but *sufficient quality time*. That is the key to knowing God. Ford Coley, a long time member of our Bible Study, had shortened the wording to "SQT," meaning "Sufficient Quality Time."

14. It is impossible to live the Christian life.

Someone has asked the question, "Is it hard to live the Christian life?" The answer is NO; it's not hard to live the Christian life. It's impossible! Why is it impossible? Because the Christian life demands perfection and we can never be perfect apart from Christ. In position I am perfect and holy, because the Spirit of Christ lives in me, but in my daily life I am far from perfect. When God looks at one of His children He sees the indwelling Christ Jesus. In order to live out who we are in Christ we must allow Him to live His life though us. That's the secret of the Christian life. Our job is to allow Him to live His life though us. We can't live it, but He can. It goes back to "The Power of Letting," and "Lord, I am willing." God wants our obedience, not our sacrifices.

15. Sound doctrine is the key to living for Christ.

Recently, son Daniel and I attended Bogue Banks Baptist Church at Atlantic Beach. When we're at the beach, Margaret and I usually attend either All Saints Episcopal Church or Bogue Banks Baptist, if we're there over Sunday. On this particular Sunday, Daniel and I heard Patrick Williams preach on, "Doctrine—The Heart of Living for Christ," based on 1 TIMOTHY 1: 3-7. In essence, he was saying unless our faith is based on sound doctrine, it will not be grounded on truth. If we don't know the doctrine of the faith we won't live our lives for Christ. This is why sound doctrine is so important. Those who lack spiritual discernment bring false doctrine into the church; therefore they drift away from the truth. The Bible is the only defense against false doctrine; therefore, we must defend the truth with God's Word. Patrick Williams was saying that Paul did not say he was thankful for the churches at Ephesus and Galatia because false teachers were within the church (not from outside the church). He was advising young Timothy to stay away from false teachers. To the church at Ephesus Paul writes, "That He might sanctify and cleanse it (the church) with the washing of water by the Word." (EPH. 5:26). Here the Word is called "water" because of it's cleansing, quenching, and refreshing qualities.

16. Play the hand you are dealt.

A number of things are not meant to be understood about life, such as why do bad thing happen to good people? Why is a baby born with an infirmity? Why does death come unexpectedly, for no apparent reason? There is so much to life we don't understand and never will. I learned some time ago the best way to approach these situations is to remember a statement I read in a "Daily Bread" devotional: "To see God's hand in everything makes life a great adventure." One of my favorite scriptures is ROMANS 8:28 which says, "For we know that God causes all thing to work together for our good for those who love God and are called according to His Purpose." Some translations say, "all things work together for good." But the best translation renders the thought that God actually "causes" all thing to work together for good. Isn't it wonderfully reassuring to realize that we have a God who is literally engineering all circumstances in the lives of His children for their good? No wonder Paul was able to "rejoice always," and "praise God in all things," even in dark times. My good friend Barbara Rabhan, at the age of 88, is an inspiring example of a modern day believer who successfully deals with her adverse circumstances. For many years she has lived with essential benign tremors, the same disease which finally led to the death of actress Katherine Hepburn. Those who visit Barbara always find her to be up-beat—rejoicing and praising her heavenly Father as she completely trusts Him to work it all out for her good. She has learned, as did the apostle Paul, to be content in all things. She says, "If this is what it took to get me where I am today, then I welcome it." What a blessing it is just to be in her presence!

17. Be a square—live a four-sided life.

Back when I was growing up, one of the popular phases used by teenagers was, "Oh, don't be a square!" To accuse someone of being "a square" was not a compliment, for to be a square was to be an odd ball, someone who didn't fit in well. But in a larger sense a square describes the four sided, ideally developed person. Jesus' growth in His earthly body gives us the pattern for our own development. "And Jesus increased in wisdom and stature, and in favor with God and men." (LUKE 2:52). He grew physically and mentally; He also grew in relation to other people and to His heavenly Father. So we can see that for us to live a fully balanced life we must develop in those same four areas: physical, mental, social and spiritual. Look after our physical body, for Paul describes it as, "the temple of God" (1 CO. 3:16). Solomon advises us to seek wisdom and to exercise our mind with Godly thoughts. The Golden Rule, "Do unto others as you would have them do unto you," gives us the standard for relating socially to others. The context of the New Testament makes it clear that we are to grow spiritually in relationship to God though His Son Jesus. Seek to be a "square" and you will live a well-balanced, godly life.

18. The importance of exercise, diet, and moderation.

Many years ago there was a television commercial emphasizing the slogan, "If you've got your health, you've got just about everything!" There's a lot of truth in that statement, even though in the long run the main emphasis in being a "square" should be on spiritual health, even more than physical health. Jesus said, "For what if he gains the whole world, and loses his own soul?" (MARK 8:36) I have found that a daily routine of proper exercise, a sensible intake of food, along with moderation in all things is the best policy. One of the best things I do each day is to spend a lengthy time doing a set of various stretching exercises (while listening to David Jeremiah on 100.3 FM weekdays at 7:00 A.M.). The objective is to stretch every part of the body, from head and neck, to shoulders and arms, to wrists and fingers, to waist and thighs, all the way down to legs, ankles, and even massaging the toes. Depending on circumstances, my general routine takes about thirty minutes. Sometimes it may be as little as fifteen or twenty minutes, with the long version being as much as forty-five minutes. I find it both fun and exhilarating, and I look forward to it each morning. I shoot for seven days a week. I also enjoy going to the "24/7" gym run by Bob Garrett, hopefully at least three days a week. The convenience of being only two minutes away from home makes it a special blessing in my life. Although I don't always do it, at my age I try to emphasize fruits, vegetables, nuts, chicken, and fish for my diet—but I sure do like a good steak topped with crab meat occasionally. Mother used to say we should always get up from the table still a little hungry. That's good advice, but most of the time it's hard to do. Brother Ely used to say the best diet is, "Don't eat as much." It seems to me the general rule for all physical activity and diet is moderation—don't go overboard with anything.

19. We have a battle raging within us—a holy war.

In our study of Romans, we learned that even though we are "new creatures in Christ" we still have a struggle with sin. The spirit of Christ lives within all believers, but the problem is we still live in fleshly bodies. The result is we have a Holy War within us between the flesh and the Spirit. The flesh is not evil in itself, for the body is neutral. We have three adversaries: the **world** (and its worldly influences); the **flesh** (and our inward desires); and **Satan** (who attacks us individually). The flesh provides the avenue by which Satan can attack us. It is as though Satan is an enemy aircraft and the flesh is the landing strip on which he comes in. Our flesh is Satan's means of approaching us. The flesh is without the ability to please God or produce righteousness. As a believer, Paul says of himself, "I want to do what is good, but I don't. I don't want to do what is wrong, but I do it anyway." (ROMANS 7:19) After zeroing in on the problem, Paul then gives us the answer: "I have discovered this principal of life—that when I want to do what is right, I inevitably do what is wrong. I love God's law with all my heart. But there is another power within me that is at war with my mind. This power makes me a slave to sin that is still within me. Oh, what a miserable person I am! Who will free me from this life that is dominated by sin and death? Thank God! The answer is Jesus Christ our Lord. So you see how it is: In my mind I really want to obey God's law, but because of my sinful nature I am a slave to sin." (ROM 7:21–25—New Living Translation) God has given us His plan for victory over the flesh. It is through His Son, Jesus Christ.

20. There's a price to be paid in living for Christ.

I heard Billy Graham say years ago, "If you were accused of being a Christian, would there be enough evidence to convict you?" Most believers find it hard to give in completely to living out who we are in Christ. We are not willing to pay the high cost of discipleship. Kent Hughes, pastor and author, gives us insight with these challenging remarks: "There is a cost to sincere service for Christ. Never share your faith, and you will never look like a fool. Never stand for righteousness on a social issue, and you will never be rejected. Never walk out of a theater because a movie or play is offensive, and you will never be called a prig. Never practice consistent honesty in business, and you will not lose the trade of a not-so-honest associate. Never reach out to the needy, and you will never be taken advantage of. Never give your heart, and it will never be broken. Never go to Cyprus and you will never be subjected to a dizzy, heart-convulsing confrontation with Satan. Seriously follow Christ, and you will experience a gamut of sorrows almost completely unknown to the unbeliever. But of course, you will also know the joy of adventure with the Lord of the universe and of spiritual victory as you live a life of allegiance to Him." The older I get, the more am I convinced that Christians need to stand firm in what we believe and not be afraid to let our thoughts be known to others.

21. Live heartily for the Lord—finish well.

In his book *Life Wide Open*, David Jeremiah advises us to live our lives "heartily" for the Lord. His basic scripture is, "Whatever you do, do it heartily, as to the Lord and not to man, knowing that from the Lord you will receive the reward of inheritance; for you serve the Lord Christ." (COL 3:23–24) Dr. Jeremiah says that "whatever" refers to every task we undertake. It includes anything we *must do* as a citizen, spouse, parent, employer, or employee. It includes anything we *choose to do*, whether it's golf or job or travel. "Whatever" also includes anything we are *gifted* or *talented* to do, whether it's preaching, teaching, piano-playing, or painting. It includes anything we are *commanded to do* by God, whether it's the Great Commission or fulfilling the Great Commandment to love God and your fellow man. It also includes whatever we are *called to do by God* for whatever reason or purpose. Finally, "whatever you do" includes fulfilling your purpose in life. The Westminster shorter catechism says, "The chief end of man is to glorify God and enjoy Him forever." This is a tall order for all of us, but yet that should be our goal in life—to live heartily for the Lord. The good news is it can be done, at least in some measure; but only through an abiding trust in Jesus Christ. Wouldn't it be wonderful and fulfilling to come to the end of our earthly existence and be able to say with the apostle Paul, "I have fought the good fight, I have finished the race, I have kept the faith."? (2 TIM, 4:7).

Conclusion

It's been a lot of fun reliving my life and trying to tell my story. I have thoroughly enjoyed the adventure. By the time this book is published, I will be well over 76 years old. My journey through this life up to this point has been, to coin a phrase from Margaret Wood Hodges, "beyond fantastic" in every way.

What is the bottom line of what I've learned, as to what we should do to get the most out of life? Luke tells it plainly, *"But seek first the kingdom of God, and all these things will be added to you."* (LUKE 12:31) What is the key to seeking the kingdom of God? The answer is in the person of Jesus Christ. Your very essence and whole spiritual life depends on your answer to one question: **"Who is Jesus?"** It has been said that if you accept Jesus as only a prophet or teacher, you have to reject His teachings, for He claimed to be God's Son, even God himself. The heartbeat of John's Gospel is the dynamic truth that Jesus Christ is God's Son, the Messiah, the Savior who existed before the foundation of the world, and shall continue to live forever. This same Jesus has invited us to accept Him and live with Him forever. When we understand who Jesus is, we are compelled to believe what He said. It's a matter of life and death. John makes it clear when he wrote, "He who has the Son has life; he who does not have the Son of God does not have life." (1 JOHN 5:12) In essence, life is all about knowing God and Jesus, and living out our lives in the light of who we are in Christ. This is the way I see it, based on what I perceive to be the truth according to the inspired Word of God—the Holy Bible.

Only God Himself knows what's in store for me as I live out the remainder of my life here on earth. Whatever it is, it's more, much more, than I deserve. In fact, I don't deserve anything. Everything I am and have comes only through God's grace and mercy. I can honestly say I look forward to the time when I will take my last breath here and make the transition into the heavenly kingdom where I will live eternally with my Lord and Savior, who sacrificed His life so that I might live.

An old Gospel hymn comes to mind, which several times Daddy mouthed the words to (with some semblance of a tune). It goes like this:

> If I have wounded any soul today,
> If I have caused one foot to go astray,
> If I have walked in my own willful way,
> Dear Lord, forgive!

During my journey through this life, I'm sure I have done things I should not have done, and have not done things I should have done. If I have offended anyone in any way, I humbly ask for forgiveness. I've already asked the Lord's forgiveness for all such transgressions. No matter how much longer He allows me to live on this earth, whether one day or 25 years, I want to leave with a clear conscience.

I close with the words of William Cullen Bryant. My prayer is that God will give me the grace and well being to follow Bryant's challenge in his poem, "Thanatopsis:"

> So live, that when thy summons comes to join
> The innumerable caravan, which moves
> To that mysterious realm, where each shall take
> His chamber in the silent halls of death,
> Thou go not, like a quarry-slave at night,
> Scourged to his dungeon, but, sustained and soothed
> By an unfaltering trust, approach thy grave,
> Like one who wraps the drapery of his couch
> About him, and lies down to pleasant dreams.